PLAYWAY
to English

Second edition

1

Teacher's Book

Günter Gerngross • Herbert Puchta

Contents

I.
Introduction

Introduction

Playway to English 1 Second edition represents an integrated body of material for teaching English starting in Year 1; its essential characteristic is learning through play. With the aid of the SMILE approach *Playway to English 1* introduces basic listening and speaking skills and engages the children in learning English.

The tried and tested **SMILE approach** is based on the following principles:

S kill oriented foreign language learning
M ulti-sensory learner motivation
I ntelligence-building activities
L ong-term memory storage through music, movement, rhythm and shyme
E xciting sketches, stories and games

What is new about *Playway to English 1 Second edition*?

Compared with the previous edition, *Playway to English 1 Second edition* is even more efficient because of the following innovations:

1. A stronger emphasis on outcome in the development of the speaking skills

With the aid of numerous exercises the pupils are systematically encouraged to speak English. An extended range of exercises and a clearer focus on communicative speaking results in the children learning to express themselves on a widevariety of topics and developing an ever expanding repertoire of communicative expressions.

2. Better possibilities for assessment and self-assessment:

Under the heading *Show what you can do*, *Playway* now offers material for self-assessment at regular intervals that the children can use to assess their progress .This is initially done under supervision but then gradually the students are encouraged to assess their progress independently.

3. New content:

- Alongside well-established content from the original edition of *Playway* there are also new songs, rhymes and stories.
- Four humorous DVD sketches about Mr Matt and his two children, Danny and Daisy, have been added. Each episode is intended to develop listening and visual comprehension in a way that is motivating and fun for the children. They bring the target language to life in an extremely entertaining way, conveying cultural information about the country and providing the children with valuable encounters with everyday English phrases and expressions used by children of the same age. In this way the sketches offer a motivating way of developing listening and speaking skills.

4. CLIL (Content and Language Integrated Learning):

The CLIL pages introduce content from the general curriculum into the English classroom. In this cross-curricular lesson the intention is not so much 'language learning' but 'learning through language'. This means, therefore, that the children work with interesting content from other areas of the curriculum that is new to them. The main aim of these lessons is to cultivate the receptive processing of language, i.e. that the children learn to understand the foreign language in new, meaningful contexts that are important for them. The cross-curricular links promote holistic 'immersion' in English and give foreign language learning additional meaning.

In *Playway to English 1 Second edition* Pupil's Book you will find CLIL activities with the following objectives:

- p. 15: Colour mixing (Investigating and naming which colours are produced when two colours are mixed together.)
- p. 29: Making a fishbowl (Following instructions to do a craft activity.)
- p. 43: Making a rainbow (Following instructions to perform an experiment to show how a rainbow is formed and being able to name the colours of the spectrum.)
- p. 57: A listening activity about health (Listening and identifying some basic ideas to maintain good health.)
- p. 71: Animals: (Predicting which animals lay eggs then listening to check their predictions.)
- In addition, in Unit 6 (*Weather*) a CLIL activity is suggested in the teacher's notes following Lesson 3 (p. 110 in the Teacher's Book) that can be used after working on the story *The Little Seed*. The activity provides a content link between the topic and Art and Natural Science.

The CLIL activities are optional and are well suited to different interests and abilities. Teachers can decide on a case by case basis which of the CLIL activities to carry out with the children according to their level and interests.

5. Steps to creativity (Word Play):

These new activities have been developed especially to give the children an opportunity to be linguistically creative with the help of set structures or models. For example, the children compose their own chant by means of set rhyming words or, with the aid of pictures, they construct a rhyme. In other sections, they are encouraged to change set expressions within a structured framework to make dialogues or role plays as they wish.

6. More user-friendliness:

A clear cross-referencing system in the Pupil's Book, Activity Book and the Teacher's Book facilitates the use of *Playway to English* in the lesson. The new active vocabulary of each activity is shown at the foot of the Pupil's Book pages. The CD icons alongside the Pupil's Book and Activity Book rubrics give the relevant audio CD track number whilst DVD section references are given alongside the teaching notes. Transcriptions of all audio CD and DVD texts are included in the teaching notes.

The components of *Playway to English 1 Second edition*

Playway to English 1 Second edition consists of a comprehensive range of teaching materials:

- Teacher's Book
- 3 Audio CDs
- Pupil's Book
- Activity Book and CD-ROM
- DVD (with the Cartoon Stories and Mr Matt Sketches)
- Cards Pack (flashcards and Story Cards)
- The Max glove puppet

Teacher's Book

The Teacher's Book provides:

- **Information on the structure, components and ways of using the material and also on the desired outcomes.** In addition there is an introduction to the teaching theory of *Playway to English 1*, the educational bases and the principles behind the use of the materials plus a discussion of important issues of classroom management.
- **Comprehensive notes on the individual units.** These notes give a clear overview of the topic in question, the desired outcomes, the learning content, the learning activities and vocabulary plus tips on possible pronunciation difficulties. The main part consists of detailed and well-tried step-by-step instructions for using the individual lesson plans in class. There are also suggestions on how to practise listening comprehension and speaking skills and sub-skills such as vocabulary and pronunciation.

Audio CDs

The three audio CDs contain all the listening exercises, action stories, Word Plays, songs and chants, dialogues and interviews plus the listening versions of the cartoon stories and scenes from the Mr Matt sketches. The songs, Word Plays and chants include karaoke versions that can be used to introduce them in stages.

Listening to a foreign language frequently and intensively is an essential requirement for the development of speaking skills. On the CD, the children hear examples of authentic pronunciation and intonation from both child and adult native speakers. Although the teacher represents the most important model for pronunciation and intonation for the children, by using the CD from the start of their learning process the children are given the opportunity to hear a variety of native speakers. In this way they can develop differentiated listening comprehension skills that are not limited to just one attachment figure (the teacher). The CD is, therefore, an ideal resource in preparing the students for meeting different variations of English.

The different types of aural comprehension activities give the children exposure to a variety of models. In the trial phase of *Playway to English 1* it was noted that, in a role play activity, some children were able to imitate the pronunciation of the characters almost perfectly. This is seldom achieved with isolated pronunciation exercises but the various activities offered in *Playway to English 1* e.g. humorous role plays that encourages the students to identify with the characters through play, emphasise the valuable connection between motivation and pronunciation.

Pupil's Book

The 80-page Pupil's Book has a wide range of illustrations that support the development of the children's listening comprehension and speaking skills.

The written word is not introduced at this level in accordance with the educational psychological theory that this prevents the interference between writing and pronunciation that might arise if the child is faced with the written word before the pronunciation is secured.

Key features and activities:

- The illustrations of the songs, Word Plays or chants help the children to quickly master the texts without the support of the written word.
- After the introduction of important words the children listen to a song, a rhyme or a chant on the CD and follow it in the book. With the aid of the pictures they learn to understand the texts and gradually to sing or say them.
- A picture dictionary with all the main vocabulary offers students the chance to revise or consolidate the learning of new words after each unit (see pp. 74–79 of the Pupil's Book). This will be more effective if the children are encouraged to actively use the dictionary through pair work games, like those outlined below:

  1) Child A points to a picture and child B names it.
  2) Child A looks at the picture dictionary for ten seconds and tries to remember as many items as possible. Then they close their eyes and tell child B as many items as they can remember.
  3) Child A names a picture and child B points to it.
  4) Both children look at the picture dictionary. Child A says the names of all the items except one. Child B has to identify and name it.

- The model presentation of dialogues with the aid of pictures has a similar function. The children look at the picture and at the same time listen to a mini-dialogue. They learn to say it themselves and also to change it in a creative way (e.g. Pupil's Book p. 49, 55, 56).
- Exercises on vocabulary revision are for playful and multi-sensory consolidation of the new words (e.g. Pupil's Book p. 11).
- Asking each other how many objects there are in puzzle pictures, counting the objects and saying how many there are.
- There are exercises that directly build upon the stories and sketches. When the children have seen a cartoon story on the DVD, for example, they then complete missing scenes in the picture story with the aid of the picture stickers (see appendix of the Pupil's Book) whilst listening to the audio version on the CD. This engages the children in an active reconstruction of the story.
- There are a wide range of activities to encourage active listening. For example, the children listen to instructions on the CD and complete a set exercise in the Pupil's Book (they draw a picture following spoken instructions, or put pictures in the correct sequence).
- There are numerous exercises that help to develop important thinking skills. For example, the children complete logical sequences by drawing a series of pictures then they 'read' out their answers (e.g. Pupil's Book p. 24).

- Regular Word Play activities give the children a valuable opportunity to use the language they have learned creatively. After practising a structured chant or rhyme, the children are then encouraged to produce their own version, therefore allowing them to engage with the language in a wholly personal, imaginative way.
- At the end of every second unit the *Show what you can do* section serves as a summary, revision and reinforcement of the main vocabulary in the topics of the preceding two units. The children may – at first with the help of the teacher and, gradually, independently – evaluate their progress for the purpose of self assessment.

Activity Book

The 64-page Activity Book offers a variety of exercises designed to consolidate the language that children have learnt and to assist them in using it creatively in individual, pair and group work. There are a wide range of activities that involve students in a number of different tasks: they listen and complete with numbers or colour; complete logical sequences by drawing pictures; draw, colour and speak, etc.

As a general guideline, the Activity Book is for use at the end of a lesson rather than at the beginning since it helps to consolidate the presented language that has been practised through various other means.

Key activities:

These are the main methodological steps that the children take when they work with the Activity Book:
- Listening to sequences of instructions that are similar to the language they have heard in the Action Stories and putting pictures in order.
- Listening to words, sequences of words, sentences or short dialogues and deciding which pictures go with what they have heard.
- Listening and comparing pictures with what they have heard and completing the pictures if things are missing.
- Looking at logical sequences, 'reading' them out and completing the sequences by drawing the missing pictures.
- Listening to stories that are slightly different from the ones they have already learnt and completing tasks based on them.
- Practising language through various games, for example *Bingo* and *Memory*.
- Looking at rows of pictures and identifying which ones are the same and which are different.
- Solving logical puzzles and other problem-solving activities and also creating similar puzzles themselves to be solved in pairs.

CD-ROM (included in the Activity Book)

This learning software contains not only vocabulary activities but also exercises for use with the songs, chants, rhymes, cartoon stories and action stories in the book, meaning that *Playway to English 1 Second edition* can be supplemented either at home or at school.

System requirements:

Operating systems: Windows 2000, XP, Vista
CPU: Pentium 800 MHz or higher
Memory: 256 MB RAM, (Vista: 512 MB RAM)
Graphics card: min. 800 x 600, 16 bit colour
CD-ROM drive: min. 16X speed
Sound card: full duplex, speakers or headphones

DVD

The DVD contains four Mr Matt sketches and six cartoon stories that present English in a way that is both humorous and culturally informative through dialogues that are relevant to the unit topic. At the centre of the Mr Matt sketches are Mr Matt and his two children, Danny and Daisy. These sequences are intended to help the children to understand English in the context of a genuine dialogue. The interaction of picture and sound offers important support for the comprehension process. The use of native speakers provides an ideal preparation for understanding English in real situations. The sketches also offer the children important pronunciation models.

In their first school year, children still have a very strong imitative way of learning pronunciation, and classroom research shows that this process is particularly effective when the pronunciation models are appropriately motivating and invite imitation.

The cartoon stories are fully animated. There are also audio versions of them on the CD. This means that the children can listen to a story several times for revision without needing to use a PC or DVD player. Furthermore, the children listen to the audio version after watching the story on the DVD when they do the text-editing exercises in the Pupil's Book, such as completing a picture story by correctly inserting the picture stickers.

Cards Pack

The pack contains 93 flashcards and 57 story cards to support work in the lesson.

Flashcards

There are flashcards for all the main vocabulary. They are an essential means of conveying the meaning of new words and they help the children to memorise them more effectively. The flashcards also eliminate the task of drawing on the board or producing home-made pictures, thus saving a lot of preparation time for the teacher. The lesson notes give numerous tips on how the flashcards can be used for the reinforcement and revision of vocabulary and in games.

A list of all the flashcards is given in the appendix of the Teacher's Book (p. 170).

Story Cards

There are story cards to accompany each of the cartoon stories in *Playway to English 1 Second edition*. After the children have watched a story on DVD, they reconstruct it with the aid of the pictures and picture stickers in the Pupil's Book, then the teacher repeats the story using story cards, mimes and gestures. Alternatively, these two stages can be reversed. The teacher revises the story with the aid of the story cards and gradually the children can join in the reconstruction of the story. Then they complete the exercise in the Pupil's Book.

The Max glove puppet

The Max glove puppet is used for the visual presentation and modelling of dialogues in the classroom. Teachers can use the puppet to act out a dialogue between two people, helping the children to understand the dialogues better. The Max puppet can also be used to ask the children questions or to act out simple dialogues with them. Short role plays where one child controls the glove puppet are also an option, after the children have seen a story on DVD, for example.

Aims

The aims of *Playway to English 1 Second edition* are:
- to let the children experience, through all the senses, that learning a foreign language is fun.
- to enable the children to experience language as a means of communication in the lesson itself.
- to enable the children to express their own wishes and needs in English.
- to develop listening comprehension and speaking skills. Reading is not introduced until later – in *Playway 2* – but is carefully prepared for with forms of practice such as copying, transcribing and rewriting. In *Playway 3* these foundations for reading and writing are methodically consolidated.
- to offer a wide range of activities that promote the learning process.
- to contribute to the development of the intellectual, social, emotional and spatial skills of the children.
- to establish foreign language learning as a positive experience for the children from the start. As they gather positive learning experiences through finding their creative side when, for example, they learn to compose short texts, rhymes and chants using the models provided and with corresponding linguistic assistance.
- to lay the foundations for an open and positive attitude to other peoples and cultures by familiarising the children with another linguistic community.
- to offer teachers concrete teaching models for an innovative and up-to-date foreign language lesson in the primary school and to support them with ideas for integrating foreign language learning into the curriculum.

Contents

Playway to English 1 Second edition is divided into ten topic areas that have been selected according to motivational and age-appropriate criteria and can also be integrated into the main curriculum as they contain elements from other subject areas.

The songs and chants, for example, can be worked on in the music lesson, the action stories and activity games can be integrated into the PE lesson and logical sequences refer to aspects of mathematics. In addition, the CLIL activities referred to above offer links to other topics.

Topics

Unit 1	Hello	Unit 6	Weather
Unit 2	School	Unit 7	Party
Unit 3	Fruit	Unit 8	Health
Unit 4	Pets	Unit 9	Food
Unit 5	Toys	Unit 10	Animals

Characters

Linda, Benny and Max appear frequently as characters in the cartoon stories and also in listening exercises in *Playway to English 1 Second edition*. Max is a fantasy figure who is friends with Benny and Linda. He also steps out of the material as a glove puppet and is used in various activities in the classroom.

Alongside them the characters of Mr Matt, Danny and Daisy from the DVD Mr Matt sketches will become familiar to the children.

Activities

The content of the units is taught with the aid of the following types of activity:
- *Cartoon Stories*
- *Mr Matt Sketches*
- *Action Stories*
- *Songs*
- *Chants*
- *Word Plays*

It has been clearly shown that information in a foreign language remains more firmly fixed in the children's memories when what they are learning appeals to them. Most information that reaches our brains via various senses is quickly forgotten. What is retained in our memories is what is relevant to us. Psychologists talk of the 'depth quality' of an experience. For teaching interesting and humorous content, stories, rhymes, songs and chants – is particularly suitable.

The activities in *Playway to English 1 Second edition* are designed to be compatible with the interests of Year 1 children and to facilitate their learning. These involve as many of the children's senses as possible.

The combination of interesting content and holistic presentation ensures that the children retain the material and have fun learning English.

Cartoon Stories and Mr Matt Sketches

It is impossible to imagine primary school lessons without stories. There is good reason for this as educational psychologists repeatedly stress the idea that stories make an essential contribution to the cultural, social and emotional development of the child:

The story form is a cultural universal; everyone everywhere enjoys stories. The story, then, is not just some casual entertainment; it reflects a basic and powerful form in which we make sense of the world and experience.[1]

In the foreign-language lesson the children learn to understand longer sequences of events with the aid of stories and gradually become accustomed to descriptive, narrative language. It has been clearly established through action research on foreign language in primary schools that stories rate particularly highly in the children's scale of preferences. Stories are strong motivators and remain very strongly anchored in the memory if they are conveyed appropriately. Moreover, they promote the children's enjoyment of theatrical presentation. The children watch the story first on DVD, then the mini-dialogues are practised and next a role play is performed.

The work with the role plays makes an essential contribution to the development of the children's speaking skills. The children's high degree of identification with the content of a story can be seen in the fact that many children succeed in imitating with surprising accuracy the pronunciation and intonation of the roles of the speakers that they have previously heard on the DVD.

---

[1] Egan, K, (1986) *Teaching as Story Telling*, Chicago, University of Chicago Press, p. 2.

Action Stories

Action stories are short stories with sentences that can be represented by actions, gestures and mimes. They are performed using the Total Physical Response (TPR) method developed by James Asher[2] to convey language with a multi-sensory approach by first aiming for intensive training of the receptive skills. As already noted above, it is critically important to develop listening comprehension skills. The closer the link between what children hear and a concrete action, the better they can remember the language that they have learned and the easier it is for them to use it productively. In the action stories the children hear a sentence and act it out immediately by imitating the teacher. The sentence is represented physically after it has been heard; in this way, listening comprehension is directly linked to action.

Action stories are a classical example of learning with all the senses. Studies on the use of Total Physical Response show that, for several reasons, this method is well suited to getting the foreign language across to children at beginners' level. The reasons for this are:

- Doing the actions with others allows the child to experience following instructions as an action game. In this game, language and action are experienced as inseparable and the meaning of the language is learned directly through the action.
- Action stories are learned in an anxiety-free environment and through play. The actions of the group provide security, particularly for those children who need a little longer to process the language; they can get their bearings by looking at other children in the group and using them as models.
- Right from the start the children learn through the action stories that they can do something in English. This is an important sense of achievement and strengthens the children's confidence in their own ability to learn a foreign language.
- The development of the children's listening comprehension skills forms an important foundation for their speaking. When working with the action stories the children should first and foremost be listening. Gradually, they will speak along with the teacher and in this way gain self-confidence in their pronunciation and intonation. The primary goal in working with action stories is developing listening comprehension. This means that the teaching/learning goal is achieved when the children can act out the sentences of an action story independently after practising it. It is not the primary goal of working with action stories to have the children immediately recite the story or even to be able to reconstruct it freely.

Songs

Songs are highly valuable for motivating children of primary school age. Singing in groups is fun and children enjoy learning a repertoire of songs during the course of the year. *Playway to English 1 Second edition* offers songs that have been written especially for the individual topics. The advantage of this is that songs consolidate the language presented and the language input can be easily monitored.

Chants

Chants are texts that are recited to a set rhythm. They offer an excellent opportunity to practise pronunciation, intonation and speech rhythm. All the chants in *Playway to English 1 Second edition* have been written especially for the individual topics. When working on a chant the children listen to it on the CD first. In the Pupil's Book the text is represented by the illustrations, so, when listening to the chant a second time, the children follow the chant in the book. In the pilot phase of *Playway to English 1 Second edition* experience showed that the pictures were very helpful for the children in mentally reconstructing the text.

Then the children watch the gestures of the teacher, imitate them and speak at the same time. Next the children listen to the first part of the karaoke section (*And now you!*) with gaps (half playback) and say the missing parts of the text. Finally, the children recite the complete text of the chant with the rhythmic support of the karaoke section.

Word Plays – creative tasks

Playway to English 1 Second edition includes tasks that carefully encourage the children to be creative in English right from the beginning. For example, in the rhyme on Pupil's Book p. 8:

> *A red bike for Linda,*
> *A green bike for Li,*
> *A yellow bike for Benny,*
> *A blue bike for me!*

First of all the children listen to the rhyme and colour the children's bikes in the appropriate colours, then the rhyme is practised intensively. Next the children look at a picture on the next page (Pupil's Book, p. 9). They are asked to colour each of the boats a different colour. This gives them the framework to compose their own rhyme using the picture as a guide. For example:

> *A green boat for Benny,*
> *A red boat for Li,*
> *A blue boat for Linda,*
> *A yellow boat for me!*

By involving as many senses as possible the rhymes are retained in the memory long-term. Research findings in primary school English lessons show that children who have forgotten parts of the text can remember them again by recalling the series of actions or the colours and the rhymes.

---

[2] Asher, J. (1988), *Learning Another Language Through Actions: The Complete Teacher's Guide Book*, Los Gatos, Ca.: Sky Oaks Publications.

Rhymes

The rhymes in *Playway to English 1 Second edition* were also written especially for the individual topics. The children can experience the rhymes in a multi-sensory way. For example a rhyme like:

> Snow, snow,
> Snowman grow.
> Oh, the sun.
> Snowman run.

is presented so that the children simultaneously listen, speak, and perform certain movements. By involving as many senses as possible, the rhymes are retained in the memory for a long time.

Research in the pre-primary English classrooms shows that children who have forgotten the text can easily remember it again by recalling the series of movements.

How to use *Playway to English 1 Second edition* in the lesson

The selection of teaching topics

There are numerous ways of using the material in *Playway to English 1 Second edition* in combination with the topics in the curriculum. The topics have been organised in such a way that the teacher can always find material and activities that link in with the topics currently being taught in the curriculum. See contents on p. 2 for the list of topics.

Lesson overviews

At the start of the teaching notes for each individual lesson there is an overview box provides a summary of the language used and lists the materials required in that lesson under the following headings:

- Vocabulary, phrases and structures
- Linguistic skills
- Cognitive, motor and social skills
- Cross-curricular integration
- Materials

Lesson plans for the school year

Lessons should always be pre-planned to take into account the situation in individual classes. The following overview gives a summary of the syllabus with suggestions for integration of the individual units of *Playway to English 1 Second edition* into the curriculum for the whole of the school year. It presents a framework that can be used as a basis for individual lesson plans.

Topics	Types of text and activities	Vocabulary, phrases and structures
1 Hello	• *I'm Max* (cartoon story) Sticker activity Mini-dialogues	• *Good morning; Hello, I'm (Max); What's your name?*
	• *What's your name?* (song) • Presenting vocabulary with flashcards Vocabulary games	• *Hello to you.* • *one; two; three; four; right; left*
	• *Stand up* (action story) Imitating and carrying out instructions Putting pictures in order	*Receptive: Stand up; Shout 'Hooray!'; Stretch; Sit down.*
	• Presenting vocabulary with flashcards Vocabulary games	• *red; yellow; green; blue; black; white* *Yes; No.* *Receptive: What colour is it?*
	• *Give me red* (chant) • Extending vocabulary Listening activity	• *Give me (red); Here you are; Yeah, alright.* • *brown*
	• Pair work: Vocabulary game • Extending vocabulary with a flashcard	
	• *A red bike for Linda* (rhyme) • Presenting vocabulary with a flashcard	• *bike*
	• Word play – Step to creativity Composing and reciting a rhyme.	• *boat*
2 School	• Presenting vocabulary with flashcards Vocabulary games	• *schoolbag; pencil; pencil case; scissors; glue; book* *Receptive: Touch (the pencil); Open/Close your eyes; What's missing?*
	• *Baby face!* (chant) • Listening activity	• *baby face; Sit down!* *Receptive: What does (Benny want)?; Thank you; Please;*
	• Pair work: Vocabulary game with stickers Practicing and performing mini-dialogues	
	• *The painting* (cartoon story) Sticker activity Retelling the story with story cards	*Receptive: Come on, Max! It's (not) very good; That's OK, Linda/Benny; Oh, no!; I'm sorry; Fantastic!; Congratulations!; Thank you.*
	• Extending vocabulary with flashcards Vocabulary game	• *orange; pink; purple*
	• Pair work: Vocabulary game • Extending vocabulary with flashcards	
	• *Smile* (action story) Imitating and carrying out instructions Putting pictures in order	• *five; six* *Receptive: Stand up; Close your eyes; Touch your nose/eyes; Smile.*
	• CLIL activity Doing an experiment (colour mixing experiment)	
Units 1–2 Show what you can do	• Matching activity • Speaking activity	*Receptive: Take a (red pencil); Write the numbers; Here we go.*

Topics	Types of text and activities	Vocabulary, phrases and structures
3 Fruit	• Presenting vocabulary with flashcards Vocabulary games Listening activity • Pair work: Vocabulary game • Presenting vocabulary through a memory game Listening and speaking activity • Pair work (word play) • *Give me more!* (chant) • *Hello!* (Mr Matt sketch) Listening activity • *I'm Danny! I'm Daisy!* (song) • *The plum* (action story) Imitating and carrying out instructions • *The greedy monster* (cartoon story) Sticker activity Retelling the story with story cards	• *apple; banana; plum; pear* • *apples; bananas; plums; pears* Receptive: *How many (apples) are there?* • *Give me more! No way! OK!* Receptive: *Hello, my name's ...; This is my boy/girl; Where are they?; Here?; Say hello; Here we are, Dad!* • *I'm Danny/Daisy; And I'm Mr Matt; Oh, no! Stop saying that you're Danny/ Daisy; Hooray!* Receptive: *Say 'Hello' to your mum; You're hungry; You're mum shows you some plums; Cut open a plum; Show the plum to your mum; Your mum says 'Eek!'.* Receptive: *A monster!; Help!; I'm thirsty!; Here you are; I'm hungry; Give me more; Just a moment.*
4 Pets	• Presenting vocabulary with flashcards Vocabulary games Listening activity • Pair work: Vocabulary game • Logical sequences • *What's this?* (chant) • *The mouse* (action story) Imitating and carrying out instructions Putting pictures in order • Extending vocabulary with flashcards Listening activity Putting pictures in order • CLIL activity Doing a craft activity (make a fishbowl)	• *dog; mouse; rabbit; duck; cat* • *What's this?; miaow; woof; squeak; quack* • *Let's play; Go away.* Receptive: *The mouse goes away; the mouse is very sad; What can I do now?; Wonderful; Abracadabra; Let's go to the show; Ladies and gentleman!;* • *ghost*
Units 3–4 **Show what you can do**	• Matching activity • Speaking activity	

Topics	Types of text and activities	Vocabulary, phrases and structures
5 Toys	• Presenting vocabulary with flashcards Vocabulary game • Revising and extending vocabulary with flashcards Picture puzzle	• teddy bear; train; plane; car; doll; computer game; ball; puzzle • seven; eight Receptive: How many (balls) are there?
	• Listen, listen! (chant)	• Listen: And there's a plane.
	• Extending vocabulary with a flashcard Listening exercise (rhyme)	• star • My (blue train).
	• Word play – Step to creativity Composing and reciting a rhyme • A dog in your car (action story) Imitating and carrying out instructions Putting pictures in order	Receptive: You're in a car; There's a dog; Stop the car and get out; The dog jumps into your car; The dog drives off; Vrooom!; You run after the car. • I've got a cool, cool, duck/dog/mouse/cat on a super bike; ting, ting; in a super car; vroom, vroom; in a super train; choo, choo; in a super plane; woo, woo; Wheel
	• My cool pets (song)	I've got (two cars), (one train), (six dolls).
	• Listening activity	Receptive: Hi, I'm (Anna); How many (cars) has (Anna) got?; How many (cars) have your got?
	• Pair work: Talking about toys	
6 Weather	• Presenting vocabulary with flashcards Listening activity vocabulary game	• rain; sun; wind; clouds; snow; It's raining/sunny/windy/cloudy/snowy.
	• Pair work: Vocabulary game	• cap; frog
	• Extending vocabulary with flashcards and realia • A cap on a cat (chant)	• A cap on a (cat); Rain, snow or sun; Caps are always fun.
	• Presenting vocabulary with flashcards and actions • Snowman grow (rhyme) • Vocabulary revision ball game Discovery picture	• snowman; grow; run snowman grow; Oh, the sun; Snowman run • cat; dog; hamster; mouse; duck; rabbit
	• Presenting vocabulary with flashcards, board drawings, and actions • The little seed (cartoon story) Sticker activity Retelling the story with story cards Optional: Role play	• bee; butterfly; flower; umbrella; a little seed; grows; What a sweet smell; Bless you! Receptive: The little seed is asleep; Hello, Bee; Hi, Butterfly; Look at the clouds; I've got an umbrella; Come with me; Aah! This is good; The little seed grows and grows; The rain stops; Thanks for the umbrella; That's OK; Careful!; Oh, dear!; Look. Here comes the sun; Fantastic!; A week later; Look at the wonderful flower.
	• CLIL activity Optional: mini-projects (Making a seed pattern; Growing cress)	Receptive: sunflower seeds; cress seeds; orange pips; apple pips; beans; peas; lentils; It's raining; Come out; Run and jump; Oh, what a rainy day!
	• It's raining (song) • Listening activity • Pair work: Vocabulary game	Receptive: What's the weather like today?; It's (very) (sunny).
	• CLIL activity Doing an experiment (make and observe a rainbow)	
Units 5–6 **Show what you can do**	• Matching activity • Speaking activity	

Topics	Types of text and activities	Vocabulary, phrases and structures

7 Party	• Presenting vocabulary with flashcards
	  Vocabulary games
	  Discovery picture
		• *sheriff; princess; bear; ghost; clown; monster; nine; ten*
		• *One cat, two cats, three cats. Four. Five cats. Six cats. Seven cats. More.*
		  Receptive: *How many ... are there?*

	• *A party for a princess* (chant) • Logical sequences • Presenting vocabulary with flashcards	• *A party for a princess, a sheriff and a dog, a bear, a cat, a monster, a ghost and a frog!* • Numbers one to ten

	• *You're a magician* (action story)
	  Imitating and carrying out instructions
	  Putting pictures in order
	• Role play
		• *cake; plate; bird; magician*
		  Receptive: *You're a magician; Get a piece of cake; A clown grabs your plate; Turn the clown into a bird; The bird flies away; Eat your piece of cake*

	• Presenting vocabulary with flashcards	• *What a lovely cake!; Here you are; Thank you; Is this your dog?; Yes, it is; Watch out!; Oh, no!* • *crocodile; prince*
	• *I'm a magician* (song)	• *Abracadabra, one, two, three!; I'm a magician; Look at me!; A ghost into a sheriff; a bear into a car; a prince into a crocodile; Oh, I'm a superstar!*

	• Speaking activity (word play)
	  Completing pictures
	  Composing and reading/singing a song	

8 Health	• Presenting vocabulary with flashcards	• *bed; tooth/teeth; knees; (a glass of) milk* Receptive: *Get out of bed; Wash your face; Clean your teeth; one, two, three; Jump – one, two, three; Have a glass of milk.*

	• *Bend your knees* (action story)
	  Imitating and carrying out instructions
	  Putting pictures in order
	• *Get out of bed* (song)
	• Presenting vocabulary with flashcards
		• *Get out of bed; Wash your face; Clean your teeth; Bend your knees; And Jump; Let's keep fit!*
		
		• *lemon; orange; ice cream; chocolate*

	• *At the Dentist* (Mr Matt sketch) Listening activity	Receptive: *I win, I think; Have an apple/a banana, Dad; No, thanks; I love chocolate/lollies/ice cream!; Bananas, oranges, a lemon; Look!; Mr fruit Face!; I'm hungry; Oh, dear ... I know... a good walk; a big ice cream, please; Here you are; Thank you; What's the matter, Dad? My tooth hurts; go to the dentist; No, not the dentist!; Don't worry; Come on; Next!; Come in; Hello; Goodbye; Take a seat; The other way!; Relax!; Nice chair!; Some music?; Yes, please; Oh, lovely!; Where's the dentist? It's me!; It's her!; open your mouth; Not today; An apple for me.*

	• Listening activity
	  Practicing and performing mini-dialogues
	  Playing a memory game
	• Role play
	• CLIL activity (health)
	  Pair work
		• *Yummy!; Tea's ready; What's the matter?; I feel sick.*
		
		• *Go and clean your teeth, Ben; Yes, Dad; Let's sing a song; Yes!; Ben, here you are; OK, sir.*
		  Receptive: *Wash your hands before meals; Wash your hands after you go to the toilet; Don't eat too many sweets; Clean your teeth after meals; Eat lots of fruit; Keep fit.*

Units 7–8 **Show what you can do**	• Matching activity • Speaking activity	

Topics	Types of text and activities	Vocabulary, phrases and structures

9 Food	• Presenting vocabulary with flashcards
	  Vocabulary games
	• Lots of spaghetti (chant)
	
	• Extending vocabulary (flashcard and drawing)
	  Listening exercise
	  Practicing and performing mini-dialogues
	• Introducing vocabulary with flashcards
	
	• The spider (action story)
	  Imitating and carrying out instructions
	  Putting pictures in order
	• Presenting vocabulary with flashcards and drawings
	• What's for breakfast? (Mr Matt sketch)
	  Listening activity
	
	• Pizza, pizza (chant)
	• Word play – Step to creativity
	  Composing and reciting a chant
	• Practicing and performing mini-dialogues
		• butter; spaghetti; chicken; cheese; chips
		
		• Lots of spaghetti/chicken on a big, big plate; With butter and cheese/ketchup and chips; Spaghetti/Chicken is great.
		• pizza; cornflakes
		  Receptive: What does Linda/Benny like?
		• I like …
		• kitchen; spider
		  Receptive: You're hungry; Go into the kitchen; Take a plate of cheese; There's a big spider on the cheese; Drop the plate; Run out of the kitchen.
		• eggs; toast; smoothie; breakfast
		  Receptive: We're hungry; What's for breakfast, Dad?; Tea and toast?; Where's our toast?; Just a minute; Sorry. No toast/eggs; A smoothie? Yes, please.; Hey, watch this!; No, Dad, please!; Don't worry; Oh, no!; No problem; There are two more eggs
		• pizza/cornflakes/apples; Yummy; I like pizza cornflakes/apples.
		• I like …
		
		• What do you like?; I like …

10 Animals	• Presenting vocabulary with flashcards
	  Vocabulary games
	• The lion is ill (cartoon story)
	  Sticker activity
	  Retelling the story with story cards
	  Role play
	• Listen to the animals (song)
	
	• The thief (Mr Matt sketch)
	
	• Listening activity
	• Listening activity
	
	• CLIL activity
	• Presenting vocabulary with flashcards
	  Listening activity
		• lion; elephant; hippo; monkey; snake
		
		• The lion is ill; the elephant/monkey/hippo/snake wants to help; Lion, lion, listen to my music; Stop it, please; What's this?; It's the elephant/…; Oh, thank you for the wonderful music.
		• Listen to the elephant/hippo/monkey/snake; What a wonderful song; One, two, three, come on, sing and dance with me!
		• left; right
		  Receptive: Can I have a banana/an orange/some popcorn, please?; Here you are; Just a minute; It's empty!; That's (very, very) strange!; Come on, Danny!; Let's go!; Back to the zoo!
		  Receptive: Open your picnic basket; A monkey grabs it and climbs a tree; The monkey's mum comes; She says 'Come down!'; The monkey comes down the tree; Have a picnic with your two friends, the monkeys.
		• whale(s); turtle(s); penguin(s); lay eggs; have babies; mouse (mice)

Units 9–10 **Show what you can do**	• Matching activity • Speaking activity	

Basic technology

Working with the flashcards

The purpose of the flashcards is to introduce important new words visually. These suggestions for using them in the lesson are based on the following educational principles:
- Conveying the meaning of new words in the foreign-language lesson should be carried out as visually as possible.
- Always apply the principle **listening precedes speaking**. The children should first of all become accustomed to the pronunciation and intonation of a word before they are asked to repeat it.
- When introducing new words use a **combination of all the senses**. Pictures, pronunciation and intonation and also motor-processing techniques complement each other and help to anchor a word in the long-term memory.
- The **anchoring of the new words** will be all the more long-lasting if the words are repeated often enough. No more than one to two minutes are needed for this. The flashcards are highly suited to such repetition stages.

The following methods have proven successful:

Introduction of vocabulary
- Show the cards in order and say the English word at the same time.
- Then stick the cards on the board. Repeat the words in order, then jumbled up, at the same time pointing to the corresponding flashcard.
- Say the words and encourage the children to point to the flashcards, e.g.: *Point to the pencil case.*
- Have the children repeat the word after you several times.
- Gradually increase the pace.

Exercises for anchoring the vocabulary in the recognition memory:
- Call one child up to the board and say the words in order. The child points to the corresponding flashcards on the board. Call another child to the board, say the words jumbled up and ask the child to point along as you speak.
- Call individual children to the front and ask them to take a card from the board and to give it to another child in the class, e.g.: *Mark, take the glue, please. Pass it to Lena.* Mark: *Here you are.* Lena: *Thank you.* When all the flashcards have been distributed around the class, say: *Stick the glue on the board.* The child with the corresponding flashcard sticks it back on the board. Continue in this way until all the flashcards are stuck back on the board.
- Call individual children out to the board. Give the following instruction: *Touch the (pencil case).* The children touch the corresponding flashcard. Then remove all the flashcards from the board. Ask the children to close their eyes. By turning off the visual channel the children can concentrate completely on the sound pattern. Say the words individually. Change your voice as you do so. Say the words loudly, quietly, in a high voice, in a deep voice, happily, sadly, angrily and encouragingly. The children just listen first of all then they repeat the word exactly as you say it.

Exercises for anchoring words in the children's productive memory
- Hold a flashcard in your hand with the reverse side to the children and ask: *What is it?* The children guess what the word is. When a child has guessed correctly, show the flashcard and reply: *Yes, it is.*
- Stick the flashcards on the board. Then say all the words in order together with the children. Clap twice between each word. Repeat the words a few times but change the activities between the individual words. For example, click your fingers, slap your thighs, stamp your feet, stand up and sit down at the next word.
- Take one flashcard after another, say the words and turn the card over so that only the reverse is visible. When all the flashcards have been turned over, ask: *Who can remember the words?* Have individual children come up, say a word and turn over the card they think is the right one.

Using the DVD sequences and the story cards

For using the cartoon story sequences on the DVD we recommend the following steps:

1st stage: Preliminary preparation of important words and phrases
Pre-teach important words or phrases beforehand if necessary – usually with the aid of the flashcards or story cards.

2nd stage: Playing the DVD sequence
Play the DVD sequence – several times if necessary.

3rd stage: Picture sticker activity
The children listen to the audio version of the story on the CD while they are completing the picture story with the picture stickers from the Appendix of the Pupil's Book.

4th stage: Evaluation
Go around the class and check whether the children have completed the picture story correctly with the stickers. Alternatively, produce a completed picture story and the children check their work independently.

5th stage: Telling the story
In further stages the story cards or Max the glove puppet can be used to practise and reinforce the story texts through play. They can also be used later on as an ideal way for regular revision of learned material.
- Tell the story with the aid of the story cards. While you are telling the story stick the cards one after the other on the board.
- Tell the story again. While you are telling the story keep stopping and asking the children with corresponding mimes and gestures to reconstruct the story with you. For example, when working on the story *The mouse* (Pupil's Book pp. 26 and 27), say: *Hello, Cat. Squeak, squeak. Let's …* Children: *… play.* Say: *No, go away. The mouse is …* Children: *… sad.*, etc.

6th stage: Story reconstruction game
- Distribute the story cards to individual children. Tell the story again. The child with the corresponding picture

comes out to the front. Finally, all the children who were given the story cards are standing in the order of the sequence of the story in front of the class. Tell the children to hold the pictures up so that they can be seen clearly by all.

- Tell the story slowly and at the same time point to the child with the corresponding picture. Stop and ask the child to complete the sentence(s). If necessary, get the other children to help. Support the children with mimes and gestures. Say: *Hello, Cat. Squeak, squeak.* Child: *...* *Let's play ...* Say: *No ...* Child: *... go away.*, etc.

Using the Mr Matt sketches

For using the Mr Matt sketches on the DVD we recommend the following steps:

1st stage: Preliminary preparation of important words and phrases
Pre-teach important words or phrases beforehand if necessary – ideally with the aid of the flashcards.

2nd stage: Playing the DVD sequence
Play the DVD sequence – several times if necessary.

3rd stage: Listening exercise
Play the listening exercise for the Mr Matt sketches on the CD (ideally) twice. In their books the children number the scenes depicted in the sketches.

4th stage: Evaluation
Go around the class and check whether the children have correctly numbered the pictures. You can also hold up your book, point to scenes and the children say the corresponding number. In high-ability groups the answers can be checked by you saying: *Picture three.* Children: *Hello! I'm Mr Matt* (see Pupil's Book p. 20).

How to use the Max glove puppet

The Max glove puppet performs a variety of functions in the lesson.
- Max should always be placed somewhere visible when you want to signal to the children that an English lesson is starting. When the children see Max, it helps them to recall the language they have already learned and this causes their previous knowledge to be activated unconsciously.
- Max can be used again and again as a model for speaking. Tell the children that he likes them to repeat what he says. The following methodology tips make the use of the Max glove puppet in the lesson particularly effective:
  - Use a distinctive voice for Max by changing your voice slightly. You can also copy the voice of Max in the film. This helps to give Max his own identity in the children's perception, i.e. it makes him seem as real as possible.
  - Take care that Max only makes mouth movements when he is speaking. When you are speaking as yourself Max should not move. This is an important aid to comprehension for the children.
  - When children speak to Max in L1 (their mother tongue) he doesn't understand them. Max should never be used in a mother-tongue lesson because he serves as an important psychological anchor for foreign language use.

How to use the action stories

The action stories are based on the Total Physical Response method through which listening comprehension is consolidated holistically through play. Here is an example for the text of an action story from the topic *Food* (Unit 9):

You're hungry.
Go into the kitchen.
Take a plate of cheese.
There's a big spider on the cheese.
Drop the plate.
Run out of the kitchen.

The following steps have proven very useful in working with the action stories.

1st stage: Listening and imitating
- Model the first statement (*You're hungry.*) and act it out by rubbing your stomach. The children imitate you.
- Model the next statement and mime it. The children imitate your actions and synchronise theirs as closely as possible with yours. Repeat this procedure for all the lines in the action story.

2nd stage: Carrying out instructions
- The sequence of instructions and actions is repeated several times until you see that the children can carry them out independently and without difficulty.
- Then give the instructions again in the correct order and the children carry them out. Do not do the actions with them. Repeat this several times until you see that the children all understand well.

3rd stage: Carrying out the instructions in jumbled order
- Give the instructions in jumbled order and the children carry them out. Do not do the actions yourself.
- A particular favourite is a game where you give each child an instruction, jumbled up and increasing in pace. The game is fun, and practises quick responses to English utterances whilst furthermore increasing the concentration of the children.

4th stage: Listening exercise
- Finally the children open the Pupil's Book. They listen to the instructions on the CD and point along in the book where the pictures are illustrated in jumbled order. Then the children put the pictures in the right order by numbering them. This serves to check and confirm whether individual children can understand the sentences in the action story.

5th stage: Evaluation
- Go around the class and check the children's work.
- Option: In high-ability classes you can put out an answer key for self-checking. The children go and check their own work themselves.
- Alternatively: Draw six boxes on the board (some action stories have four or six pictures/boxes) that represent the page in the Pupil's Book. Have the children tell you the numbers. Write the numbers in the boxes.

Using the songs

The following steps have proven very successful when used with the songs.

1st stage: Preliminary preparation and playing the song on the CD
Option: Introduce the new words with the aid of the flashcards. If necessary, reinforce important phrases with appropriate actions/gestures or drawings on the board. Play the song twice. The children follow in the book.

2nd stage: Reinforcing the text
Facilitate the understanding of the text with corresponding actions or gestures and encourage the children to imitate you. Say the lyrics – several times if necessary in the rhythm of the song.

3rd stage: Singing along
Ask the children to stand in a circle. Hum the tune of the song. Gradually the children join in with you and hum along. When they are all humming, start to sing the words. Sing the song together with the children a few times along with the CD.

4th stage: Singing to the karaoke version of the CD
Sing the song together with the children using the karaoke version of the CD. Sing the song and do the actions.

Using the rhymes

The rhymes in *Playway to English 1 Second edition* have been carefully constructed so that they can be worked on using the multi-sensory method; the children listen to the rhyme, speak and carry out certain movements at the same time. The following steps have proven very useful in practice:

1st stage: Play the rhyme on the CD and present its content in gestures
Play the rhyme on the CD and, at the same time, present its content with the aid of appropriate gestures and actions or point to the corresponding pictures in the book.

2nd stage: Reinforcing the text (1)
Play the rhyme for a second time. Do the corresponding actions to it again or point along in the book. At first the children just watch. Say the rhyme line by line with the support of actions and encourage the children to copy you. Practise the chant with the children one line at a time by saying it out loud and doing the appropriate actions. The children repeat after you and imitate your actions.

3rd stage: Reinforcing the text (2)
The children open their books. Say the lines of the text in random order and the children point to the corresponding pictures in the book.

4th stage: Presentation
Invite any children who feel confident about it to recite the rhyme. The children can also do this in pairs. High-ability groups can also say the rhyme to the playback version of the CD.

5th stage: Step to creativity (only relevant for Word Plays)
Some of the rhymes are used as Word Plays. In that case, the original rhyme gives the children the framework to compose their own rhyme using the pictures in the Pupil's Book as a guide.

Using the chants

All the chants in *Playway to English 1 Second edition* have been written especially for the individual topics and have been carefully constructed so that they can be worked on using the multi-sensory approach. The following steps offer a basic structure for working on the chants:

1st stage: Play the chant on the CD and prepare the comprehension of the text
Play the chant on the CD and carry out appropriate actions to facilitate the comprehension of the text.

2nd stage: Reinforcing the text (1)
Play the chant a second time on the CD and have the children point along in the book. The text is represented by the illustrations in the Pupil's Book. Say the text line by line. The children do the actions.

3rd stage: Reinforcing the text (2)
Practise the chant with the children by giving two 'instructions' and miming them. The children imitate your actions and repeat after you. Practise the chant in this way one verse at a time, then get the children to repeat the verses rhythmically and mime them.

4th stage: Listening exercise
Play the chant on the CD. The children number the pictures accordingly in the book. This serves to check and confirm whether they can understand the lines of the chant.

5th stage: Using the first playback version of the CD
(And now you!)
Play the CD. The children point to the corresponding pictures in the book and join in the verses. Play the half playback version on the CD. The children point along in the book and recite the missing parts of the text.

6th stage: Using the karaoke version of the CD
(One more time!)
The children now say the whole text to the karaoke section on the CD. Finally, divide the children into two groups. Allocate sections of the chant that can be said by each group; the teaching notes for specific chants offer some suggestions as to how this could be done, e.g. one group takes the part of the speaker with the teacher and the other group repeats. The group that is not speaking carries out the instructions. Repeat this several times.

Developing speaking skills

The development of the children's ability to express themselves in English represents an important aim in the educational concept of *Playway to English 1 Second edition* and in its method of use. Foundations for speaking are first and foremost laid by the children getting to know and understand various sorts of texts (action stories, songs, chants, sketches, stories, listening exercises) important words, chunks of language, phrases and sentences and absorbing and storing many of them by way of text-editing exercises. A wide range of exercises serves to consistently build up and systematically extend the children's linguistic expressions. A distinction must be made between so-called 'pre-communicative' and 'communicative' exercises in the course. In the pre-communicative exercises the focus is on the language work. The exercises provide preparation for later communicative exercises. Communicative exercises, on the other hand, are distinguished by the fact that they offer opportunities for speaking that the children want or have to use to express themselves.

*Examples for **pre-communicative exercises** in Playway to English 1 Second edition*

- **Matching**
  On p. 11 of the Pupil's Book, after the introduction of the key sentences, e.g.: *The (pencil) and the (glue), please*, the children listen to the CD and match the phrases to the corresponding pictures. Through the act of matching linguistic utterances to pictures the children's stock of linguistic actions is extended – albeit only receptively at first. This language is used later in pair work mini-dialogues that then help to store the language in the children's stock of productive language, e.g. Child A: *The book, please.* Child B: *Here you are.*

  On p. 29 of the Activity Book the children listen and colour numbered shapes. They then follow jumbled lines to match these shapes with toys and they colour and number the toys accordingly. When the matching activity is complete, the results are used in a communicative activity where the teacher asks about the toys, colours and numbers, e.g.: *What colour is the (car)?* and *What's number (five)?*

- **Completing**
  In Unit 10, the children watch a cartoon story on the DVD (*The lion is ill*). After listening several times and reconstructing the story with the story cards the children look at a picture summary of the story in the Pupil's Book (pp. 66 and 67). They then complete the pictures with the picture stickers whilst listening to the story on the audio CD.

  On Activity Book p.19, the children listen to a dialogue and identify which frames have part of their picture missing. They then complete the frames by drawing the missing details according to what they hear. Having done this, the children practise the dialogue in pairs with the completed pictures a prompts.

*Examples of **communicative exercises** in Playway to English 1 Second edition*

- **Games**
  Speaking can be practised through games in a way that is very motivating and appropriate for children. For example,

on p. 24 in the Pupil's Book the children start by looking at the pictures of the animals on the topic *Pets*. After working on the animal vocabulary, the children work in pairs and check whether they have remembered the names of the animals through a vocabulary game.

On p. 41 of the Activity Book the children play a memory game in pairs whereby each has to remember the colour the other has used to fill in the numbers one to ten by asking the question: *What colour is number (eight)?* They then go on to play an information gap guessing game with numbers and colours.

- **Interviews**
  Using set phrases children ask each other questions or give information about themselves as, for example, on p. 61 in the Pupil's Book where, as a model for the pair work activity, the characters Linda and Benny say what food they like, e.g.: *Linda: I like spaghetti, cornflakes, … .*

  In Unit 5, the children draw pictures of the toys in the main vocabulary set and colour them (Activity Book p. 33). They then present them to the class as their own, e.g.: *I've got a blue car, two yellow planes and a red doll.* They then go on to do a pair work in which they ask each other: *What have you got?*

- **Dialogues and scenes**
  We recommend that dialogues should be listened to several times first of all and then, in high-ability groups, practised well. Children also like performing such dialogues in front of the class. They first of all re-enact the model dialogues. Then the children should be asked to gradually change the dialogue based on an example given by the teacher. Before acting them out the children should be given the opportunity to memorise them well and consider how they might personalise the dialogue. Just small changes are sufficient, for example, on p.55 of the Pupil's Book *Two bananas, please.* instead of the phrase given in the book *Three lollies, please.* shows the children that the point is not to recite language but that they learn to use language communicatively themselves.

The use of the English in the here-and-now of the lesson

Increasingly, conversation in class should be carried out in English. It will start off with the teacher speaking English and the children understanding and carrying out what the teacher says. With the appropriate skills it will, however, also be possible to motivate the children to try saying something communicatively themselves in English which goes beyond the pre-communicative or communicative exercises described above. You can support the children in this by whispering words or groups of words as prompts whenever necessary. It is also important to emphasise that learning foreign languages and making mistakes belong inseparably together.

Working with *Show what you can do*

- This self-assessment section appears after every two units. It serves the purpose of consolidating the most important words; the ones that are set as compulsory in the syllabus. The children listen to the CD and match the words to the pictures by numbering them in the colours given on the recording.

- The speaking and colouring activity represents a further stage in the self-assessment in that the children only colour the frame of the pictures if they can **say** the corresponding words in English.
- Children and parents should be aware that the words in the self-assessment are to be mastered as productively as possible, i.e. that the children can use the words from the self-assessment with as few errors as possible.

Observations from the psychology of learning on the early learning of foreign languages

Requirements of foreign-language learning for very young learners

When children start learning English at primary school as a rule they not only already know a few English words but also have a range of basic skills that enable them to learn a new language. These skills have been gained in the process of learning their mother tongue. Learning a foreign language at school builds on these foundations and further develops the skills:

The ability to grasp meaning
Before toddlers know the exact meanings of individual words they are able to understand the sense of complete utterances. Intonation, mime, gesture, and the connection between what is said and their environment helps them to decode what they have heard. In the foreign-language lesson this skill needs to be activated. By doing so, already in very early stages of the foreign-language lesson, the children experience a sense of achievement.

The ability to manage with limited linguistic means
Children often play with language and try to extend their often very limited linguistic options by transferring what they have learned to other contexts and through new creations. Often, for example, L1 words are spoken with an English accent if a child cannot find the right word in English. Observing this gives the teacher insight into important processes in the learning of languages.

The ability to learn indirectly
Primary school children are not very interested in grammatical structures, the system of pronunciation or other formal aspects of language. They are fascinated by a story and try to understand it. They gain pleasure from the sound of new words that the teacher introduces and love copying them. They enjoy chants and songs and enthusiastically do the actions to them when they speak or sing. They want to find the answer in a guessing game and eagerly use the structure that the teacher has introduced when they do this. They act out scenes from a story in class imitating the voices of the characters that they are playing so well that their pronunciation comes very close to the models that they have previously heard on the DVD or CD. In all these cases, and in many others, the children are unconsciously learning important linguistic skills. Here language is not an end in itself but a natural means of reaching communicative goals.

The ability to learn through fantasy and imagination
Children know that role play is a game. At the same time they identify so strongly with the story that it is as if it were actually real. The boundary between make-believe and reality is blurred. Children can better make the foreign language their own in such situations. In this way, the foreignness of the new language is gradually diminished.

The ability to interact and to speak
Children have a natural need to communicate with each other and to adults. This may not always be easy, especially when teachers or parents want to encourage them to listen. However communication is also an important basic skill on which the ability to interact in a foreign language can be built.

Learning languages as a holistic process

Language is communication. By using language we can understand others and make ourselves understood. For many adults learning a foreign language, the conscious explanation of its formal aspects is important. They want to understand how the language works and what rules it follows; they want to know, for example, how different verb tenses are formed and how they are used and try to use their cognitive knowledge about language as an aid to learning a foreign language systematically. Children learn a foreign language in a different way. They pick it up as a holistic process. The **development of listening comprehension** forms one of the important bases of this process. Children learn to understand what they hear, speculating at first about what it might mean. In this process, mime and gesture, realia and other visual aids such as pictures and drawings on the board play an important part in assisting comprehension. Thus, from the beginning, the children can understand the teacher's request to *Stand up.* because the teacher stands up the first time the phrase is used and asks the children to imitate through mime and gesture. When subsequently the teacher gives the same instruction time and again, the children will gradually be able to do it without any prompting. What a child assumes a phrase or question might mean is verified through constant repetition. An anxiety-free atmosphere and a pleasant learning environment are created by praising children for having correctly understood and by patiently helping them when they have misunderstood.

The content of what the children are offered in the new language is of crucial importance in motivating them to work out the meaning of what they hear. If this content is meaningful, interesting, exciting or funny they will be more motivated to try to understand. The pleasure in their ability to understand, for example, a story in the foreign language, increases their self-esteem and heightens their **motivation to learn**.

The same is true for **developing speaking skills**. Songs, rhymes and chants give children the opportunity to gain experience with pronunciation and intonation, through play and without anxiety. The children also practise and repeat important words and expressions in ways that are fun and subconsciously store them in their memories. Stories (cartoon stories and Mr Matt sketches) are as valuable an aid in the development of speaking skills when learning a foreign language as they are in the acquisition of the mother tongue. The children memorise important expressions. They learn to understand connections and they can try out simple utterances in communicative contexts in the role plays.

The SMILE approach®

In developing the **SMILE approach**® we were guided by the following basic principles which are based on accepted findings in research in the psychology of learning:

➤ **Skill-oriented learning**
M
I
L
E

Recent findings in the psychology of learning clearly show that the development of foreign-language skills does not take place independently of general cognitive development. For example, when children are engaged in deciphering the meaning of a sentence that they have heard spoken by the teacher they draw on abilities that they also need for handling tasks in other areas of life. These abilities include solving problems, establishing causal relationships, drawing conclusions based on analogy, etc. For this reason it makes sense to integrate early foreign-language learning into the curriculum as far as possible. This is congruent with the learning style of children of this age group which is still very holistic. Integrating the foreign-language lesson and the curriculum in this way develops the child's general intellectual skills and they promote each other reciprocally.

S
➤ **Multi-sensory learner motivation**
I
L
E

You need only watch children at play to understand the significance of learning through all the senses. *Playway to English 1 Second edition* aims to constantly activate all the senses as far as possible. This is based on the following concepts of the psychology of learning:

- When our pupils take in information, they do so through the senses: they learn what they see, hear and do.
- The auditory reception of information correlates with the so-called left side of the brain activities. Processing information kinaesthetically – by concrete activity is closely connected to the processing part that is often attributed to the right side of the brain. The visual reception of information can be controlled by either the left or the right side of the brain.
- The better the individual senses are integrated into the presentation of information stage the better the children's reception of the information (multi-sensory reception).
- The reception of information activates the neurological systems (visual, auditory, kinaesthetic) in the processing of information when thinking and remembering. During these processes a multi-sensory activation of the brain heightens children's ability to pay attention and concentrate and to store linguistic information in their long-term memories.
- The fact that most children have different learning styles and have a preference for one sensory channel over another (and can therefore also have weaknesses in one or two sensory channels) underlines the importance of a teaching methodology that takes account of the differing sensory needs of different learners and aims to strike a balance between visual, auditory and kinaesthetic presentation, processing and practice of linguistic information.
- Children love stories (narrative texts) and humorous sketches (dialogues). These stories and sketches remain firmly in the memory when presented in an appropriate multi-sensory way. Words, parts of sentences and sentences (chunks of language) can thus be fixed in the long-term memory.

S
M
➤ **Intelligence-building activities**
L
E

'Intelligence' is a collective term that covers a range of different human abilities which are all independent of each other. Researchers into intelligence speak of a multiplicity of 'intelligences'.
Howard Gardner, for example, claims that there are seven different areas of intelligence, i.e. 'multiple intelligences'.[3] Modern research into intelligence also clearly indicates that intelligence is not a gift with which human beings are born and which then stays with them for the rest of their lives in the form of a higher or lower IQ (intelligent quotient). Even though the inherited element is not inconsiderable, intelligence is quite clearly influenced by the learning process. Simply put, it can be said that intelligence can be learned. Learning a foreign language at an early age helps develop and stimulate a child's intelligence in a number of ways. All the intelligences named by Howard Gardner are stimulated by the **SMILE** approach:

Area of intelligence	Activation in *Playway to English 1 Second edition* by:
Linguistic intelligence	• Systematically developing the ability to decode the meaning of a foreign language through a great variety of different kinds of text. • Developing the child's hearing of phonemes by exercises in phonetic and articulatory differentiation. • Promoting the pleasure in playing with language. • Promoting unconscious discovery of laws of language. • Offering associative aids to noting vocabulary and phrases.

---

[3] Gardner, H, (1983) *Frames of Mind: the Theory of Multiple Intelligences.* Basic Books.

Area of intelligence	Activation in *Playway to English 1 Second edition* by:
Musical intelligence	• Promoting the ability to differentiate rhythm through chants and rhymes. • Promoting the ability to differentiate tunes through songs.
Interpersonal intelligence	• Developing basic social skills as an intrinsic principle: learning to listen to each other, tolerance of language errors, patience, etc. • Promoting empathy through role play. • Promoting the ability to work in pairs by cooperative tasks.
Kinaesthetic intelligence	• Using the whole body when working on the language through action stories, songs and action games. • Developing fine motor skills through various types of activities: picture stickers, drawing, colouring and craft activities.
Visuospatial intelligence	• Developing visuospatial perception through picture searches (discovery pictures). • Promoting the visual memory through picture puzzles.
Mathematical-logical intelligence	• Developing mathematical-logical intelligence through exercises where the children sort and match. • Encouraging logical perception through logical sequences and activities requiring putting things in order.
Intrapersonal intelligence	• Encouraging the ability to reflect as a basis for one's own speaking.

S
M
I
E
➢ **Long-term memory storage through music, movement, rhythm and rhyme**

It is well known that adults can remember rhymes and songs they learned in the earliest stages of childhood. The reason these songs are so well retained is because children learn them using actions and movement. The ability to grasp and carry out rhythmic structuring can almost be seen as an expression of the level of language development of a child. The central function of the rhythmic differentiation ability for the unity of the perception and understanding of language is important for the storage of word and writing content and also of sentence patterns.'

S
M
I
L
➢ **Exciting sketches, stories and games**

When learning, motivation is highly dependent on whether the learners identify with what they are learning. When children can identify closely with what has been learned it leads to them remembering it better. They remember phrases, parts of sentences and often whole sentences (so-called chunks of language) holistically. Good foreign-language learners are characterised by the fact that they can repeatedly transfer such chunks of language to other contexts and thus so to speak practise and consolidate the foreign language through play. A learner who identifies with a foreign language makes this foreign language more easily 'their own'. This reduces the 'foreignness' of the foreign language. This principle also plays an important role in the acquisition of good pronunciation. Role plays are a natural component of a child's everyday life. In role play children develop their identity. Identifying with the foreign language and with foreign-language roles and characters in role play in the class helps build up a good pronunciation and intonation.

Learning a language through play is more than just fun and games

'That is by no means to say that learning too must be through play in all these cases. It can also remain associated with effort even during a game...'.[4] Early foreign-language learning is anything but laborious swotting of vocabulary, difficult puzzling over structures or anxiety-ridden battling with correctness of language. Foreign-language learning should not have negative connotations at any age – and yet for some adults it has those associations. *Playway to English 1 Second edition* makes it possible for children to enjoy foreign-language learning from the very beginning by involving them in games, songs, chants, role plays, puzzles and craft activities. For children these activities are fun, and yet they are involved in serious learning as they are doing them. Because of the many elements of play, children seem to completely forget that they are learning. They are so fascinated by the stories, role plays, songs and activities that they seem to take in the language effortlessly and remember it well. The children often cannot wait to be allowed to recite a rhyme or a short dialogue in a role play in front of the class.

The importance of constant revision

Revision is vital for learning a foreign language. This is clearly established in the psychology of learning. The acquisition of a foreign language makes it necessary to acquire a whole range of complex skills that can be summed up, in terms of cognitive psychology, under the heading of *procedural knowledge*. This is a multitude of intertwining cognitive process skills acquired as a complex whole and cannot be compared with the simple learning of facts (declarative knowledge). One of the essential prerequisites for establishing procedural knowledge is that its acquisition requires significantly more time and is stimulated by constant regular practice over a long period of time. Like driving a car, procedural knowledge is established by regular revision.[5] Therefore it is beneficial to revise with the children repeatedly in very short bursts during the lesson. This can be very enjoyable for them; it becomes a demonstration of their own capabilities and thus an essential confirmation of their learning success. It shows you and the children how the foreign language grows and gradually moves into the 'possession' of the children. The applause of the class community and praise from the teacher are not only an outward sign of progress made; they also strengthen the children's self-confidence and increase their motivation.

Playway to English 1 Second edition offers you numerous options for revision:
- Revising the songs and chants regularly.
- Revising the rhymes and also having them recited by individual children.
- Carrying out regular vocabulary revision with the aid of the flashcards.
- Using the DVD or story cards to revise the stories.
- Having the children perform role plays of the stories that lend themselves to it.

Classroom management

The teacher's tasks

In the process of teaching English the teacher has a number of different tasks:
- Conveying linguistic input (in part with the aid of media) and checking that this input has been understood.
- Using the mother tongue (L1) in small doses.
- Establishing routines.
- Encouraging the children to express themselves in the foreign language.
- Reacting to the children's errors in a methodologically correct way.
- Encouraging the children to learn independently.
- Adapting the seating arrangement to suit the type of activity.

Checking comprehension

When we learn a foreign language we are constantly exposing ourselves to the risk of not understanding everything that we hear or see. We try to understand messages holistically and work out what is not understood from the context. In class, the teacher tries to help the children understand as much as possible by conveying the information through different sensory channels (auditory, visual and motor). Watching children when they are performing tasks gives the teacher clues as to how much they have understood. Three patterns of behaviour frequently observed among teachers checking comprehension are **counterproductive**.
These are:
- Constantly translating individual words. This makes the children feel that they can only understand the foreign language when they know every single word. For example, when you teach the sentences in the action story in Unit 8 (*Health*), *Get out of bed.*, *Wash your face.*, etc. ... you teach the children to understand the sentences as an integral whole. Translating individual words would be absurd and would hinder the learning process. In contrast, translation in the following case is appropriate. The teacher says: *Touch the pencil.*, etc. to establish whether the children have mastered the English terms for school items. A child hits every object named. At this point the teacher cannot distinguish whether the child is displaying aggressive behaviour, wants attention or has not understood. The teacher goes to the child and says *Touch the book.* S/he gives the L1 equivalent for *touch* and shows the child the action once again.

---

[4] Hans Scheuerl, (1990) Das Spiel [*Play*], Volume 1, Beltz, p. 176.

[5] cf. J. R. Anderson, (1983) *The Architecture of Cognition*, Harvard, University Press.

- The question *Do you understand?* is in most cases counterproductive. Children prefer to say yes to a question rather than go into explaining what they have not understood. It is much more useful to maintain eye contact and watch closely how the children behave and this will enable you to determine whether further aids to comprehension are needed.
- The following pattern of behaviour can frequently be observed during lessons. The teacher gives an instruction in English and then translates it into the L1. The reason for this may be that the teacher is unsure whether or not the children really understand the instruction in English. As soon as the children realise that each instruction is also given in L1, they hardly bother to listen to the English instruction any more. It is therefore recommended that you speak in short sentences, give the children time to think, repeat the instructions patiently and help by using mimes and gestures or, in some cases, support the instructions by drawing on the board or using pictures.

The role of the mother tongue (L1)

In the first months of the children's contact with the foreign language, giving explanations, instructions etc. in the child's first language cannot be avoided. The aim, however, over the course of the school year is to increase the use of the foreign language in conducting the classroom activities. By constantly using classroom phrases it is easy to gradually move over to the foreign language for regular routines. So the children very soon react, e.g. to the request *Let's do an action story.*, by standing up and putting their chairs away to make room for the actions, and to the request *Now work in pairs.*, by moving closer together.

Although the aim is to reduce the use of the mother tongue, there are always situations where it is necessary to translate single words or phrases because they cannot be represented by gestures, pictures, realia, etc. It is unavoidable to explain, for example, the phrase *Let's ...* in *Let's make a ...* with a mother tongue equivalent when it first comes up. *Let's ...* cannot be represented with gestures, pictures, realia etc., and the children must be prevented from coming up with their own interpretation. In contrast, when introducing the word book it is pointless to add a translation in addition to showing an actual book. The meaning is made clear by the object. To sum up, the following ground rule should determine the use of the mother tongue. Use as much English as possible and only as much of the mother tongue as is absolutely necessary.

An observation on the children's names

In primary schools there is a tradition of giving the children English names in the English lesson. **Two arguments** for this are usually given:
- Children like to slip into another role.
- When the teacher says for example *Gerd, can you help me, please.*, the articulatory basis is the native language – the child's name – and the teacher then switches into English with the next word.

We are inclined to support the following counterarguments in favour of retaining the child's own name:
- Playing a part in a role play means that a child takes on the identity of a character for the duration of the game. However, Klara becomes Sue in the English lesson, she does not take on another identity. Only the name is changed. The child stays the same person despite the fact that she has been given or has assumed another name.
- The children – and sometimes also the teacher – keep forgetting the English names of their classmates. This leads to confusion in group work and when working with a partner.
- If children are to learn to communicate in the foreign language, then this also means that they should state their own feelings, state of health, preferences etc. When, for example, the teacher encourages Sue (who is actually called Klara), to name her favourite food, Klara talks about herself. Sue's identity is not present.
- If Klara meets another child in the holidays and this child can only communicate in English, if she is asked her name she will answer Klara and not Sue.

Routines

English lessons involve constantly changing classroom scenarios. The children watch and listen to a story and show that they have understood it by putting pictures in order. They learn a song. They practise and revise a rhyme that they already know well. They ask each other for words in pair work, etc.

Alongside these changing scenarios, other processes are constantly taking place at the socio-emotional level. One child is being disruptive, another is trying to get the teacher's attention, a third is explaining an exercise to their partner, another is looking for their pencil or borrowing a rubber, etc.

The teacher tries to guide these processes verbally and non-verbally. The important thing is that the teacher begins to develop routines around all these complex processes using English to an ever-increasing degree.

CLASSROOM LANGUAGE

General instructions:
Let's start.
Listen.
Stand up.
Sit down.
Can you come here?
Can you come to the front?
Show me a/the ... .
Bring me a/the ... .
Give me a/the ... .
Put it here/there.
Open/close the door/window ... .
Stop now.
Pay attention.
Stop eating.
Put it in the bin.

Working with vocabulary:
Say the word.
All together.
Say it after/with me.
Say it again.
Now in groups.

Working with the Pupil's Book:
Look at the picture/pictures.
Write the numbers.
Work in/get into pairs.
Colour the ... .
Open your books (at page) ... .

Working with Songs, Rhymes und Chants:
Sing along.

Giving praise:
Great!
Well done.
Yes, that's right.
What a lovely drawing!
Good./Very good.

Language the children use:
Good morning.
Goodbye.
Hello.
Can I have the (scissors)?
I don't know.
I don't understand.
Can I go to the toilet?
Check, please.
It's my turn.
Sorry!
Thank you.
I can't find my ... .
I haven't got ... .
What's ... in English?

Dealing with linguistic errors

What errors do children make when acquiring a foreign language? Basically, we differentiate between errors that occur in understanding and errors in reproduction or production of language. The errors that can be made at the reproduction stage or in the production of language occur at the levels of pronunciation and intonation, vocabulary and grammar. Three examples may illustrate this:

- In a role play one child says to the other *Go away*. During the performance several children do not succeed in pronouncing the [w] in *away* correctly. The teacher does not interrupt the role play. Even after the role play she does not dwell on the fact that three particular children have made this pronunciation mistake but she practises the [w] with the whole class with other words they already know and points out the exact position of the mouth. It would be naïve to assume that this compensatory practice would have the effect of clearing up problems with the [w] once and for all. The correct pronunciation of sounds and sound combinations, and also the intonation are the result of long practice. Adequate opportunities to hear English in motivating situations, the teacher's good example and short activities that are carried out again and again help the learners to improve their pronunciation and intonation.
- While performing a mini-dialogue a child says: *Here.* instead of *Here you are.* The teacher does not interrupt but practises the phrase again before other pairs present the dialogue.
- When working out a puzzle a child says: *Four cat.* The teacher repeats: *Right, four cats.* Unlike during a role play, a rhyme or chant where it would be disruptive for the teacher to interrupt the course of the lesson, in this example they acknowledge the correct content of the child's utterance positively and adds the linguistic correction.

Making mistakes is unavoidable when trying to make progress in a foreign language. For this reason, when the teacher corrects the child the tone and context must be clearly helpful so that the child perceives it as such. Correcting in a negative way is counterproductive. The result is that the children no longer dare to speak. Mistakes that occur during activities with the objective of producing correct language (drills, etc.) are corrected immediately. The teacher does not make corrections during role plays and other situations where the children are trying to be linguistically creative. The teacher will show interest in what the child is communicating.

Should certain errors occur repeatedly in these stages then the teacher should consider what activities could be effective in improving the linguistic accuracy as a follow-up.

Learning to learn

Learning to learn can, in its initial stages, start to be developed in the first year of primary school. The aim is for children to gradually gain slight awareness of how they understand what is presented to them, what helps them remember words, phrases and texts and whether or not the pace of the lesson is appropriate for them. In order to achieve this aim, it is important to talk with the children about goals and about their own learning. That does not mean that the teacher takes the position of knowing everything, but that the aim is to take on board what the children say and talk about and what is particularly helpful or hinders their learning progress.

The seating arrangement

Although it is unrealistic to expect the tables in the classroom to be moved round for short periods of English teaching, the following points should, if possible, be considered with respect to the seating arrangement:
- Tables and chairs should be arranged in such a way that the children have enough room in their places to be able to move.
- Ideally there should be space in the classroom to allow the performance of role plays.
- All children should have a clear view of the board.
- If a DVD player is used, the children should have the possibility of being able to sit on the floor in front of the 'stage' like a puppet show.

The role of the parents

In general, the parents of primary school children have a very positive attitude towards the early learning of a foreign language and also want to actively support their children's language development.

It is recommended that at a parents' evening the following points are made:
- The children's early experiences of learning the foreign language should be positive ones. Through these experiences they gain self-esteem and motivation and lose their shyness about expressing themselves in a foreign language.
- Parents should not expect their children to be able to speak English right from the start. Children should first learn to understand linguistic utterances and later be able to respond orally in simple language.
- Using *Playway to English 1 Second edition* in foreign-language lessons will develop the children's intellectual, social, emotional and motor skills.
- Learning a foreign language at an early age stimulates an open-minded attitude towards other people and cultures.
- Point out that it is very important to praise children for the slightest progress in learning. If a child comes home and says *'Today we learned 'yes' and 'no'.'*, they should receive recognition for it.
- If children would like to show what they can do at home, parents should listen patiently and show interest. Errors are a sign of progress in learning. It is quite normal for children to make a lot of errors at the beginning.

- Parents should not ask their children to translate an English sentence into their mother tongue. The children learn the foreign language holistically. They may be able to understand the content of many sentences and phrases but not be able to translate them into the mother tongue.
- Parents should not be disappointed if their child cannot yet say something that has been learned. Some children start talking earlier than others. Parents can support their children in learning English with *Playway to English 1 Second edition* in the following way:
  - Rhymes, songs and chants can be revised. The pictures in the Pupil's Book can be used for support.
  - Parents can play at 'school' with their children and take on the role of the pupil. Children take great pleasure in teaching their parents in the foreign language. On the following page you will find a photocopiable master for an OHP slide that explains foreign-language learning with *Playway to English 1 Second edition* in more detail. You can use this OHP slide for parents' evenings.
  - Parents can do the exercises on the CD-ROM with their children.

Photocopiable master:

Characteristics of early foreign language learning

This is how children learn in practice:

- They grasp the meaning of new words with the aid of flashcards.

- They learn correct pronunciation by imitating English native speakers on the CD and DVD.

- They extend their vocabulary through play with the aid of targeted exercises.

- They learn to understand and carry out short action stories.

- They learn songs, rhymes and rhythmic chants.

- They watch short DVD sequences with simple storylines (cartoon stories) and humorous sketches (Mr Matt).

- They learn to perform simple dialogues/role plays in class.

- They learn to assess their learning/progress/knowledge/ vocabulary and their ability themselves by means of regular self-assessment activities.

- They also gradually learn to understand about other topics on the curriculum in the foreign language (CLIL).

II.
Lesson plans

 Unit 1
Hello

 Unit 2
School

 Units 1–2
Show what you can do

 Unit 3
Fruit

 Unit 4
Pets

 Units 3–4
Show what you can do

 Unit 5
Toys

 Unit 6
Weather

 Units 5–6
Show what you can do

 Unit 7
Party

 Unit 8
Health

 Units 7–8
Show what you can do

 Unit 9
Food

 Unit 10
Animals

 Units 9–10
Show what you can do

Playway to English

Lyrics: Gerngross/Puchta
Music: Lorenz Maierhofer
© Helbling, Rum/Innsbruck

Pictograms in the Teacher's Book:

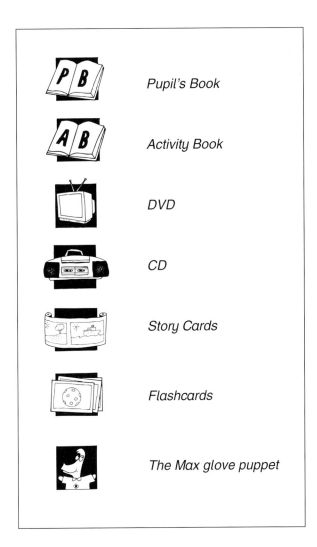

Pupil's Book

Activity Book

DVD

CD

Story Cards

Flashcards

The Max glove puppet

Teacher's Book • Playway to English 1 Second edition

L E S S O N   1

Vocabulary, phrases and structures:
Good morning; What's your name?; Hello, I'm Max/Benny/Linda/...

Linguistic skills:
Understanding a story (*I'm Max*) from the DVD and the CD.
Asking names.
Introducing oneself.

Cognitive, motor and social skills:
Completing a picture story with stickers.
Pair work: Saying a mini-dialogue.

Cross-curricular integration:
Topic: Learning how to behave in a social setting.

Materials:
DVD (*I'm Max*); *Pupil's Book*, p. 4, ex. 1; glove puppet Max; CD 1/2; picture stickers from the appendix of the *Pupil's Book*

Warm-up

- Greet the children in English:
  Hello/Good morning. I'm Mrs/Mr/Ms ... .
- Motivate the children to want to learn English by telling them all the things they can expect: songs, rhymes and funny stories.
- Give the children some time to flick through their Pupil's Books and arouse their curiosity.

Note: As a warm-up, ask the children for English words that they already know.

❶ Watch the story.
Cartoon Story: *I'm Max*

- Show the children the DVD sequence *I'm Max* twice.

DVD script: *I'm Max*

Max:	Hello.
Linda and Benny:	Hello.
Linda:	What's your name?
Max:	Aaaaaaah... M...m...m...
Benny:	Martin?
Max:	M...m...
Linda:	Mike?
Max:	M...m...m...
Benny:	Max?
Max:	Yes. Yes. I'm Max. Max. What's your name?
Benny:	I'm Benny.
Max:	And what's your name?
Linda:	I'm Linda.

❶ Listen and stick.
Listening exercise: Sticker activity CD 1/2

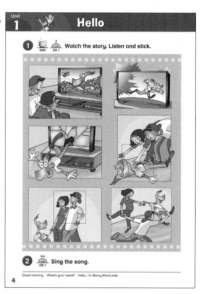

- Ask the children to find the picture stickers for this unit and show them where to look. They then look at p. 4 in their Pupil's Books.
- Play the audio version of the story twice (CD 1/2). The children follow it in the book and complete the missing scenes in the picture story with the stickers. Go around the class and check that all the pictures are in the right place.

Note: Use English as you are going up and down the aisles. Keep repeating: *Let me check. Yes. Very good/Excellent. Now stick in the pictures.*

Mini-dialogues

- Put on the glove puppet Max and change your voice to speak as Max: *Hello, I'm Max.*
- Go round the class with the puppet. Ask the children for their names and greet them. *What's your name? – Martin. – Hello, Martin.*
- Gradually the children take over the role of Max. The children take the puppet and ask other children their names.

L E S S O N 2

Vocabulary, phrases and structures:

Hello to you!
Receptive language: *Where's Linda/Benny/Max?*

Linguistic skills:

Sing a song (*What's your name?*).

Cognitive, motor and social skills:

Paying attention while speaking in unison, singing
and clapping to the right beat.
Paying attention to pauses in clapping.
Singing a song.
Looking for characters hidden in a picture.
Practising fine motor skills.

Cross-curricular integration:

Music
Art

Materials:

glove puppet Max
CD 1/3–4; *Activity Book*, p. 4, ex. 1; coloured
pencils; (optional) props for the characters Linda
and Benny in the role play

Revision

- Greet some of the children with the puppet. Then hand
the puppet to a child. She/He continues to greet others in
Max's voice: *Good morning. I'm Max. What's your name?*

❷ Sing the song.

Song: *What's your name?*
CD 1/3–4

What's your name?

Lyrics: Gerngross/Puchta
Music: Lorenz Maierhofer
© Helbling, Rum/Innsbruck

- Play the song (CD 1/3) and sing along yourself.
- Read the words out slowly several times and have the
children speak along.
- Play the song again and clap three times after the
second *What's your name?* Ask the children to clap
along. Say: *Come on. Clap your hands.*
- Sing the song with the children using the karaoke version
(CD 1/4).
- Cast three children in the parts of Benny, Linda and Max.
They either say or sing the line: *I'm Linda/Benny/Max.*
- Choose three children and have Max ask their names:
What's your name? – I'm Peter. If necessary, whisper
cues to help them.
- Sing and clap the verses along with all the children as
the three children with roles sing or recite their parts on
their own.

Option: Give the children who are playing Benny, Linda and Max
a prop each to distinguish their character, e.g. a cap for
Benny and a T-shirt for Linda. Max is played by the glove
puppet.

❶ Look and say. Colour Linda, Benny and Max.

Discovery picture

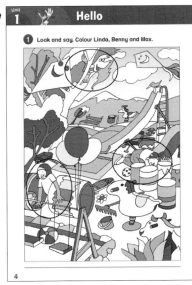

- Ask the children to open their Activity Books at p. 4.
- Tell the children to find where Linda, Benny and Max are
hidden in the picture. Give the children sufficient time for
this step.
- If the children cannot find Linda, Benny and Max,
suggest that they look at the picture from different
angles. Show them the best way to do this.
- When the children have found the characters, ask them:
Where's Linda/Benny/Max? Get the children to hold up
their books and point at the spot where Benny is hidden.
Prompt them to say: *Here.*
- The children colour the characters in the picture.

L E S S O N 3

Vocabulary, phrases and structures:

one; two; three; four; right; left
Receptive language: *stand up; stretch; shout: 'Hooray!'; sit down*

Linguistic skills:

Understanding and naming the numbers one to four.
Understanding and naming quantities of one to four.
Counting rhythmic sequences of numbers.
Understanding instructions in an Action Story (*Stand up*).
Understanding instructions on the CD and matching with the pictures in the book.

Cognitive, motor and social skills:

Counting.
Counting rhythmically.
Pair work: Practising the numbers.
Matching instructions with actions.
Understanding and carrying out jumbled instructions.

Understanding instructions on the CD and numbering pictures in the correct order.
Understanding instructions on the CD and ticking the corresponding pictures in the book.

Cross-curricular integration:

Music
Mathematics: Numbers one to four
Sport

Materials:

CD 1/4
Tambourine; *Flashcards* 1–4; CD 1/5; *Pupil's Book*, p. 5, ex. 3; (optional) answer key for self-checking; CD 1/6; *Activity Book*, p. 5, ex. 2

Revision

- Play the karaoke version (CD 1/4) and sing the song *What's your name?* together with the children.

Introduction of vocabulary

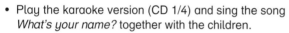

one, two, three, four

- Introduce the numbers one to four by counting them on your fingers. Show the flashcards with the numbers and elicit the language from the children. Repeat this several times and stick the flashcards on the board.
- Say a number. The children show the corresponding number on their fingers.
- Now say, e.g.: *Show me the number two.* A child comes out and points to the corresponding flashcard.

Pronunciation tip: For the pronunciation of the [θ] in *three* the children should have the tip of their tongue between their teeth. Avoid saying an [s].

Exercises for anchoring words in the children's productive memory

- Speaking rhythmically: Count from one to four on your fingers and say the words at the same time.
- The children count aloud with you.
- Say the following sequence four times, one after the other, stressing the next higher number each time:
  One, two, three, four
  One, **two**, three, four
  One, two, **three**, four
  One, two, three, **four**
- Say the number sequence again. This time the children clap their hands during the counting. They clap louder on the number stressed.
- Show a number of fingers (one to four) and the children say the correct number.

Pair work:

- Child A shows a quantity and child B says the number.
- Child A touches child B's back with a number of fingers (one to four) and child B tries to guess the correct number of fingers.

In the gymnasium: Circulate among the children to the rhythm of the tambourine. Stop suddenly and shout out a number between one and four. The children should get together in groups of two, three or four or stand on their own. Then take up the rhythm again with the tambourine.

Action Story: *Stand up*

Listen and imitate

- Ask the children to stand in a circle or stand up in their places.
- Give the first instruction and at the same time demonstrate through mime/gesture. Say: *Stand up.* Stand up at the same time. The children imitate your action.
- Say: *Stretch.* – Stretch.
- Say: *Shout 'Hooray!'* – Shout 'Hooray!'.
- Say: *Sit down.* – Sit down.
- Keep repeating this until you see that the children have a good grasp of the instructions and the actions that go with them.

Note: Tell the children that they do not need to repeat your instructions. However, if the children cannot stop themselves repeating, let them.

Carrying out instructions

- Tell the children that you are now going to give the same instructions but **not** carry them out yourself. Give the same instructions as above in the same order. Say: *Stand up.* The children do the action. Do **not** do any of the actions yourself but give positive feedback (e.g. by nodding your head) when the children carry out the instruction correctly.
- Continue with the rest of the instructions in the same way.
- Keep repeating this until you see that the children can carry out the instructions without difficulty. Gradually increase the tempo.

Carrying out the instructions in a different order

- Say that you are going to give the instructions jumbled up and the children are to carry them out. Do **not** do any of the actions yourself.
- Now give the instructions as above but in random order. Say, e.g.: *Shout 'Hooray!'./Stand up./…*
- Keep repeating this until you see that the children can carry out the instructions without difficulty.
- Call on individual children and give each of them one of the instructions to carry out, in any order.

❸ **Listen and point.**
  Write the numbers.

Action Story: *Stand up* **CD 1/5**

Tapescript:

| Stand up. | Shout 'Hooray!'. |
| Stretch. | Sit down. |

- The children open their Pupil's Books at p. 5. The four pictures are printed in random order. Give the children sufficient time to look at the pictures.
- Play the Action Story (CD 1/5). The children point to the appropriate pictures.
- Tell the children to put the pictures in the correct order by numbering them. Number 1 is already done.

- Now play the Action Story again. The children look for the corresponding picture and number the pictures in order.
- Go around the class and check the children's work.

Option: In high-ability classes you can put out a completed Action Story for self-checking. The children go and check their own work themselves.

Alternative: Draw four boxes on the board that represent the page in the Pupil's Book. Ask the children to call out the answers. Write the numbers in the boxes.

❷ **Listen and tick (✓).**
Listening exercise CD 1/6

- Ask the children to look at the first pair of pictures on p. 5 in the Activity Book. Say: *One. Stand up. Sit down.* Repeat two or three times and get the children to point at the corresponding pictures. Proceed with the other pairs in the same way: *Two. Stretch. Shout 'Hooray!'., Three. Sit down. Stretch., Four. Sit down. Stand up.*
- Tell the children that they are going to listen to the CD and that they should put a tick in the box of the corresponding picture of each pair.
- Play CD 1/6. The children tick the appropriate pictures in the book.

Tapescript:

One. Stand up.	Three. Stretch.
One. Stand up.	Three. Stretch.
Two. Shout 'Hooray!'	Four. Sit down.
Two. Shout 'Hooray!'	Four. Sit down.

- The children listen again and check.
- Draw a grid on the board.
  1 ☐ ☐
  2 ☐ ☐
  3 ☐ ☐
  4 ☐ ☐
- Say the words: *left/right* several times. Ask the children to repeat and point at the appropriate side.
- Ask the children: *Number one. Left or right?* Point to each box. Look at them questioningly and prompt them to give you the right answer.

LESSON 4

Vocabulary, phrases and structures:

Vocabulary revision: numbers one to four
What is it?; Yes; No; Give me red/yellow/green/ blue/black/white; Here you are; Yeah, all right.

Linguistic skills:

Learning the meaning and pronunciation of the new words.
Understanding new words (colours) from the CD.
Naming colours.

Chanting rhythmically in unison and individually with the support of pictures (*Give me red*).

Cross-curricular integration:

Music

Materials:

Flashcards 1–4
Flashcards 5–10; coloured pencils; glove puppet Max; *Pupil's Book*, p. 6, ex. 4; CD 1/7–8

Revision

- Give the instructions from the Action Story (*Stand up*) from the previous lesson.
- Revise the numbers one to four with the flashcards.

Introduction of vocabulary

red; yellow; green; blue; black; white

- Introduce the colours with the help of the flashcards. Show the flashcards in order and repeat the word several times. Have the children repeat it after you.
- Stick the flashcards on the board. Point to the flashcards in any order and have the children name the corresponding colour.

Exercises for anchoring the vocabulary in the recognition memory

- Say the colours in any order. Ask the children individually to point to the corresponding colour on the board, e.g.: *Peter, come out. Point to red.*
- Ask the children to hold up pencils of the corresponding colours: *red, yellow, ...*

Exercises for anchoring words in the children's productive memory

- Ask the children to close their eyes. Say the colours. First the children just listen. Then say each word individually and change your voice: loud, quiet, high, deep, happy, sad or angry. The children repeat the word exactly as you say it.

Comment: By turning off the visual channel the child can concentrate completely on the sound pattern. Accurate listening and imitating of different sound qualities is good training for listening and sound. It supports the memorizing of the pronunciation in the long-term memory.

- Hold a flashcard in your hand with the reverse side to the children and ask: *What colour is it?*
- The children guess what colour it is: *Red? – No.– Blue? – Yes.*
- When a child has guessed correctly, show the flashcard.

Option: Use the glove puppet. One child takes the glove puppet, points to a face-down flashcard and asks: *What colour is it?*

Pronunciation tip: Pay attention to the pronunciation of **b**lue [b]. The [r] in *red* and *green* needs particular practice. The children learn the pronunciation primarily through imitation.

❹ **Listen and point. Say the chant.**
Chant: *Give me red* **CD 1/7–8**

Tapescript:

Give me red.	*Give me blue.*
Here you are.	*Here you are.*
Give me yellow.	*Give me black.*
Here you are.	*Here you are.*
Give me green.	*Give me white.*
Here you are.	*Yeah, all right.*

- The children open their Pupil's Books at p. 6 and look at the pictures.
- Play the chant (CD 1/7). Point to the pictures so that all the children can see. Then play the chant again. Now the children point to the appropriate pictures in the book.

- Practise the chant with the children in sections by saying it out loud and making the appropriate gestures. The children imitate your actions and say it after you. Use the corresponding flashcards (*red, yellow, green, blue, black, white*) as visual support.
- Play the first part of the recording (*And now you!* CD 1/8) several times and say the chant with the children. The children point to the corresponding pictures in the book as they say the chant.

- Play the karaoke version of the chant (*One more time!* CD 1/8). The children look at the words in the Pupil's Book and chant rhythmically.
- Divide the class into two groups, A and B. One group is lead by you, one group by the glove puppet. The pictures in the book act as support.
- Ask the groups to stand in two rows. Each pair, **A** and **B** face each other and recite the chant:
  A: Give me red.
  B: Here you are.
  A: Give me....

L E S S O N 5

Vocabulary, phrases and structures:

Vocabulary revision: Numbers one to four; colours
brown

Linguistic skills:

Learning the meaning and pronunciation of the new word.
Understanding colours from the CD.
Naming colours.

Cognitive, motor and social skills:

Understanding numbers and colours from the CD and pointing along in the book.
Pair work: Playing a vocabulary game.

Cross-curricular integration:

Mathematics: Number range one to four

Materials:

CD 1/8; *Flashcards* 1–10
Flashcard 11; CD 1/9; *Pupil's Book*, p. 7, ex. 5–6

Revision

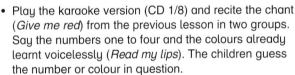

- Play the karaoke version (CD 1/8) and recite the chant (*Give me red*) from the previous lesson in two groups. Say the numbers one to four and the colours already learnt voicelessly (*Read my lips*). The children guess the number or colour in question.
- Hand out the flashcards to individual children. Name a colour or number and the child with the corresponding flashcard comes out and sticks it on the board.
- Start a clapping rhythm, e.g.: xx xxx and the children follow it.
- Call out ten children. They say the number words and colours out loud in the order that they are on the board. After each word the other children clap in the practised rhythm, e.g.:
  blue xx xxx
  three xx xxx
  yellow xx xxx
  etc.

Vocabulary extension

brown

- Introduce the colour brown with the aid of the flashcard. Make sure the children have the opportunity to repeat the word several times.

❺ Listen and point.

Listening exercise CD 1/9

- The children open their Pupil's Book at p. 7 and look at ex. 5.
- Hold up your book and point to a colour. The children say the corresponding word.
- Play the listening exercise twice (CD 1/9). The children listen and point to the corresponding colours in the book.

Tapescript:

blue	white
red	black
green	brown
yellow	

❻ Look and say.
Vocabulary game: Pair work

- Demonstrate the pair work (Pupil's Book, p. 7 ex. 6) with a child.
- Point to a colour in ex. 5. The child says the corresponding word. Then have the child point to a colour in the book and you name the word.
- The children work in pairs. Child A points to a colour and child B names it. Then they swap roles.
- During this exercise go around the class and help if necessary.

L E S S O N   6

Vocabulary, phrases and structures:
Vocabulary revision: colours
Give me yellow; Here you are; please; thank you

Linguistic skills:
Understanding dialogues from the CD.

Cognitive, motor and social skills:
Understanding dialogues from the CD and colouring pictures accordingly.
Pair work: Mini-dialogues.

Cross-curricular integration:
General knowledge: Motivation to speak 'Being polite and helpful'.
Art

Materials:
Flashcards 5–11
coloured pencils; CD 1/10; *Activity Book*, p. 6, ex. 3–4; glove puppet Max

Revision
- Hand out the flashcards to individual children. Name a colour and the child with the corresponding flashcard comes out and sticks it on the board.
- Make sure each child has their set of the following coloured pencils on their desk: yellow, blue, black and green.
- Call out the colours one after the other and ask the children to hold up the appropriate pencils.

❸ Listen and colour.
Listening exercise CD 1/10

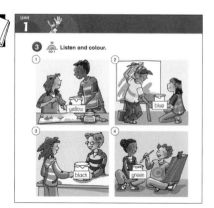

- Then they open their Activity Books on p. 6 and look at the four pictures in ex. 3. Tell the children that they are to colour in the paint cans in each of the four pictures according to what they hear on the CD.
- Play CD 1/10. First the children only listen to the CD.

Tapescript:

Speaker:	One.
Girl:	Give me yellow, please.
Boy:	Here you are.
Girl:	Thank you.

Speaker:	Two.
Boy:	Give me blue, please.
Girl:	Here you are.
Boy:	Thank you.

Speaker:	Three.
Girl:	Give me black, please.
Boy:	Here you are.
Girl:	Thank you.

Speaker:	Four.
Boy:	Give me green, please.
Girl:	Here you are.
Boy:	Thank you.

- Play the CD again. The children first of all mark the cans in the corresponding colour as they listen. They can colour them in completely after listening.
- Go around the class and help if necessary.
- The children now colour the cans.
- To check the answers ask the children, e.g.: *One. (Two/…) What colour is it?* Individual children answer: *Yellow. (Blue/…)*

❹ Say and colour.
Pair work: Mini-dialogues

- Ask the children to look at the pictures in ex. 4 on p. 6 in their Activity Books.
- Take the glove puppet. Present the dialogue while saying it with the glove puppet as dialogue partner.
  Teacher: *Give me (green), please.*
  Glove puppet: (Hands over the green pencil) *Here you are.*
  Teacher: *Thank you.* (Pretend to colour can 1 in your book green.)

- Repeat this exchange until you see that all the children have understood the dialogue.
- Max asks as many children as possible for different colours. If necessary, prompt the children quietly with: *Here you are.*
- Ask the children to do ex. 4 in their Activity Books. Child A asks: *Give me (red), please.* Child B hands over the red pencil and says: *Here you are.* Child A answers: *Thank you.* and colours in can 1 in the picture. They continue with cans 2 and 3 in the same way. Then they swap roles.
- During this exercise go around the class and help if necessary.

Note: Do not move the glove puppet when you are speaking but only when the puppet is speaking.

L E S S O N   7

Vocabulary, phrases and structures:
a red/... bike for Linda/me...; boat

Linguistic skills:
Understanding the meaning and pronunciation of the new words.
Understanding a rhyme from the CD.
Chanting rhythmically in chorus and individually with the support of pictures (*A red bike for Linda*).
Learning and reciting fluently a self-composed rhyme.

Cognitive, motor and social skills:
Speaking in the rhythm of a group.
Practising a rhyme and reciting it.
Colouring in pictures in corresponding colours and composing one's own rhyme (*word play*).
Reciting one's own rhyme.

Cross-curricular integration:
Music

Materials:
Flashcards 1–11
Flashcards 12–13; *Pupil's Book*, pp. 8–9, ex. 7–8; CD 1/11–12; coloured pencils

---

Revision

- Revise the colours and the numbers with the flashcards.

Vocabulary extension

bike

- Introduce the word *bike* with the aid of the flashcard and appropriate gestures. Show the flashcard and repeat the word several times. Have the children repeat it after you.

❼ **Listen and colour. Say.**

Rhyme: *A red bike for Linda*
CD 1/11

- The children look at p. 8 in their Pupil's Book.
- Point to the pictures of the children in turn. Say: *Linda – Li – Benny – me.* At *me* point to yourself.
- Then point to the paint pots at the bottom of the page and have individual children name the corresponding colours.
- Play the rhyme once (CD 1/11). The children point to the paint pot and the corresponding bike. Demonstrate this exercise with the first line of the rhyme.

Tapescript:

A red bike for Linda,
A green bike for Li,
A yellow bike for Benny,
A blue bike for me!

- The children have a red, green, yellow and blue pencil on the desk in front of them. Play the rhyme again. The children first mark the bikes in the corresponding colour and then colour them in completely after they have listened.
- Practise the rhyme thoroughly line by line with the children.
- The children can practise the rhyme in pairs and volunteers or individual children then recite the rhyme in front of the class.
- Able groups can also try to recite their version to the karaoke version (CD 1/12).

Introduction of vocabulary

boat

- Introduce the word *boat* with the aid of the flashcard.
- Then hold the flashcard in your left hand and take a flashcard for a colour e.g. *red* in your right hand. Say: *A red boat (for me!)* Have the children repeat it after you several times. Use the flashcards to make the sentences: *A green/yellow/blue boat for me/Max/Li...* and ask the children to say the corresponding sentences.

❽ **Colour and say.**

Speaking exercise:
Step to creativity (Word Play)

- The children look at p. 9 in their Pupil's Books.
- They have red, green, yellow and blue pencils on the desk in front of them. Tell the children that they are to colour in each boat in a different colour and thus make up their own rhyme. Give the children sufficient time for this work. While they are doing this, go around the class and watch that the children are only colouring each boat in one colour.
- Afterwards the children learn the text of the rhyme they have composed off by heart. Show the children the best way to do this. Hold up your book with coloured-in boats. Recite the rhyme and point along in the book. Then go around the class and help if necessary.
- Individual children present their rhymes to the class. Remember to give them appropriate applause (Say: *Let's give them a big hand!*).

Option: High-ability children can also recite their rhyme to the karaoke version (CD 1/12).

L E S S O N   8

Vocabulary, phrases and structures:

Boat number one is red/...
Receptive language: *What colour's boat one/boat number one?; What colour is it?*

Linguistic skills:

Understanding instructions from the CD.
Completing logical sequences.

Cognitive, motor and social skills:

Understanding instructions from the CD and colouring in pictures accordingly.
Completing logical sequences by drawing.
Creating own logical sequences and checking logical sequences with a partner.

Cross-curricular integration:

Art

Materials:

CD 1/12
CD 1/13; *Activity Book*, p. 7, ex. 5–6; coloured pencils

Revision

- Get individual children to present their rhymes from the previous lesson to the class. Remember to give them appropriate applause (Say: *Let's give them a big hand!*).

Notes: High-ability children can also recite their rhyme to the karaoke version (CD 1/12).

❺ Listen and colour.

Listening exercise CD 1/13

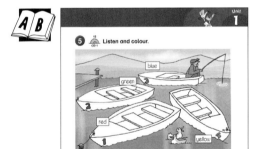

- The children have a red, a green, a yellow and a blue pencil on the desk in front of them. Name the colours one after the other and the children hold up the appropriate pencil.
- Ask the children to look at the picture in ex. 5 on p. 7 in their Activity Books. Tell the children that they are to listen to the CD and to colour the boats accordingly.
- Play CD 1/13 twice and the children first of all mark the boats in the corresponding colour and then colour them in completely after they have listened.

Tapescript:

Boat number one is red.
Boat number one is red.

Boat number two is green.
Boat number two is green.

Boat number three is blue.
Boat number three is blue.

Boat number four is yellow.
Boat number four is yellow.

- Check the answers by asking the children: *What colour's boat one/two/...* or *Boat one. What colour is it?* The children answer: *Red./Green./etc.*

❻ Look and colour. Say.

Logical sequences

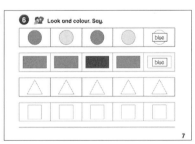

- Demonstrate this exercise by drawing a logical sequence of coloured shapes on the board, e. g. green – blue – green – blue – <blank>.
- Read out the sequence together with the children while pointing along on the board. Say: *green, blue, green, blue....* Then look at the children questioningly and elicit the missing colour: *Green.* Say: *Right.* Complete the sequence on the board.

- Ask the children to open their Activity Books at p. 7 and to look at the pictures in ex. 6.
- Hold up your book and work on the first line together with the children.
- Get them to read out the sequence with you while you point along in your book. Say: *blue, yellow, blue, yellow...* When pointing at the blank shape, look at the children questioningly and elicit the missing colour: *Blue.* The children then colour the blank circle blue.
- The children complete the next sequence of shapes individually.
- Get them to read it out to check the answers.

Pair work

- The children create their own logical sequences individually by colouring the triangles in the third row. Tell them to leave blank one or two shapes in each of the rows. Give them sufficient time for this step. Go around the class and help if necessary.
- Now they work in pairs, complete each others' rows and read out the sequences to one another.
- They then do the same with the row of squares.

L E S S O N 9

Vocabulary, phrases and structures:

Vocabulary revision: colours; *bike; boat*

Linguistic skills:

Understanding instructions from the CD and matching with the pictures in the book.

Cognitive, motor and social skills:

Understanding instructions on the CD and ticking the corresponding pictures in the book.
Practising fine motor skills by colouring shapes.

Cross-curricular integration:

Art
Mathematics: Recognising shapes.

Materials:

Flashcards 5–13
CD 1/14; *Activity Book*, pp. 8–9, ex. 7–8; coloured pencils

Revision

- Revise the words for colours, *boat* and *bike* with the flashcards.
- Play *What's missing?* with the flashcards. Put the flashcards on the board. The children close their eyes. (*Close your eyes.*) Take away one flashcard from the board. The children open their eyes. (*Open your eyes.*) Ask: *What's missing?* The children name the missing object or colour. You can also take away two flashcards at the same time.

❼ **Listen and tick (✓).**

Listening exercise CD 1/14

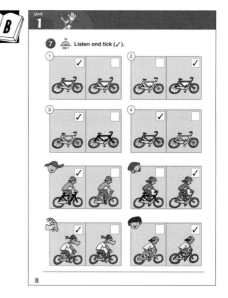

- Ask the children to look at the first pair of pictures in ex. 7 on p. 8 in their Activity Books. Then say: *A green bike./A blue bike.* and get the children to point to the corresponding picture.
- Proceed with the other pictures in the same way. Notice that instead of numbers there are pictures of Benny/Linda/Max/Li in the lower part of p. 8. Name the characters and say: *Benny. A black bike/...*, etc.
- Tell the children that they are to listen to the CD and put a tick in the box of the corresponding picture of each pair.
- Play CD 1/14. The children tick the appropriate pictures.

Tapescript:

One. A green bike.
One. A green bike.

Two. A brown bike.
Two. A brown bike.

Three. A yellow bike.
Three. A yellow bike.

Four. A red bike
Four. A red bike

Benny. A black bike.
Benny. A black bike.

Linda. A blue bike.
Linda. A blue bike.

Max. A white bike.
Max. A white bike.

Li. A red bike.
Li. A red bike.

- The children listen again and check.
- Draw a grid on the board.

  1 ☐   2 ☐
  3 ☐   4 ☐

  Benny Linda
  ☐   ☐

  Max   Li
  ☐   ☐

- Say the words: *left/right* several times. Ask the children to repeat and point at the appropriate side.
- Ask the children: *Number one. Left or right?* Point to each box. Look at them questioningly and prompt them to give you the right answer.

❽ Look and colour.
Discovery picture

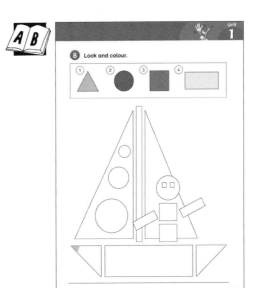

- The children open their Activity Books on p. 9 and look at the coloured shapes in ex. 8. Say the colours one after the other and the children point to the appropriate colour. Ask the children: *What colour's number one/...?* They answer: *Green./...*
- The children need red, green, yellow and blue pencils.
- Ask them to look at the shapes on the lower part of the page. Tell them that they are to use the shapes at the top as a guide and colour in the shapes accordingly.
- Demonstrate one example. Hold up your book. Point, e.g. at a triangle. Ask: *What colour is it?* Get the children to check in the row of coloured shapes above and give you the appropriate answer: *Green.*
- Give the children sufficient time to colour in all the shapes. Go around the class and help if necessary.
- To check the children's work, hold up your book again. Point at one shape after the other and the children say the correct colour.

Teacher's Book • Playway to English 1 Second edition **41**

L E S S O N   1

Vocabulary, phrases and structures:

schoolbag; pencil; pencil case; scissors; glue; book; baby face; sit down

Linguistic skills:

Learning the meaning and pronunciation of the new words.
Saying words for school items.
Understanding a chant (*Baby Face!*) from the CD.

Cognitive, motor and social skills:

Understanding new words from the CD and pointing to the corresponding pictures in the book.
Listening to a chant on the CD, pointing along in the book and chanting rhythmically in unison and individually.
Playing a quick recognition game with flashcards.
Playing a game in a group.

Cross-curricular integration:

Topic: We go to school.
Music

Materials:

Flashcards 14–19; CD 1/15–16 *Pupil's Book*, p. 10, ex.1; (optional) mask from the appendix of the *Teacher's Book* p. 171

Revision

- Revise the colours learnt in Unit 1. Say: *Point to something blue.* Get the children to point to something in the classroom that is blue. Continue with the other colours in the same way.

Introduction of vocabulary

schoolbag; pencil; pencil case; scissors; glue; book

- Show the *book* flashcard. Open an imaginary book and read it.
- Now say the word *book* several times and ask various children to imitate your gestures.
- Show the *pencil case* flashcard and say: *pencil case.* At the same time mime opening a pencil case and taking out a pencil then closing the pencil case.
- Introduce the next word – *scissors* – with the flashcard. Make cutting movements with your index and middle fingers.
- Say the word *scissors* several times and ask various children to imitate your gestures.
- Introduce the words *pencil, schoolbag* and *glue* with mimes in the same way.

Exercises for anchoring the vocabulary in the recognition memory

- Say a word, e.g.: *pencil case,* and ask a child to respond with the corresponding gesture (*Do it.*). Practise all the other words in this way.
- The children put a pencil case, glue stick/glue, scissors, a pencil and a Pupil's Book on the desk in front of them and put their schoolbag next to their chair. Say: *Touch the pencil.* Demonstrate by touching a pencil.
- Practise the other words in the same way.

Exercises for anchoring words in the children's productive memory

- Say the words noiselessly. Move your lips as if you were really saying the words (*Read my lips.*). The children read the words from your lips and say them out loud.
- Show the flashcards or the school items in quick succession. The children name the objects.

Pronunciation tip: Take care with the pronunciation of *schoolbag.* It is important that the pronunciation of the [æ] is as open as possible.

Note: Ensure that the tempo of the vocabulary work is quite brisk and is characterized by a quick change of exercises. However, every child must have sufficient time to reflect if necessary.

❶ Listen and point. Say the chant.

Chant: *Baby Face!* CD 1/15–16

- The children open their Pupil's Books at p. 10 and look at the pictures. If you decide to use the mask (see appendix p. 171 in the Teacher's Book), photocopy enough for each child to have one.
- Introduce the word *baby face* by pointing at the picture in the Pupil's Book or the mask.
- Play the chant (CD 1/15). The children listen.

Tapescript:

*Schoolbag, pencil, pencil case,
scissors, glue, book, Baby Face!
Sit down.*

- Play the chant a second time and encourage the children to point to the pictures in their books.

- Now stand in a circle. Practise the chant, reciting and accompanying your words with gestures, e.g. miming using the school objects. The children imitate your actions and join in the chant.
- Recite the chant again and, as you say each school object, move around the circle and point at each child in turn. The child named last – *Baby Face!* – holds the mask (see appendix p. 171 in the Teacher's Book) in front of his/her face or makes a baby face expression and drops out of the game. Repeat.
- Play the first part of CD 1/16 (*And now you!*) and point to the children around the circle in turn. Play the game again with the students chanting along.
- Play the karaoke section (CD 1/16). The children play the game whilst you watch and monitor. Every child that says: *Baby Face!* holds up the mask to their face or makes a baby face expression before sitting down.

L E S S O N   2

Vocabulary, phrases and structures:
Receptive language: *What has (Benny) got?*; *What have you got?*; *Put your book in your schoolbag*; *Put your pencil case in your schoolbag*; *Put your scissors in your schoolbag*; *Go to school.*

Linguistic skills:
Understanding the meaning of the new questions.
Solving a puzzle: Finding out which object belongs to whom.
Answering questions.
Understanding instructions on the CD and matching with the pictures in the book.

Cognitive, motor and social skills:
Colouring in objects and answering questions about them.
Drawing oneself and one of one's own school items in the book and giving information about it.

Matching instructions with actions.
Understanding and carrying out jumbled instructions.
Understanding instructions on the CD and numbering pictures in the correct order.

Cross-curricular integration:
Art
Sport

Materials:
Flashcards 5–11; 14–19; CD 1/16
Activity Book, p. 10, ex. 1; coloured pencils;
CD 1/17; *Activity Book*, p. 11, ex. 2; (optional) answer key for self-checking

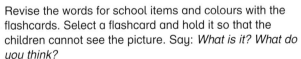

Revision
- Revise the words for school items and colours with the flashcards. Select a flashcard and hold it so that the children cannot see the picture. Say: *What is it? What do you think?*
- Stand in a circle and revise the chant *Baby face!* from the previous lesson with the karaoke section of CD 1/16.

❶ Colour and say.
Matching activity

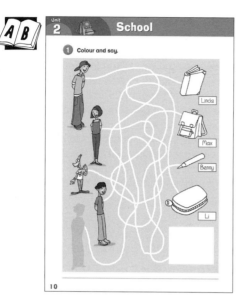

- Hold up p. 10 of your Activity Book. Say the names of the children on the left hand side of the book as you point to them in order: *Benny, Linda, Max, Li* and *me*. At *me* point to yourself and indicate to the children that they should also point to themselves. Then name and point to the school items on the right-hand side of the page.
- Say the name of one of the children from the book and one of the school items. The children point as quickly as possible to the character and the corresponding object.
- The children have coloured pencils in front of them on the desk. Explain to them that they are to colour each object on the right hand side of the Activity Book in only one colour each.
- With a coloured pencil the children then draw along each of the lines from Benny, Linda, Max, Li and the silhouette. The children use different colours for each one.
- Then ask the children individually: *What has Benny got?* Child: *A pencil.* Teacher: *What colour is it?* Child: *Green.* Help if necessary by whispering to the child.
- The children draw their own face in the silhouette and one of their school objects in the empty frame at the bottom of the page. They then colour the object in one colour.
- Ask individual children: *(Maria), what have you got?* (Maria): *A (yellow schoolbag).* etc.

Pre-teaching key phrases

Put your book in your schoolbag; Put your pencil case in your schoolbag; Put your scissors in your schoolbag; Go to school.

- Ask the children to stand in a circle or stand up in their places.
- Say the first sentence and at the same time demonstrate through mime and gesture. Say: *Put your book in your schoolbag.* Mime putting a book in a schoolbag. The children imitate your action.
- Proceed with the other phrases in the same way.

- Keep repeating this until you see that the children can mime the actions that go with the sentences without difficulty.
- Call on individual children and give each of them one of the sentences to mime.

❷ Listen and write the numbers.
Listening exercises CD 1/17

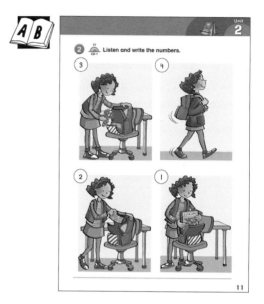

Tapescript:

Put your book in your schoolbag.
Put your pencil case in your schoolbag.
Put your scissors in your schoolbag.
Go to school.

- The children open their Activity Books at p. 11. Give them sufficient time to look at the pictures.
- Play CD 1/17 twice. The children listen and number the pictures accordingly. Number one is already done as an example.
- To check the children's work, ask: *What number is 'Go to school?'*? Child: *Four.*

Option: In high-ability classes you can put out an answer key for self-checking. On a sheet of paper draw four boxes with circles that represent the page in the Activity Book. Write the correct numbers in the circles. The children go to the key and check their own work themselves.

Alternative: Draw four boxes on the board that represent the page in the Activity Book. Have the children tell you the answers. Write the numbers in the boxes.

L E S S O N   3

Vocabulary, phrases and structures:

Vocabulary revision: School items and colours
*the pencil and the glue/...; The (glue), please;
Here you are; Thank you.*
Receptive language: *What does Benny/... want?*

Linguistic skills:

Understanding a dialogue from the CD.
Naming objects.

Cognitive, motor and social skills:

Understanding dialogues from the CD and ticking
the corresponding pictures in the book.
Sticking the picture stickers in the spaces provided.

Pair work: Playing a vocabulary game.
Following the rules of the game.
Pair work: Mini-dialogues

Cross-curricular integration:

General knowledge: Speaking motivation 'being
helpful'.

Materials:

Flashcards 5–11; 14–19
Pupil's Book, p. 11, ex. 2–3; CD 1/18; picture
stickers from the appendix of the *Pupil's Book*

Revision

- Revise the words for school items and colours with the
flashcards.
- Play *What's missing?* with the flashcards. Put the
flashcards on the board. The children close their eyes.
(*Close your eyes.*) Take away one flashcard from the
board. The children open their eyes. (*Open your eyes.*)
Ask: *What's missing?* The children name the missing
object. You can also take away two flashcards at the
same time.

❷ Listen and tick (✓).
Listening exercise CD 1/18

- Ask the children to open their Pupil's Books at p. 9.
- Point to the first pair of pictures in ex. 2 and say: *Look
at Benny and Max.* Then say: *The pencil and the glue.*
Repeat this several times. Then ask the children to point
to the pencil and glue in the three pictures of school
items next to Benny and Max.
- Proceed in the same way with the other two situations
(Linda and Max; Max and Benny).
- Explain the listening exercise to the children. They
must listen carefully and find out which objects Benny,
Linda and Max would like. In each case they tick the
corresponding picture.
- Play the recording twice (CD 1/18). The children listen
and tick the correct answers.

Tapescript:

Benny and Max.
Benny: *Max?*
Max: *Yes, Benny.*
Benny: *The pencil and the glue, please.*
Max: *The pencil and the glue.*
Benny: *Thank you.*

Linda and Max.
Linda: *Max?*
Max: *Yes, Linda.*
Linda: *The pencil case and the scissors, please.*
Max: *The pencil case and the scissors.*
Linda: *Thank you.*

Max and Benny.
Max: *Benny?*
Benny: *Yes, Max?*
Max: *The schoolbag and the book, please.*
Benny: *The schoolbag and the book.*
Max: *Thank you.*

- Check the answers by asking: *Look at Benny and
Max. What does Benny want?* Look at the children
questioningly. One child answers, e.g.: *The pencil and
the glue.* If necessary, whisper the right answer. Say:
Yes, well done. or *No, sorry.*

❸ Stick and say.
Pair work: Vocabulary game

- Ask the children to look at ex. 3 on p. 11. Name the school objects in the picture in any order. The children point to the appropriate pictures in the book.
- The children choose two picture stickers of school objects from the appendix of the Pupil's Book and stick them in the first double frame. They do the same with the two other double frames.
- Demonstrate the game with a volunteer. Name one pair of objects that you have stuck in your book, e.g.: *scissors and schoolbag.* The child must point to the corresponding picture stickers in your book.
- Swap roles and play again.
- The children play the game in pairs.

Additional task for high-ability groups: Child A names the objects and their colours that she/he has stuck in one of the double frames in his/her book, e.g.: *a blue pencil case and a green pencil.* Child B now points to the corresponding picture stickers in child A's book. Then they swap roles.

Pair work: Mini-dialogues

- Demonstrate the dialogue with a child. Give the child the school item flashcards.

  Teacher: *The glue, please.*
  Child: *Here you are.* (He/She passes you the glue flashcard.)
  Teacher: *Thank you.*

- Have the children repeat the dialogue until they are confident.
- Divide the class into pairs. The children place the school objects in front of them on the desk. Child A asks for an object (*The scissors, please*), child B hands over the object (*Here you are*). Child A says thank you. (*Thank you.*) Then they swap roles.
- During this exercise move around the class and help if necessary.

L E S S O N   4

Vocabulary, phrases and structures:

Vocabulary revision: school items, colours *orange; pink; purple; I hate it; I'm sorry.*
Receptive language: *The painting; Come on, Max!; OK; Blue and green/red/yellow; It's not good; It's very good; Oh, no!; I'm sorry; That's OK, Linda/ Benny; I hate my picture; Fantastic; Congratulations!; Thank you.*

Linguistic skills:

Understanding a story *(The painting)* from the DVD, from the CD and from narration by the teacher.
Learning the meaning and pronunciation of the new words and phrases.

Cognitive, motor and social skills:

Following the sequence of events in a story in dialogue form.
Completing a picture story with picture stickers.
Pair work: Playing a vocabulary game.

Cross-curricular integration:

Curriculum area: Speaking motivation 'Art'.

Materials:

soft ball
Flashcards 5–11; 20–22; *Story Cards* 1–9; *Pupil's Book,* pp. 12–13, ex. 4–5; DVD *(The painting)*; CD 1/19; picture stickers from the appendix of the *Pupil's Book*; (optional) completed picture story for self-checking

---

Revision

- Revise the words for school objects by throwing a soft ball to a child and saying, e.g.: *Book.* The child who catches the ball says another school object and throws the ball to another child. Also review the colours in this way.

Pre-teaching phrases

I hate it; I'm sorry.

- Make the meaning of the new phrases clear through appropriate gesture and mime.

❹ Watch the story.

Cartoon Story: *The painting*

• Show the children the DVD sequence *The painting* twice.

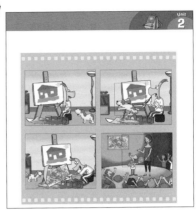

DVD script: *The painting*

Linda:	Come on, Max!
Max:	OK.
	OK. Blue and green.
	It's not good.
Linda:	It's very good, Max!
	Oh, no! I'm sorry!
Max:	That's OK, Linda.
Max:	OK. Red.
	It's not good.
Benny:	It's very good, Max!
	Oh, no! I'm sorry!
Max:	That's OK, Benny.
Max:	OK. Yellow.
	It's not good.
Dog:	Bow-wow, bow-wow!
Max:	I hate it!
	Aaaaah!
	Fantastic!
Headmistress:	Congratulations!
Max:	Oh, thank you.
Children:	Max!

• Ask the children to find the picture stickers for this unit and show them where to look. The children then look at pp. 12 and 13 of their Pupil's Books.
• Play the audio version of the story twice (CD 1/19). The children complete the missing scenes in the picture story with the picture stickers while they are listening.
• Go around the class and check the children's work.

Option: Place a completed picture story on the teacher's desk. When the children have finished, they check their work themselves.

❹ Listen and stick.

Listening exercise:
Sticker activity CD 1/19

Telling the story

• Now tell the story again with the aid of the story cards. As you are telling the story, stick the cards on the board.
• If you tell the story several times, you can gradually prompt the children to say it with you. Indicate the first picture and say, e.g.: *Come on, Max …*
• Now encourage the children by gestures to say with you: *OK …, etc.*

Note: Act as director and keep helping the children along by whispering prompts if they get stuck when speaking. In high-ability classes the story can also be performed as a role play.

Vocabulary extension

orange; pink; purple

• Revise the colours from Unit 1 and introduce the new ones with the flashcards. Get the children to repeat the new colours several times.
• Play *What's missing?* with the flashcards. (See Lesson 3 Revision.)

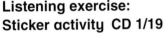

❺ Say.

Pair work: Vocabulary game

- Ask the children to open their Pupil's Books at p. 13 and look at ex. 5. Say the school things plus the corresponding colours, e.g.: *a blue book.* The children point along in the book.
- Tell the children that they have to learn the school things and their colours by heart. Give them sufficient time for this step. Then the children work in pairs. Each pair has one book.

- Demonstrate the exercise with a child in front of the class.
  Say, e.g.: *Glue.*
  Child: *Green.*
  Teacher: *Pink and white.*
  Child: *Pencil case.*
- The children work in pairs and play the game. Child A says an object *(scissors)* and child B says the corresponding colour *(red)*. Child A says a colour *(orange)*. Child B says the corresponding school object *(pencil)*, and so on.
- They swap roles and play again.
- During this exercise go around the class and help if necessary.

L E S S O N 5

Vocabulary, phrases and structures:

five; six
Receptive language: *Stand up; Close your eyes; Touch your nose; Open your eyes; Listen; Smile.*

Linguistic skills:

Understanding instructions in an Action Story (*Smile*).
Understanding instructions from the CD and matching with the pictures in the book.

Cognitive, motor and social skills:

Matching instructions with actions.
Understanding and carrying out jumbled instructions.

Understanding instructions from the CD and numbering pictures in the correct order.

Cross-curricular integration:

Sport

Materials:

DVD (*The painting*); *Pupil's Book*, pp. 12–13, ex. 4 *Flashcards* 23, 24; CD 1/20; *Pupil's Book*, p. 14, ex. 6; (optional) answer key for self-checking

Revision

- Revise the story *The painting* from the previous lesson. (DVD and pp. 12–13 in the Pupil's Book).

Vocabulary extension

five; six

- Introduce the new numbers with the flashcards.
- Count from one to six on your fingers and say the words at the same time. Repeat several times.
- The children count along with you.
- Show a number of fingers from one to six and the children say the correct number.

Action Story: *Smile*
Listen and imitate

- Ask the children to stand in a circle or stand up in their places.
- Give the following instructions and at the same time demonstrate through mime/gesture.
  Stand up.
  Close your eyes.
  Touch your nose.
  Touch your eyes.
  Open your eyes.
  Smile.
- Keep repeating this until you see that the children have a good grasp of the sentences and the actions that go with them.

Carrying out instructions

- Tell the children that you are now going to give the same instructions but **not** carry them out yourself. Now give the same instructions as above in the same order.
- Say: *Stand up.* The children carry out the action. Do **not** do any of the actions yourself but give positive feedback (e.g. by nodding your head) when the children carry out the instruction correctly. Continue the rest of the instructions in the same way.
- Keep repeating this until you see that the children can carry out the instructions without difficulty. Gradually increase the tempo.

Carrying out the instructions in a different order

- Say that you are going to give the instructions jumbled up and the children are to carry them out. However, do **not** do any of the actions yourself.
- Now give the instructions as above but in random order. Say, e.g.: *Touch your nose. Stand up.*, etc.
- Keep repeating this until you see that the children can carry out the instructions without difficulty.
- Call on individual children and give each of them an instruction to carry out.

❻ Listen and point. Write the numbers.

Action Story: *Smile* CD 1/20

- The children open their Pupil's Books on p. 14. The six pictures are printed in random order. Give the children sufficient time to look at the pictures.

- Play the Action Story (CD 1/20). The children point to the appropriate pictures in the book.

Tapescript:

Stand up.
Close your eyes.
Touch your nose.
Touch your eyes.
Open your eyes.
Smile.

- Explain to the children that they are to put the pictures in the correct order by numbering them. Number one is already done.
- Now play the Action Story again (CD 1/20). The children look for the second picture and write in the corresponding number, and so on.
- Go around in the class and check the children's work.

Option: In high-ability classes you can put out an answer key for self-checking. On a sheet of paper draw six boxes with circles that represent the page in the Pupil's Book. Write the correct numbers in the circles. The children go and check their own work themselves.

Alternative: Draw six boxes on the board that represent the page in the Pupil's Book. Have the children tell you the answer. Write the numbers in the boxes.

L E S S O N   6

Vocabulary, phrases and structures:

Receptive language: *Congratulations, Sue!; Thank you; Oh, I'm sorry; That's OK; I hate yellow; Your picture is/This colour's fantastic; I think my picture's not good; It's very good.*

Linguistic skills:

Understanding sentences and mini-dialogues from the CD.

Cognitive, motor and social skills:

Understanding sentences and mini-dialogues from the CD and colouring circles in the book accordingly.

Cross-curricular integration:

Curriculum area: Speaking motivation 'Art'.

Materials:

Story Cards 1–9
CD 1/21; *Activity Book*, p. 12, ex. 3; (optional) answer key for self-checking

Revision

- Give the instructions from the Action Story (*Smile*) from the previous lesson.

❸ Listen and colour.

Listening exercise CD 1/21

- Ask the children to open their Activity Books at p. 12 and look at the pictures.
- Tell the children that they will hear individual sentences or short dialogues on the CD and are to match them to the corresponding pictures in the book by colouring the circles accordingly. Half of the circle of the first picture is already coloured brown.
- Play CD 1/21 once. The children listen and look at the pictures in the book.

Tapescript:

Speaker:	Brown.
Boy:	Congratulations, Sue!
Girl:	Thank you!

Speaker:	Green.
Boy:	Oh, I'm sorry.
Girl:	That's OK.

| Speaker: | Red. |
| Girl: | I hate yellow! |

Speaker:	Blue.
Girl:	Your picture is fantastic. Wow!
Boy:	Thank you.

Speaker:	Yellow.
Girl:	The picture's not good.
Boy:	It's very good, Sandra!

| Speaker: | Black. |
| Girl: | This colour's fantastic! |

- Play the CD again. The children first mark the circles in the pictures in the corresponding colours while listening. They then complete the circles.
- Go around the class and check the children's work.

Option: In high-ability classes you can put out an answer key for self-checking. On a sheet of paper draw six boxes with circles that represent the page in the Activity Book. Colour the circles according to the tapescript. The children go to the key and check their own work themselves.

Alternative: Draw six boxes on the board that represent the page in the Activity Book. Have the children tell you the answer. Colour the circles.

L E S S O N   7

Vocabulary, phrases and structures:

Receptive language: *Here you are; Have a hot dog; Come on, give it to me; Ah. A fantastic picture; My picture!; Stop; Woof!; Look at the dog; It's very good, Max; It's not good; Now blue and green*

Linguistic skills:

Understanding a story from the CD.
Following the sequence of events of a story in dialogue form.

Cognitive, motor and social skills:

Putting a story into the right order by numbering pictures accordingly.

Cross-curricular integration:

Curriculum area: Speaking motivation 'Art'.

Materials:

Story Cards 1–9 *(The painting)*
CD 1/22; *Activity Book*, p. 13, ex. 4; (optional) answer key for self-checking

---

Revision

- Use the story cards to reconstruct the story *The painting* together with the children.

❹ Listen and write the numbers.

Listening exercise CD 1/22

- The children open their Activity Books at p. 13. Explain that the pictures make a story but that they are printed in the wrong order.
- Give the children sufficient time to look at the pictures.
- Play the story once (CD 1/22). The children listen and look at the pictures.

Tapescript:

Linda:	Come on, Max!
Max:	OK.
	OK, red and yellow.
Max:	It's not good.
Benny:	It's very good, Max.
	Come on.
Max:	OK. Now blue and green.
	It's not good.
Linda:	It's very good, Max.
	Come on.
Linda:	Look at the dog!
Max:	Hehehehehehe!
Dog:	Woof! Woof!
Max:	Stop. Stop!!!!
	My picture!
Hot dog man:	Ah. A fantastic picture.
	Come on, give it to me.
	Here you are. Have a hot dog.
Dog:	Woof! Woof!

- Play the CD again. The children listen to the story and put the pictures in the correct order by numbering them from one to six.
- Go round the class and check the children's work.

Option: In high-ability classes you can put out an answer key for self-checking. On a sheet of paper draw six boxes with circles that represent the page in the Activity Book. Write the correct numbers in the circles. The children go to the key and check their own work themselves.

Alternative: Draw six boxes on the board that represent the page in the Activity Book. Have the children tell you the answers. Write the numbers in the boxes.

L E S S O N   8

Vocabulary, phrases and structures:

Vocabulary revision: instructions *(Stand up; Stretch; Shout: 'Hooray!'; Sit down; Give me red/yellow/...; Put your book in your schoolbag; Put your pencil case in your schoolbag; Put your scissors in your schoolbag; Go to school; Close your eyes; Touch your nose; Open your eyes; Listen; Smile.)*

Linguistic skills:

Understanding instructions from the CD.
Giving instructions.

Cognitive, motor and social skills:

Understanding instructions from the CD and ticking the corresponding pictures in the book.
Pair work: Giving instructions and acting them out.

Materials:

Activity Book, p. 13, ex. 4
Activity Book, p. 14, ex. 5; CD 1/23; (optional) answer key for self-checking

Revision

- Use Activity Book p.13 to revise the story from the previous lesson.
- Revise the following instructions together with the children by saying the sentences and doing the corresponding actions. The children copy your actions:

  Stand up.
  Sit down.
  Stretch.
  Close your eyes.
  Open your eyes.
  Touch your nose.
  Touch your eyes.
  Smile.

- Tell the children to perform the various actions. For example, say: *Max says, 'Close your eyes.'* The children obey your instructions, but only when you begin them with: *Max says...* If you give an instruction without saying: *Max says...* first, the children must not carry it out. Anyone who does it is 'out'.

❺ Listen and tick (✓).

Listening exercise CD 1/23

- Ask the children to look at the first pair of pictures on p. 14 of their Activity Books. Then say: *One. Stand up.* Get the children to point to the corresponding picture and repeat after you. Continue with the other instructions on the tapescript in the same way.
- Tell the children that they are to listen to the CD and put a tick in the box of the corresponding pictures of each pair.
- Play CD 1/23 twice. The children tick the appropriate boxes.

Tapescript:

One. Stand up.
One. Stand up.

Two. Touch your nose.
Two. Touch your nose.

Three. Sit down
Three. Sit down.

Four. Smile.
Four. Smile.

Five. Stretch.
Five. Stretch.

Six. Open your eyes.
Six. Open your eyes.

- The children then listen again and check. Go around the class and check the children's work.
- Now say a number and elicit the instructions from the children.

Option: In high-ability classes you can put out an answer key for self-checking. The children go to the key and check their own work themselves.

Alternative: Draw six pairs of boxes on the board that represent the page in the Activity Book. Have the children tell you the answers. Write the numbers in the boxes.

Pair work

- The children get together with a partner. Child A gives an instruction. Child B acts it out. Then they swap roles.
- Go around the class and help if necessary.

Teacher's Book • Playway to English 1 Second edition   **53**

L E S S O N   9

Vocabulary, phrases and structures:

Vocabulary revision: colours; school things
Receptive language: *What colour's his (pencil)?*
What have you got?

Linguistic skills:

Saying school objects and their colours.
Saying what Max has got.
Answering questions.

Cognitive, motor and social skills:

Remembering and naming objects.
Drawing oneself, colouring school objects in the
book and giving information about them.

Materials:

Flashcards 5–11; 20–22
Activity Book, p. 15, ex. 6–7;

Revision

- Hold up a flashcard with the back of the card facing
the children and ask them: *What colour is it?* Tell the
children to guess which word it could be: *Green? – No.*
Yellow? – Yes! That's right.
- When the children have made the correct guess, show
them the flashcard.
- Mouth the words by moving your lips as if you were
actually speaking, but do not say the words. Encourage
the children to read the words from your lips and say
them aloud.

❻ Look and remember. Say.

Memory training and speaking exercise

- Ask the children to open their Activity Books at p. 15. Tell
them to look at the picture in ex. 6 for half a minute and
try to remember the colour of the school objects.
- The children then close their books.
- Ask: *Look at Max's school things. What colour's his*
pencil case? Child: *(It's) green.*
- Continue with the other school objects in the same way.
Help the children to answer through whispering cues if
necessary.
- Alternatively, ask: *What has Max got?* and prompt the
children to say: *A green pencil case./A green and orange*
book, etc.

❼ Colour and say.

Speaking exercise

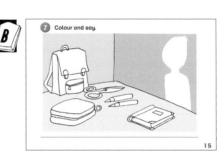

- Ask the children to look at Activity Book ex. 7. Tell them
to draw their face in the silhouette and colour in the
school objects. Make sure that they don't use more than
two colours per object.
- Give the children sufficient time for this step and go
around the class to help if necessary.
- When the children have finished colouring, ask, e.g.:
(Andrew), what have you got? Prompt the child to
answer, e.g.: *A blue and red schoolbag.*, etc.

C L I L:
Content and Language Integrated Learning

Objective:

Training of perceptive faculty.
Understanding/Recognising what happens when mixing colours.

Materials:

Pupil's Book, p. 15, ex. 7; coloured pencils, a paint box, a brush, a cup of water, a tissue for each child; a sheet of white paper for each child

Revision

- Revise the colours. Show a red/pink/brown/etc. pencil and ask the children to name the colour. (*Say the colours.*)

❼ Look and guess. Colour.
Experiment

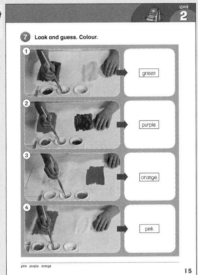

- Prepare the room with the painting things and give out a sheet of white paper to each child.
- Ask the children to guess what happens when you mix the colours blue and yellow.
- Say: *Take some blue. Blue. OK.* Apply some blue paint to a sheet of white paper.
- The children do the same and apply some blue to their sheet of paper.
- Say: *Now, yellow. Mix blue and yellow. What colour is it?* Add yellow to the blue on your sheet and encourage the children to do the same. The children mix blue and yellow. Look at them questioningly and prompt them to answer: *Green.*
- Continue with the other three experiments in pictures 2, 3 and 4 on Pupil's Book p.15.
- Clear away the painting things but let the children keep their experiments on the desk. Ask the children to open their Pupil's Books at p. 15 and say: *Number one. What colour is it? Can you remember? Yes, green. That's right. Now, number two…* and elicit the answers.
- The children colour in the blank spaces in the book accordingly.
- Go round the class and check the children's work.

Option: Ask the children: *What about black and white?* These cannot be made by mixing together other colours. But let the children find out what happens if you add black or white to any other colours. Demonstrate on a sheet of paper.
If you add black to a colour you darken it. If you add white, you lighten it.

L E S S O N   1

Vocabulary, phrases and structures:
Checking of vocabulary acquisition.

Linguistic skills:
Understanding and saying the key vocabulary from Units 1–2 on the topic areas *Hello* and *School*.

Cognitive, motor and social skills:
Matching words and phrases from the CD to the corresponding pictures in the book.
Numbering these words/phrases in the corresponding colours.
Checking answers in an answer key.
Self-evaluation

Materials:
CD 1/24–25; *Pupil's Book*, pp. 16–17, ex. 1–2; coloured pencils; answer key for self-checking

Self-evaluation

Option: Divide *Show what you can do* into two lessons.

Note: For notes on the basic methodology of this section, see *Show what you can do* on p. 18 of the introduction.

❶ **Listen and write the numbers.**
Listening exercise: Matching exercise CD 1/24

- Tell the children that they will now find out which of the words on Pupil's Book p. 16 they can already understand well and which words they can say.
- The children now check independently whether they can match the words they hear to the corresponding pictures. They have a red, a green and a blue pencil in front of them on the desk.
- Play CD 1/24. The children write the numbers one to six in the appropriate colours in the circles for each picture. The first picture has already been numbered.
- Go around the class and help the children as necessary.
- Put out a completed sheet and let the children come out and check their results independently.

Tapescript:

Speaker 1: Take a red pencil. Write the numbers. Take a red pencil. OK? Here we go.

Number one: schoolbag.
Number one: schoolbag.

Number two: touch.
Number two: touch.

Number three: boat.
Number three: boat.

Number four: glue.
Number four: glue.

Speaker 2: Take a green pencil. Write the numbers. Take a green pencil. OK? Here we go.

Number one: smile.
Number one: smile.

Number two: pencil.
Number two: pencil.

Number three: bike.
Number three: bike.

Number four: eyes.
Number four: eyes.

Speaker 1: Take a blue pencil. Write the numbers. Take a blue pencil. OK? Here we go.

Number one: book.
Number one: book.

Number two: picture.
Number two: picture.

Number three: scissors.
Number three: scissors.

Number four: pencil case.
Number four: pencil case.

❶ Say and colour.
Speaking exercise

- Ask the children to look at the pictures again. Explain that if they can say the correct words for the pictures, they colour the frames in the corresponding colours.
- When the children have coloured the frames, give them an activity from Units 1 or 2 of the Teacher's Resource Pack to work on while you go around and check the individual answers to the colouring activity. Ask individual children to say the colours, e.g.: Teacher: (*Lena*). (Lena): *boat – red.* Teacher: (*Daniel*). (Daniel): *book – blue.*
- Divide the class into groups of four or five to do this if it is easier to move from group to group to check their work.

❷ Listen and write the numbers.
Listening exercise: Matching exercise CD 1/25

- Tell the children that they will now find out which of the phrases on Pupil's Book p. 17 they can already understand well and which of them they can say.
- The children now check independently whether they can match the phrases they hear to the corresponding pictures. They have a red and a green pencil in front of them on the desk.
- Play CD 1/25. The children write the numbers one to four in the appropriate colours in the circles for each picture. The first picture has already been numbered.
- Go around the class and help the children as necessary.
- Put out a completed sheet and let the children come out and check their results independently.

Tapescript:

Speaker 1: Take a red pencil. Write the numbers. Take a red pencil. OK? Here we go.

Number one: Stretch.
Number one: Stretch.

Number two: I'm sorry.
Number two: I'm sorry.

Number three: Close your book.
Number three: Close your book.

Number four: I hate it.
Number four: I hate it.

Speaker 2: Take a green pencil. Write the numbers. Take a green pencil. OK? Here we go.

Number one: Sit down.
Number one: Sit down.

Number two: Open your book.
Number two: Open your book.

Number three: Shout.
Number three: Shout.

Number four: Here you are.
Number four: Here you are.

❷ Say and colour.
Speaking exercise

- Ask the children to look at the pictures again. Explain that if they can say the correct words for the pictures, they colour the frames in the corresponding colours.
- When the children have coloured the frames, give them an activity from Units 1 or 2 of the Teacher's Resource Pack to work on while you go round and check the individual answers to the colouring activity. Ask individual children to say the colours, e.g.: Teacher: (*Tom*). (Tom): *I'm sorry – red.* Teacher: (*Sandra*). (Sandra): *Here you are – green.*
- Divide the class into groups of four or five to do this if it is easier to move from group to group to check their work.

L E S S O N 1

Vocabulary, phrases and structures:

apple; banana; plum; pear; two apples/bananas/plums/pears
Receptive language: *What is it?; Yes; No; How many apples/... are there?*

Linguistic skills:

Learning the meaning and pronunciation of the new words.
Understanding words from the CD.
Recognising and naming quantities of one to six.
Plural-*s*.

Cognitive, motor and social skills:

Responding to words with gestures.
Matching flashcards to the corresponding words.
Understanding words from the CD and pointing to the corresponding pictures in the book.
Guessing words.
Recognising quantities, circling and naming them.
Pair work: Playing a vocabulary game.

Cross-curricular integration:

Mathematics

Materials:

Flashcards 1–4; 23–24
Flashcards 25–28; CD 1/26; Pupil's Book, p. 18, ex. 1; Activity Book, p. 16, ex. 1; (optional) glove puppet Max

Revision

• Revise the numbers from one to six with the flashcards.

Introduction of vocabulary

apple; banana; pear; plum

• Show the *apple* flashcard and say: *Apple.* Then stick the flashcard on the board. Introduce the other words in the same way.
• Say: *Apple.* and show an imaginary apple in your hand. The children imitate you. Continue with the other words using the following gestures:

banana – hold an imaginary banana in one hand and make a movement with the other hand as if you were peeling it.

plum – show an imaginary plum with your thumb and index finger.

pear – with both hands make the outline of a pear.

Pronunciation tip: It is important that the pronunciation of [æ] in *apple* is very open. Take care with the pronunciation of *pear* [eə].

Exercises for anchoring the vocabulary in the recognition memory

• Say a word and ask the children to respond with the corresponding gesture.
• Give the instruction: *Touch the pear.* A child comes to the board and touches the appropriate flashcard. Continue in this way with the other words.

❶ Listen and point.

Listening exercise CD 1/26

Tapescript:

apple
banana
plum
pear

• The children listen to the words (CD 1/26) and point to the corresponding fruit in the Pupil's Book, p. 18 (ex. 1).
• Play the CD several times. The children point to the appropriate pictures as they listen.

Exercises for anchoring words in the children's productive memory

- Ask the children to close their eyes.
  Say the words. At first the children just listen. Then say each word individually and change your voice: loud, quiet, high, deep, happy, sad or angry. The children repeat the word exactly as you say it.
- Play the words once again (CD 1/26). The children point to the corresponding fruit in the Pupil's Book and try to say it with you.
- Say the words a few times together.
- Hold a flashcard in your hand with the reverse side to the children and ask: *What is it?*
- The children guess what the word is: *Banana? – No.– Pear? – Yes.*
- When a child has guessed correctly, show the flashcard.

Note: The linguistically correct question would be: *A banana?* or *Is it a banana?* In this early phase one word questions *(Banana?)* are acceptable.

Option: Use the glove puppet. One child puts on the glove puppet, points to the back of a flashcard and asks: *What is it?*

Note: By turning off the visual channel the child can concentrate completely on the sound pattern. Accurate listening and imitating of different sound qualities is good training for listening and sound. It supports the memorising of the pronunciation in the long-term memory.

❶ Listen and point.

Pair work: Vocabulary game

- The children work in pairs with one Pupil's Book. Child A says a word and child B points to the corresponding fruit on p. 18 (ex. 1). Then they swap roles.
- Demonstrate the exercise first with a child in front of the whole class and then have two children act it out before you go on to the general pair work.

Note: Pair work increases the children's willingness to speak in a foreign language.

Pre-teaching key phrases

How many (apples) are there?; Plural *-s*

- Draw two apples, three bananas, four plums and five pears on the board. If you are able to, close the board so the students can no longer see the fruit. If you cannot, get the students to put their heads down on their desks and to close their eyes. Make sure no students are still looking at the board.
- Ask: *How many apples are there? Do you remember?* Prompt the children to say: *Two.* Say: *Right, there are two apples.* Continue with the other fruit in the same way.
- Focus on the plural *-s.* Say: *Listen. One apple. Two apples. One plum. Two plums.* Continue in this way for the other fruit. Then repeat, encouraging the children to join in with you. Say, e.g.: *One pear. Four pears.*

❶ Think and draw.
Recognising quantities

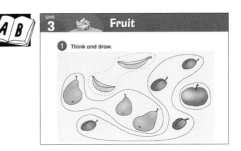

- Ask the children to take a pencil and circle the various quantities of fruit in ex. 1 on p. 16 of the Activity Book.
- Ask: *How many bananas are there?* Hold your book up and point to the two bananas. Pretend to circle them with a pencil. Ask again: *How many bananas are there?* The children answer accordingly: *Two (bananas).* Help the children with the plural as necessary.
- Give the children enough time to find the remaining quantities and circle them. Go around the class and help if necessary.
- Check the answers by asking: *How many apples/pears/ plums are there?* Children: *One (apple)/three (pears)/* etc.

Answer key:
one apple
two bananas
three pears
four plums

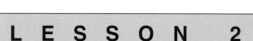

L E S S O N 2

Vocabulary, phrases and structures:
Vocabulary revision: fruit; numbers

Linguistic skills:
Counting rhythmic sequences of numbers.
Recognising and being able to name quantities of
one to six.
Naming the number of fruit found in a hidden
picture game.

Cognitive, motor and social skills:
Counting rhythmically.
Finding fruit in a hidden picture game.

Practising fine motor skills.
Awareness of the plural -s.
Pair work: Recognising quantities of fruit

Cross-curricular integration:
Mathematics
Art

Materials:
Flashcards 25–28
CD 1/27–28; *Pupil's Book*, p. 18, ex. 2; *Activity
Book*, p. 16, ex. 2; coloured pencils

Revision

- Count aloud from one to six on your fingers, saying the numbers rhythmically.
- Ask the children to count along with you.
- Say the following sequence six times in a row, and each time emphasise the next higher number as follows:

  one, *two, three, four, five, six*
  one, **two**, *three, four, five, six*
  one, two, **three**, *four, five, six*
  one, two, three, **four**, *five, six*
  one, two, three, four, **five**, *six*
  one, two, three, four, five, **six**

- Revise the fruit with the flashcards.
- Draw apples ◌, bananas ◌, plums ◌ and pears ◌ in quantities of one to six on the board. Say: *Show me two apples.* A child comes up to the board and points at the pair of apples, and so on.

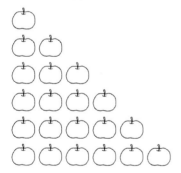

❷ Listen. Say and draw.

Listening and speaking exercise CD 1/27

- Ask the children to open their Pupil's Books at p. 18. Give them a few seconds to look at the first picture in ex. 2. Then they close their books.
- Draw one of each fruit on the board and ask: *How many (apples) are there? Do you remember?* The children answer accordingly. Write the numbers they guess alongside each fruit.
- Play CD 1/27. When they have listened, ask the children to call out the numbers they heard on the CD. Correct them on the board, if necesssary. Play the CD as many times as necessary for the children to do this.

Tapescript:

*Dad: Four apples, two bananas, three pears
       and a plum.*
Girl: Thanks, Dad.

- The children open their books again. Play the CD one more time for them to listen and look at the picture.

Step to creativity (Word Play)

Pair work: Recognising quantities of fruit CD 1/28

- Ask the children to look at the second picture in their Pupil's Book, p. 18, ex. 2.
- Child A asks child B for some fruit e.g.: *A plum, one banana, four apples and three pears, please.* Child B draws the fruit into his/her empty plate in the second picture and says: *Here you are.* Then they swap roles.
- Play the karaoke version of the Word Play beat on CD 1/28 and encourage the students to say their own words to the rhythm using the drawings in their books. Demonstrate with a student's book or create an example for the board.

- The children look at the picture in their Activity Book, p. 16, ex. 2. Tell them to find out how many apples/plums/… are in the picture. Let the children work with a partner to find the fruit. Say, e.g.: *Look for the apples.*
- When the children have found the six apples in the picture, ask them to colour in six apples in the corresponding row below the picture, using the colour next to it. Now ask the children to look for the other hidden fruit and to colour in the same number of fruit accordingly.
- When the children have coloured the fruit, check the answers by asking, e.g.: *How many (apples) are there?* Help the children to answer: *Six apples/Two bananas/Five pears/Four plums.*
- Let them practise the plural *-s* by rhythmically saying the sequence in unison: *Six apples, four plums…*, etc.

❷ Count, colour and say.

Discovery picture

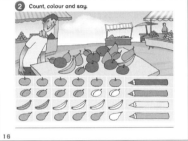

L E S S O N   3

Vocabulary, phrases and structures:
*One apple, two apples, three apples, four;
Give me more, give me more!*

Linguistic skills:
Saying a chant *(Give me more)* rhythmically.
Saying mini-dialogues.

Cognitive, motor and social skills:
Maintaining a rhythm in the group.
Pointing to rows of pictures while speaking rhythmically.
Saying a chant rhythmically in two groups.

Cross-curricular integration:
Music
Topic: Speaking motivation 'sharing'.

Materials:
Flashcards 5–11; 20–22; 25–28
CD 1/29–30; *Pupil's Book*, p. 19, ex. 3; glove puppet Max

Revision

- Revise colours and the fruit with the flashcards. Put them on the board and give the children a few seconds to look at the pictures. Ask the children to close their eyes. Turn the flashcards over so that they face the board.

- Tell the children to open their eyes. Point at one of the flashcards. Ask the children to guess which fruit/colour it is. Say: *What is it? Can you remember?*

③ Listen and point.
   Say the chant.

Chant: *Give me more!*

- Play the chant (CD 1/29). Hold your book up and point along in your book.
- Present the chant again, this time saying it with the glove puppet as dialogue partner.

   Glove puppet: *One apple, two apples, three apples, four.*
   You: *Give me more, give me more!*
   Glove puppet: *One plum, two plums ..., etc.*

Tapescript:

Group: *One apple, two apples, three apples, four.*
Child: *Give me more, give me more!*
Group: *One plum, two plums, three plums, four.*
Child: *Give me more, give me more!*
Group: *One pear, two pears, three pears, four.*
Child: *Give me more, give me more!*
Group: *No way!*
Child: *OK!*

- Play the chant again (CD 1/29). The children point along in their Pupil's Books.
- Practise the chant with the children in sections by chanting it rhythmically and making the appropriate gestures. The children imitate your actions and say it after you. Use the corresponding flashcards *(apple, plum, pear)* as visual support.
- Play the first part of CD 1/30 *(And now you!)* and say the chant with the children several times line by line. The children point to the corresponding pictures in the book as they say the chant.
- Play the karaoke section of CD 1/30 *(One more time!)* and ask the children to look at the page in the Pupil's Book and chant along in time.
- Finally, divide the class into two groups to play the roles. One group is lead by you and the other by the glove puppet. The pictures in the book act as support.

Note: Do not move the glove puppet when you are speaking but only when the puppet is speaking.

L E S S O N   4

Vocabulary, phrases and structures:
Vocabulary revision: fruit

Linguistic skills:
Understanding instructions from the CD.

Cognitive, motor and social skills:
Understanding instructions from the CD and ticking the corresponding pictures in the book.

Materials:
Flashcards 25–28; CD 1/30
CD 1/31; *Activity Book*, p. 17, ex. 3; (optional) answer key for self-checking

Revision

- Place the fruit flashcards on your desk. Get individual children to come up to the desk and revise the following mini-dialogue:

   You: *Give me the apples, please.*
   Child: *Here you are.* (Picks up the *apples* flashcard and hands it over to you. Help through whispering cues.)
   You: *Thank you.*

   Repeat the dialogue several times with other fruit items and get the other children to speak after you.

- Play the karaoke section of the chant (*Give me more*, CD 1/30) with the children in two groups, as in the previous lesson.

❸ Listen and tick (✓).
Listening exercise CD 1/31

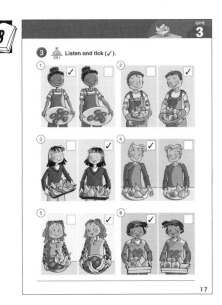

- Ask the children to look at the pictures on p. 17 in their Activity Books.
- Then say: *Give me six plums/three pears and two bananas/..., please.* Get the children to point to the corresponding pictures in the book.
- Tell the children that they are to listen to the CD and to put a tick in the box of the corresponding picture of each pair.
- Play CD 1/31 twice. The children tick the appropriate pictures in the book.

Tapescript:

Speaker: One.
Boy: Give me six plums, please.
Girl: Here you are.
Boy: Thank you.

Speaker: Two.
Girl: Give me five apples, please.
Boy: Here you are.
Girl: Thank you.

Speaker: Three.
Boy: Give me three pears and two bananas, please.
Girl: Three pears and two bananas. Here you are.
Boy: Thank you.

Speaker: Four.
Girl: Give me an apple and three pears, please
Boy: An apple and two pears?
Girl: No, an apple and three pears.
Boy: OK. An apple and three pears. Here you are.
Girl: Thank you.

Speaker: Five.
Boy: Give me three plums and two bananas, please.
Girl: No problem. Three plums and two bananas. Here you are.
Boy: Thank you.

Speaker: Six.
Girl: Give me two apples and three pears, please.
Boy: two apples, and one, two, three pears. Here you are.
Girl: Thank you.

- The children then listen again and check. Go round the class and check the children's work. You can also check the children's answers by asking them: *Number one. How many plums are there?* The children say the appropriate number of fruit.

Option: In high-ability classes, put out an answer key for self-checking. On a sheet of paper draw six pairs of boxes that represent the page in the Activity Book. Tick the correct box in each pair. The children go to the key and check their own work themselves.

Alternative: Draw six pairs of boxes on the board that represent the page in the Activity Book. Point to the first pair of boxes. Say: *Left or right?* The children say the answers. Tick the corresponding boxes on the board.

L E S S O N   5

Vocabulary, phrases and structures:

I'm Danny; I'm Daisy; And I am Mister Matt; Oh, no! Stop saying that; You're Danny; OK; Hooray, hooray, hooray!
Receptive language: *Hello! My name's …; You can call me Mr Matt; OK? I'm Mr Matt!; Say 'Hello, Mr Matt!'; After three. One, two, three!; Sorry; Very good!; Nice to meet you; What's your name?; One, two, three! Louder!; This is my boy/girl; Where are they? Here we are, Dad; My girl, Daisy.*

Linguistic skills:

Understanding a sketch *(Hello!)* from the DVD.
Understanding mini-dialogues (scenes from the sketch) from the CD.
Understanding and singing a song *(I'm Danny! I'm Daisy!)* from the CD.

Cognitive, motor and social skills:

Understanding mini-dialogues from the CD and numbering pictures in the correct order.
Singing a song *(I'm Danny! I'm Daisy!).*
Paying attention to the right beat while speaking in unison and singing.
Option: Acting out a role play.

Cross-curricular integration:

Topic: Learning how to behave in a social setting.
Music

Materials:

CD 1/4
DVD *(Hello!)*; CD 1/32–35; *Pupil's Book*, p. 20, ex. 4–5; *Activity Book*, p. 18, ex. 4

Revision

• Play the karaoke section of the song *What's your name?* from Unit 1 and sing with the children. (CD 1/4).

❹ **Watch the story.**

Mr Matt sketch: *Hello!*

• Show the children the DVD sketch *Hello!* twice. Tell the children that they should particularly listen out for what the people in the film are called.

DVD script: *Hello!*

Mr Matt:	Hello! My name's Matthew Morris
Danny:	Hello!
Mr Matt:	And … … this is my girl.
	Oh!
	This is my girl
	Where are they?
	Here?
	No!
	Here?
	No!
Danny and Daisy:	Here we are, Dad!
Mr Matt:	My girl, Daisy. Say hello!
Girl:	Hi! I'm Daisy!
(They start singing.)	
Danny:	I'm Danny!
Daisy:	I'm Daisy!
Mr Matt:	And I am Mr Matt!
Danny:	Danny!
Daisy:	Daisy!
Mr Matt:	Oh, no! Stop saying that!
Mr Matt:	You're Danny! You're Daisy!
Danny and Daisy:	OK, OK, OK!
Danny:	I'm Danny!
Daisy:	I'm Daisy!
All three:	Hooray, hooray, hooray!

• After watching the DVD ask the children:

What's the boy's name? (Danny)
What's the girl's name? (Daisy)
What's the man's name? (Mr Matt)

❹ Listen and write the numbers.
Listening exercise CD 1/32

- The children open their Pupil's Books at p. 20 and look at the pictures. Tell the children that they will now hear individual sentences or short dialogues on the CD and are to match them to the corresponding pictures in the book. Picture 1 has already been numbered.
- Play the listening exercise twice (optional) (CD 1/32). The children listen and write the corresponding numbers in the circles provided in the book.

Tapescript:

Announcer:	Picture one.
Mr Matt:	This is my boy, Danny. Say hello.
Danny:	Hello!
Announcer:	Once again. Picture one.
Mr Matt:	This is my boy, Danny. Say hello.
Danny:	Hello!
Announcer:	Picture two.
Mr Matt:	Where are they?
Announcer:	Once again. Picture two.
Mr Matt:	Where are they?
Announcer:	Picture three.
Mr Matt:	Hello! I'm Mr Matt.
Announcer:	Once again. Picture three.
Mr Matt:	Hello! I'm Mr Matt.
Announcer:	Picture four.
Danny and Daisy:	Here we are, Dad!
Announcer:	Once again. Picture four.
Danny and Daisy:	Here we are, Dad!

- Hold your book up. Point to the first picture and ask: *What number is it?* Children: *Three.*

❺ Sing the song.
Song: *I'm Danny! I'm Daisy!*
CD 1/33–34

Lyrics: Gerngross/Puchta
Music: Matt Devitt
© Helbling, Rum/Innsbruck

- Stand in a circle with the children. Play the song several times (CD 1/33) and present the words through corresponding actions. The children do the actions with you.
- Say the words several times rhythmically in unison with the children.
- Then sing the song together to the full recording (CD 1/33) and then to the karaoke section (CD 1/34).

❹ Listen and write the numbers.
Listening exercise CD 1/35

- Ask the children to open their Activity Books at p.18.
- Play CD 1/35. The children listen and look at the pictures in the book.

Tapescript:

Woman: *Where are they?*
Children: *Here we are, Mum!*
Woman: *This is my girl, Lara.*
Woman: *This is my boy, James.*

- Play the CD again. The children number the corresponding pictures one to four.
- Check the children's work. Say, e.g.: *Here we are, Mum!* and the children say the appropriate number.
- The situation can also be acted out.

L E S S O N   6

Vocabulary, phrases and structures:

Receptive language: *Say 'Hello!' to your mum; You're hungry; Your mum shows you some plums; Cut open a plum; Show the plum to your mum; Your mum says 'Eek!'; Hi, Mum; Hello, dear; I'm hungry, Mum; Have a plum; Look.*

Linguistic skills:

Understanding instructions in an Action Story (*The plum*).
Understanding instructions/a dialgoue on the CD and matching with the pictures in the book.

Cognitive, motor and social skills:

Matching instructions with actions.
Understanding and carrying out jumbled instructions.
Listening to the CD and completing a picture story with drawings.
Option: Acting out a role play.

Cross-curricular integration:

Topic: Speaking motivation 'A healthy snack'.

Materials:

Flashcards 25–28; CD 1/34
CD 1/36–37; *Pupil's Book*, p. 21, ex. 6;
Activity Book, p. 19, ex. 5

Revision

- Place the fruit flashcards on your desk. Get children to come up to your desk in pairs to revise the following mini-dialogue:
  Child A: *Give me the bananas, please.*
  Child B: *Here you are.* (Picks up the *bananas* flashcard and gives it to child A.)
  Child A: *Thank you.*
  Then the children swap roles.
- Play the karaoke section and sing the song *I'm Danny! I'm Daisy!* from the previous lesson with the children (CD 1/34).

Action Story: *The plum*
Listen and imitate

- Ask the children to stand in a circle or stand up in their places.
- Say the following sentences and at the same time demonstrate through mime/gesture:
  Say 'Hello!' to your mum. – Hello!
  You're hungry.
  Your mum shows you some plums.
  Cut open a plum.
  Show the plum to your mum.
  Your mum says 'Eek!'
- Keep repeating this until you see that the children have a good grasp of the sentences and the actions that go with them.

Carrying out instructions

- Tell the children that you are now going to give the same instructions but **not** carry them out yourself. Give the same instructions as above in the same order. Say: *Say 'Hello!' to your mum. – Hello!* The children do the action. Do **not** do any of the actions yourself but give positive feedback (e.g. by nodding your head) when the children carry out the instruction correctly.
- Continue with the rest of the instructions in the same way.
- Keep repeating this until you see that the children can carry out the instructions without difficulty. Gradually increase the tempo.

Carrying out the instructions in a different order

- Say that you are going to give the instructions jumbled up and the children are to carry them out. Do **not** do any of the actions yourself.
- Now give the instructions as above but in random order. Say e.g.: *Show the plum to your mum*, etc.
- Keep repeating this until you see that the children can carry out the instructions without difficulty.
- Call on individual children and give each of them one of the instructions to carry out, in any order.

**⑥ Listen and point.
Write the numbers.**

Action Story: *The plum* CD 1/36

⑤ Listen and draw.

Listening exercise CD 1/37

Tapescript:

Say 'Hello!' to your mum. – Hello!
You're hungry.
Your mum shows you some plums.
Cut open a plum.
Show the plum to your mum.
Your mum says 'Eek!'.

Tapescript:

Jack:	*Hi, Mum.*
Mum:	*Hello, dear.*
Jack:	*I'm hungry, Mum.*
Mum:	*Have a plum.*
Jack:	*Mum?*
Mum:	*Yes?*
Jack:	*Look!*
Mum:	*Eek!*

- The children open their Pupil's Books at p. 21. The six pictures are printed in random order. Give the children sufficient time to look at the pictures.
- Play the Action Story (CD 1/36). The children point to the appropriate pictures.
- Tell the children to put the pictures in the correct order by numbering them. Number 1 is already done.
- Now play the Action Story again. The children number the pictures in order.
- Go around the class and check the children's work.

Option: In high-ability classes you can put out an answer key for self-checking. On a sheet of paper draw six boxes with circles on them that represent the page in the Pupil's Book. Write the correct numbers in the circles. The children go and check their own work themselves.

Alternative: Draw six boxes on the board that represent the page in the Pupil's Book. Have the children tell you the answers. Write the numbers in the boxes.

- Present the dialogue as a role play as follows. Changing your voice say: *Hi, Mum!* and answer as Mum with: *Hello, dear.,* and swap places. In this way develop the whole dialogue and act it out several times in front of the class.
- Then encourage one child to take on the role of Jack. Whisper cues to help. Then ask another child to take on the role of Mum. You take the part of Jack. In this way act out the dialogue in front of the class with several children.
- Ask the children to open their Activity Books at p. 19 and look at the picture story. Explain that the two pictures at the top of the page are missing from two of the frames.
- Tell the children to listen to the dialogue (CD 1/37) and to complete the picture story by drawing the missing elements in the blank spaces (in frames 4 and 6).
- Play CD 1/37 twice. The children listen and draw accordingly.
- Go around the class to help if necessary. Check the children's work.
- The children practise the dialogue in pairs.
- Finally, volunteers act out the dialogue as a role play in front of the whole class. Ask the class to applaud the actors: *Let's give them a big hand!*

LESSON 7

Vocabulary, phrases and structures:

Receptive language: *I'm thirsty; Here you are; I'm hungry; Give me more; Just a moment; Help!*

Linguistic skills:

Understanding a story (*The greedy monster*) from the DVD, from the CD and from narration by the teacher.
Gradually joining in with the narration.

Cognitive, motor and social skills:

Following the narrative structure of a story.
Representing a time sequence visually.
Option: Acting out a role play.
Completing a picture story with stickers.

Cross-curricular integration:

Topic: Speaking motivation 'Going shopping'.
Art

Materials:

CD 1/30
DVD (*The greedy monster*); CD 1/38; *Pupil's Book*, pp. 22–23, ex. 7; *Story Cards* 10–21; picture stickers from the appendix of the *Pupil's Book*; (optional) answer key for self-checking

Revision

- Ask volunteers to act out the dialogue *The plum* from the previous lesson in front of the whole class.
- Revise the chant *Give me more*. Split the class into two groups and chant to the karaoke section of CD 1/30.

❼ Watch the story.

Cartoon Story:
The greedy monster

- Show the children the DVD sequence *The greedy monster* twice.

DVD script: *The greedy monster*

Linda and Benny:	Mmmmh! Mmmmh! Aaahhhhh!
Monster:	Grrrrrrrrrrrrrrrrrrr!
Benny and Linda:	A monster! Help!!!!!
Monster:	Grrrrrrrrrrrr! I'm thirsty!
Benny:	Here you are.
Monster:	Aaahhhhh!
Monster:	Grrrrrr! I'm hungry.
Linda:	Ohhh! Here you are.
Monster:	Mmmmh! Yum yum! Mmmmh! Give me more!
Max (in the house):	Oh. Mmh ... ah! Heeheehee!
Monster:	Give me more! Grrrrrrrr!
Linda:	Ohhh! Ohhh!
Monster:	Give me more!
Max:	Just a moment!
Monster:	Eh?
Max:	Here you are!
Monster:	Aaahhh! Mmmmhhhh! Atishoo! Atishoo! Help! Help!
Max, Linda, Benny:	Heeheehee! Hahaha! Heeheehee!

- Ask the children to call out words or phrases they remember.

❼ Listen and stick.

Listening exercise: Sticker activity
CD 1/38

- Ask the children to find the picture stickers for this unit and show them where to look. They then look at pp. 22 and 23 in their Pupil's Books.
- Play the audio version of the story twice (CD 1/38). The children complete the missing parts in the picture story with the stickers while they are listening.
- Go around the class and check the children's work.

Option: Place a completed picture story in the classroom. The children go and check their own work themselves.

Telling the story

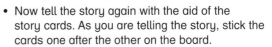

- Now tell the story again with the aid of the story cards. As you are telling the story, stick the cards one after the other on the board.
- If you tell the story several times, you can gradually prompt the children to say it with you. Indicate the first picture and say, e.g.: *Linda and Benny are eating fruit.*
- Point to the second picture and say: *A monster comes and says…* Elicit the expression: *I'm thirsty.* from the children. Help if necessary by whispering a prompt.
- Point to the third picture and say: *Benny says …* Elicit: *Here you are.,* etc.

Note: In high-ability classes the story can also be performed as a role play after appropriate intensive practice.

L E S S O N 8

Vocabulary, phrases and structures:

Vocabulary revision: *I'm thirsty; Here you are; I'm hungry.*
I want more; Just a moment; Yuck. Help!

Linguistic skills:

Understanding sentences and mini-dialogues from the CD and linking them with the pictures in the book.

Cognitive, motor and social skills:

Associating illustrations with what they hear on the CD and numbering them accordingly.
Option: Acting out a role play.

Cross-curricular integration:

Topic: Speaking motivation 'Healthy food'.

Materials:

CD 1/38; *Pupil's Book*, pp. 22–23, ex. 7; *Story Cards* 10–21
CD 1/39; *Activity Book*, p. 20, ex. 6; (optional) answer key for self-checking

Revision

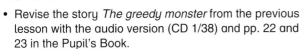

- Revise the story *The greedy monster* from the previous lesson with the audio version (CD 1/38) and pp. 22 and 23 in the Pupil's Book.
- Then tell the story again with the aid of the story cards. As you are telling the story, stick the cards one after the other on the board and prompt the children to say it with you. Indicate the first picture and say, e.g.: *Linda and Benny are eating fruit.* Point to the second picture: *A monster comes and says…*

❻ Listen and write the numbers.

Listening exercise CD 1/39

- Get the children to look at the pictures on p. 20 in the Activity Book. Tell them that they are in random order and that the children are to put them in the correct order by numbering them.
- Play the CD (CD 1/39). The children listen and look at the pictures in the book.

Tapescript:

Boy and Girl:	*A monster! Help!*
Monster:	*I'm thirsty.*
Boy:	*Here you are.*
Monster:	*I'm hungry.*
Girl:	*Here you are.*
Monster:	*I want more.*
	Give me an apple.
Girl:	*Just a moment.*
	Here you are.
Monster:	*Yuck. Help!*

- Play the CD again. The children listen and number the pictures accordingly. Go around the class and help if necessary.
- Check the answers by asking, e.g.: *What number's 'Just a moment. Here you are.'?*
- Then say a number and the children say the corresponding sentence/s. Help through whispering cues. Repeat the sentence/s and get all the children to repeat after you.
- The story can also be acted out as a role play. The children get together in threes and practise the dialogues. Go around the class and help if necessary. Volunteer groups act the story out as a role play in front of the class.

Option: In high-ability classes you can put out an answer key for self-checking. On a sheet of paper draw six boxes with circles on them that represent the page in the Activity Book. Write the correct numbers in the circles. The children go to the key and check their own work themselves.

L E S S O N 9

Vocabulary, phrases and structures:	Cognitive, motor and social skills:

Vocabulary, phrases and structures:

Two plus one is three/...

Linguistic skills:

Learning and understanding the meaning of new words.
Formulating simple addition sums in English.
Naming the amount of fruit.

Cognitive, motor and social skills:

Doing simple addition.
Checking the results with a partner.
Discovering hidden fruit and colouring it accordingly.

Cross-curricular integration:

Mathematics: Addition of numbers one to six

Materials:

Activity Book, p. 21, ex. 7–8; coloured pencils

Revision

- Get the children to act out the role play from the previous lesson.

Pre-teaching key phrases

One plus three is four.

- Write individual figures on the board in the form of a sum, e. g. 1 + 3 = ...
- Say: *One plus three is ...* and elicit the answer. Children: *... four.* Say: *Yes, that's right.* Complete the addition on the board. Say: *One plus three is four.* The children repeat after you.
- Continue with several simple addition sums that you do together with the children in the same way as above.

❼ Do the sums. Say.

Addition

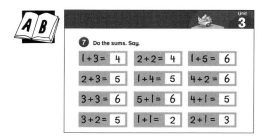

- Ask the children to open their Activity Books on p. 21 and do the sums in ex. 7 on their own. Say: *Now do the sums.*
- Give the children sufficient time for this work. Go around the class and help if necessary.
- Check the sums by writing them on the board in figures. As you do this, say the sums together with the children.
- Alternatively, the children check the answers in pairs and take turns to read out one of the sums to their partner.

❽ Look and colour. Say.

Discovery picture

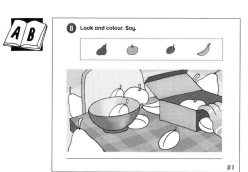

- Tell the children to look carefully and find the hidden fruits in the picture in ex. 8 on p. 21 of their Activity Books. Ask them to colour the fruits according to the small pictures below the rubric. They should colour the pears red, the apples green, etc
- To check the children's work say: *OK. What have you got?* The children answer accordingly: *two apples, three pears,* etc.
- Alternatively ask: *How many (bananas) are there?* The children answer: *One.*

Answer key:
one banana
two apples
three pears
four plums

L E S S O N   1

Vocabulary, phrases and structures:

dog; mouse; rabbit; duck; cat; hamster
Receptive language: *Touch the (cat); Show the (rabbit); What's missing?*

Linguistic skills:

Learning the meaning and pronunciation of the new words.
Understanding words from the CD.

Cognitive, motor and social skills:

Associating sounds with animals.
Responding to words with gestures.
Matching flashcards to the corresponding words.

Understanding words on the CD and pointing to the appropriate pictures.
Playing a vocabulary game with rhythmic clapping.
Pair work: Playing a vocabulary game.

Cross-curricular integration:

Topic: Animals

Materials:

DVD *(The greedy monster)*; *Story Cards* 10–21; *Flashcards* 29–34; CD 2/1; *Pupil's Book*, p. 24, ex. 1

Revision

- Show the story *The greedy monster* from the previous unit (DVD). Together with the children, reconstruct the story with the story cards.

Introduction of vocabulary

dog; mouse; rabbit; duck; cat; hamster

- Present the new words with the flashcards. Hold up the flashcards one by one and say the word.
- Then say the words again and for each one make the corresponding animal sound and a gesture or mime for each animal: *miaow; woof; squeak; quack;* etc.

Exercises for anchoring the vocabulary in the recognition memory

- Stick the flashcards on the board. Say one of the animals. Ask a child to touch the corresponding flashcard, e.g.: *(Thomas), touch the cat.*, etc.
- Hand out the flashcards to individual children. Say, e.g.: *Show the rabbit/...to (Julia)*. The child with the corresponding card shows it to (Julia), and so on.

❶ Listen and point.
Listening exercise CD 2/1

Tapescript:

cat
dog
hamster
mouse
duck
rabbit

- The children listen to various noises or animal sounds (CD 2/1) and point to the corresponding animal in the Pupil's Book, p. 24 (ex. 1). Then they hear the word.
- Play the listening exercise a second time and the children point along in the book.
- Then whisper one of the words to a child. The child must mime the corresponding animal. Whoever knows the English word for the animal may mime the next animal.

Exercises for anchoring words in the children's productive memory

- Put the flashcards on the board. Together with the children say the words one after the other in the order of the flashcards on the board. Clap between the individual words, at first three times, then twice, then once:

  cat x x x dog x x x hamster x x x ...
  cat x x dog x x hamster x x ...
  cat x dog x hamster x mouse x duck x rabbit

- Jumble the flashcards on the board. Give the children a few minutes to memorise them.
- Play *What's missing?* with the flashcards (see Unit 1, Lesson 9, Revision).

❶ Then say and point

Vocabulary game: Pair work

- Each pair has one Pupil's Book open at p. 22. They look at the picture in ex. 1. Child A names an animal and child B points it. Then they swap roles.
- Demonstrate the exercise first with a child in front of the class before the children work in pairs.

Note: Pair work increases the time the children spend speaking English and makes an important contribution to social learning.
Gradually introduce certain phrases that the children can use to express what they want in English.
Examples: *Once more, please; Let's play it again; It's my turn; Can we play the game again?*

L E S S O N   2

Vocabulary, phrases and structures:

Is it a cat/...?; No, sorry; Yes; one mouse; two dogs; three cats; four rabbits
Receptive language: *How many ... are there?*

Linguistic skills:

Guessing animals.
Saying the number of animals found in a hidden pictures puzzle.
Speaking rhythmically: Plural *-s*.

Cognitive, motor and social skills:

Following the rules of a game.
Recognising animals in a picture puzzle and identifying the number of them.

Option: Pair work: Looking for animals in a picture puzzle.
Keeping to a specified rhythm.
Paying attention to the Plural-*s*.

Cross-curricular integration:

Mathematics: Naming quantities.
Art.

Materials:

Flashcards 29–34; glove puppet Max
CD 2/2; *Activity Book*, p. 22, ex. 1; coloured pencils

Vocabulary revision

dog; mouse; rabbit; duck; cat; hamster

- Say the words noiselessly. Move your lips as if you were really going to say the words. The children say the word (*lip reading*).
- Put on the glove puppet. Ask a child to choose a flashcard without showing Max the animal. Max guesses what is on the card. He says: *Is it a ...?* The child answers: *No, sorry.* or *Yes.*
- Play the guessing game again. Give six children a flashcard each. Each child looks briefly at the flashcard and then holds it so that the other children cannot see the card. The other children try to guess the word.

Note: Rehearse the expressions needed beforehand with the class by saying and repeating several times. Whisper if a child cannot recall the phrase: *Is it a ...?.*

Revision of the phrase

How many ... are there?

- Play a guessing game with the children. Briefly show some coloured pencils and then hide them behind your back. Ask: *How many (red) pencils are there?* Have the children guess. When a child has guessed correctly, show the pencils. Repeat the game several times.

❶ Look and colour.

Discovery picture

- Look at the picture puzzle on p. 22 of the Activity Book with the children. Tell them that they are to find out how many cats, dogs, etc. are hidden in the picture. First have the children look together for one type of animal e.g. for the dogs. Say: *How many dogs are there?* Children: *Two.*

- When the children have found the (two) dogs hidden in the picture, tell them that they are to colour in two dogs in the row of dogs. The children colour in two dogs in the second row in red as indicated by the coloured pencil.
- The children look for all the hidden animals and colour in the correct number of animals in the relevant row in the corresponding colour.

Option: The exercise can also be done as pair work. The social aspect of helping each other comes particularly into play here.

❶ Listen and point.

Listening exercise CD 2/2

- Now play the recording twice (CD 2/2). The children listen and point to their answers in the book. In this way they can check their answers themselves in the Activity Book.

Tapescript:

Four rabbits,
two dogs,
three cats,
three ducks,
two hamsters,
one mouse.

- Ask the children: *How many animals are there?* Help the children with their answers: *Two rabbits....*, etc.
- Finally, for rote learning of the plural-*s*, have them speak the lines from the CD rhythmically in unison: *Four rabbits, two dogs, three cats, three ducks, two hamsters, one mouse.*

L E S S O N   3

Vocabulary, phrases and structures:

Vocabulary revision: animals/pets; colours; numbers; plural-*s*
Receptive language: *What is it?*

Linguistic skills:

'Reading' logical sequences and completing them. Giving answers.

Cognitive, motor and social skills:

Completing logical sequences by drawing.
Option: Pair work: Checking answers.
Matching animals with coloured shapes by numbering.

Cross-curricular integration:

Mathematics: Logical sequences; recognising shapes
Art

Materials:

Flashcards 29–34
Pupil's Book, p. 24, ex. 2; *Activity Book*, p. 23, ex. 2; (optional) answer key for self-checking

---

Revision

- Draw six pictures of different quantities (from one to six) of each animal on the board, e.g. five rabbits, three ducks, etc.

Note: The irregular plural 'mice' has not yet been taught, so only draw one mouse.

- Point to one of the pictures and say the incorrect quantity of animals, or, if you think the class can manage it, say the incorrect quantity and the incorrect animal, e.g. point to three ducks. Say: *Four ducks?* Look at the children questioningly to elicit the answer: *(No!) Three ducks.* Continue like this for all the pictures.
- If the children need help, point to the picture and say, e.g.: *How many (ducks) are there?* Children: *Three!*

❷ Think and draw.
Logical sequences

- The children open their Pupil's Books at p. 24 and look at ex. 2.
- Work on the first line together with the children. Hold up your book. Point in order to the pictures and say them together: *Rabbit – duck – rabbit – duck – rabbit...*
- Point to the last empty box and look questioningly at the children. Elicit the word *duck*. The children draw a duck in it.
- The children complete the remaining lines individually.
- Check the answers as a class by having the children read out the lines.
- Finally, the children can also read out the lines to each other as pair work.

Answer key:

*rabbit – duck – rabbit – duck – rabbit – duck – rabbit – duck – rabbit – **duck***

*mouse – rabbit – hamster – mouse – rabbit – hamster – mouse – rabbit – hamster – **mouse***

*cat – dog – dog – cat – dog – dog – cat – dog – dog – **cat***

*duck – duck – mouse – duck – duck – mouse – duck – duck – mouse – **duck***

❷ Look and write the numbers.
Matching activity

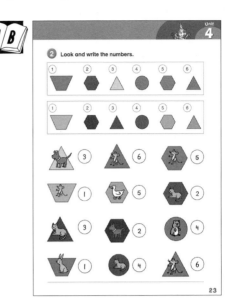

- Hold up your Activity Book so that the children can see the shapes at the top of p. 23. Point at one shape after the other and get the children to say the numbers from one to six plus the appropriate colour: *one – blue; two – red*; etc.
- Then point at the shapes in random order and the children call out the numbers plus colours again.
- Now point at the animals on the lower part of the page. The children name the animals.
- Explain to the children that they need to match the shape and colour of the animal frames with the shapes at the top of the page. Then they are to write the corresponding number in the circle provided in each of the pictures.
- Demonstrate the exercise. Hold up your book and point to the first shape in the top row and at number 1. Say: *Look. One. Blue.* Look at the pets in picture frames. Point at the rabbit in the picture with the blue trapezium frame. Pretend to write the number 1 in the circle of that picture.
- Now the children try to match the shapes to the frames. Go around the class and help if necessary.
- Finally, check the children's work as a whole class. Say, e.g.: *One. Blue. What is it?* Prompt the children to say: *Rabbit.*, etc.

Options: In high-ability classes you can put out an answer key for self-checking. Photocopy the page from the Activity Book and complete the answers. The children go to the key and check their own work themselves.
When the children have finished, get them to work with a partner and compare their answers.

L E S S O N 4

Vocabulary, phrases and structures:
What's this?; miaow; woof; squeak; quack

Linguistic skills:
Understanding a chant (*What's this?*) from the CD.
Chanting rhythmically.

Cognitive, motor and social skills:
Keeping to a rhythm.
Pointing to the right pictures while speaking rhythmically.
Chanting in two groups.
Understanding instructions on the CD and numbering pictures in the book.
Accompanying a chant with percussion instruments.

Cross-curricular integration:
Topic: Animal noises
Music

Materials:
CD 2/3–4; *Pupil's Book*, p. 25, ex. 3; glove puppet Max; percussion instruments

Revision
- Mime one of the animals from the previous lessons and ask the children to guess. The child who guesses the animal correctly may mime the next animal.

Preliminary preparation of phrases
- Imitate an animal noise, e.g.: *Woof, woof* and ask: *What's this?* The children name the animal, and so on.
- Then say: *Mouse.* The children give the corresponding animal noise: *Squeak, squeak.* Continue with the other animals in the same way.

❸ **Listen and write the numbers. Say the chant.**
Chant: *What's this?* CD 2/3–4

Tapescript:

What's this? What's this?
Miaow, miaow.
A cat, a cat.
A cat, miaow.

What's this? What's this?
Woof, woof, woof, woof.
A dog, a dog.
A dog, woof, woof.

What's this? What's this?
Squeak, squeak, squeak, squeak.
A mouse, a mouse.
A mouse, squeak, squeak.

What's this? What's this?
Quack, quack, quack, quack.
A duck, a duck.
A duck, quack, quack.

- Play the chant once as a model (CD 2/3). The children just listen.
- Ask the children to open their Pupil's Books at p. 23. Play the chant again.
- The children number the individual verses by looking at the pictures and writing the numbers one to four in the circles provided.
- Circulate and check the children's work.
- Practise the chant in sections with the children by saying it out loud and making the appropriate gestures. The children imitate your actions and say it after you. Use the corresponding flashcards (*cat, dog, mouse, duck*) as visual support.
- Play the first part of CD 2/4 (*And now you!*) and say the chant with the children several times line by line. The children point to the corresponding pictures in the book as they say the chant.

- Play the karaoke section of CD 2/4 (*One more time!*) and ask the children to look at the page in the Pupil's Book and chant along in time.
- Now divide the class into two groups to recite the chant. One group is lead by you, one group by the glove puppet. The pictures in the book act as support.
- Play the karaoke section again (*One more time!*). Use the various percussion instruments for supporting the rhythm and as instrumental representation of the animal noises. Some children support the continuous rhythm by constant regular drumming in the background. Others represent the animal noises in sound.

Variation 1: Divide the speaking roles or the musical support among various children or groups.

> A: What's this? What's this?
> B: Miaow, miaow.
> A: A cat, a cat.
> A and B: A cat, miaow.

Variation 2: Four groups of four or five children each represent one of the animals in the chant. The individual groups stand with their instruments in one corner of the room. The rest of the children stand in the middle and ask: *What's this?* The other groups answer accordingly.

Pronunciation tip: It is important the [ð] in *this* is voiced. With their fingers in their ears the voiced nature can be demonstrated as the children can feel a vibration.

L E S S O N   5

Vocabulary, phrases and structures:

Vocabulary revision: animals/pets; fruit; school objects
What is it?; Is it a (mouse)/...?; Yes, it is; No, it isn't.

Linguistic skills:

Completing logical sequences.
Guessing.

Cognitive, motor and social skills:

Completing logical sequences by drawing.
Pair work: Creating logical sequences
Pair work: Playing a guessing game.
Practising fine motor skills.
Drawing

Cross-curricular integration:

Art

Materials:

percussion instruments
Flashcards 14–19; 25–28; 29–34; *Activity Book,* p. 24, ex. 3–4; glove puppet Max

---

Revision

- Recite the chant *What's this?* from the previous lesson with four groups of four or five children each representing one of the animals. The individual groups stand with their instruments in one corner of the room. The rest of the children stand in the middle and ask: *What's this?* The other groups answer accordingly.

Exercises on phrases

- Practise the phrases *What is it?; Yes, it is; No, it isn't.* with the flashcards of school objects, fruit and pets. Model the activity with the glove puppet.
Take a flashcard. Don't show it to the children or Max. Ask: *What is it?* Prompt Max to answer with: *Is it a mouse/banana/book ...?* Answer: *Yes, it is.* or *No, it isn't.* Show Max and the children the picture to confirm your answer. Repeat the game with another card.
- Play the game again. This time the children take Max's role. Prompt them to guess the picture with: *Is it a ...?*

❸ Look and draw.
Logical sequences

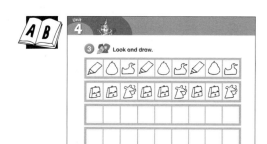

- Ask the children to open their Activity Books at p. 24 and to look at the pictures in ex. 3.
- Hold up your book and work on the first line together with the children.
- Get them to read out the sequence with you while you point along in your book. Say: *pencil, pear, duck, …* When pointing at the last square, which is blank, look at the children questioningly and elicit the missing item *duck*. The children then draw a duck in the square.
- The children complete the next sequence of pictures individually.
- Check the answers as a class by getting the children to read out their sequences.

Pair work: Logical sequences

- The children create their own logical sequences individually by drawing animals in the two blank rows in ex. 3.
- Tell them to leave blank one or two boxes in each of the rows. Give them sufficient time for this step. Go round the class and help if necessary.
- In pairs, the children complete each others' rows and say the sequences to one another.

❹ Draw. Work in pairs.
Guessing game: Pair work

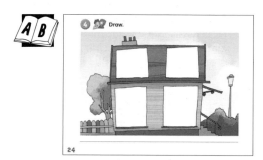

- The children work in pairs. Each child draws an animal in one of the windows of the house in ex. 4 on page 24 of the Activity Book. They should not show their drawing to their partner and should close their book or cover the drawing when they have finished.
- Before the children work in pairs, demonstrate the exercise with a child in front of the class. Draw an animal in one of the windows in your book and hide the page from the child. Ask: *What is it?* Encourage the child to guess, e.g.: *Is it a (duck)?* Answer: *No, it isn't.* or *Yes, it is.* Accept the answers: *Yes* or *No, (sorry)* if the child is struggling with *Yes, it is./No, it isn't.*
- The children work in pairs and repeat the activity. When child B has found out what the animal is, child A shows the picture and it is child A's turn to guess the animal in child B's house.
- Then both partners draw a second animal in one of the windows of their house and carry on with the game in the same way until there are animals in all four windows.
- When the children have finished the game, they can colour in their animals.

L E S S O N 6

Vocabulary, phrases and structures:

Let's play; No, go away!
Receptive language: *The mouse is (very) sad; The mouse goes away; Let's go to the show; Wonderful; Abracadabra; Super; You're the (dog).*

Linguistic skills:

Understanding a story (*The mouse*) from the DVD and the CD and from narration by the teacher. Gradually joining in with narration.
Mini-dialogues and (optional) acting out a role play.

Cognitive, motor and social skills:

Following the sequence of events of a story.
Completing a picture story with stickers.
Option: Checking independently by means of an answer key.

Cross-curricular integration:

Topic: Speaking motivation 'Being excluded from a community'.

Materials:

Percussion instruments
DVD (*The mouse*); CD 2/5; *Pupil's Book*, pp. 26–27, ex. 4; picture stickers from the appendix in the *Pupil's Book*; *Story Cards* 22–33; props for a role play (optional) picture story answer key for self-checking; (optional) masks for the role play; (photocopiable master in the appendix of the *Teacher's Book* p. 172–174)

Revision

- Recite the chant (*What's this?*) again together with the children. Use percussion instruments (See Lesson 4, ex. 3). Divide the children into groups for the speaking roles or the musical support.

Pre-teaching new phrases

Let's play; Go away.

- Put up on the board the story cards that illustrate the sentences *Let's play.* and *Go away.*
- Make the meaning of the sentences clear through appropriate gestures and say the phrases a few times. Get the children to imitate your movements and repeat after you.

❹ Watch the story.

Cartoon Story: *The mouse*

- Show the children the DVD sequence *The mouse* twice.

DVD script: *The mouse*

Mouse:	Hello, dog. Squeak, squeak. Let's play.
Dog:	No, go away. Woof, woof.
Storyteller:	The mouse goes away.
Mouse:	Hello, cat. Squeak, squeak. Let's play.
Cat:	No, go away. Miaow!
Storyteller:	The mouse is sad.
Mouse:	Hello, rabbit, hello, hamster. Squeak, squeak. Let's play.
Rabbit and hamster:	No, go away.
Storyteller:	The mouse is very sad.
Mouse:	Oh, I'm so sad. What can I do now? Oh, what's this? Wonderful. Abracadabra, one, two, three. Ooooooh!
Dog:	Woof, woof! Let's go to the show.
Hamster and cat:	Yes.
Mouse:	Ladies and gentlemen. Welcome to the show. Abracadabra, one, two, three. Tada.
All the animals:	Super!
Dog:	A duck!
Mouse:	Thank you. Thank you very much. Squeak, squeak.

❹ Listen and stick.

Listening exercise:
Sticker activity CD 2/5

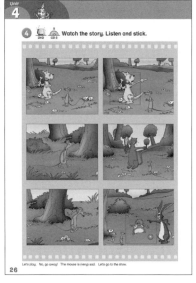

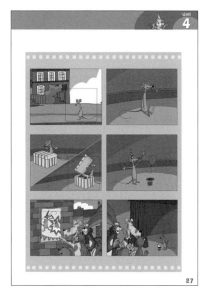

- Ask the children to find the picture stickers for this unit and show them where to look. They then look at pp. 26–27 in their Pupil's Books.
- Play the audio version of the story twice (CD 2/5). The children listen and stick the picture stickers in the corresponding blank spaces.
- Circulate and check the children's work.

Option: Place a completed picture story in the classroom. The children go and check it independently.

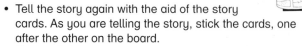

Telling the story

- Tell the story again with the aid of the story cards. As you are telling the story, stick the cards, one after the other on the board.
- If you tell the story several times, you can gradually prompt the children to say it with you. Point to the first picture and say, e.g.: *Hello dog. Squeak, squeak. Let's play.*
- Gesture for the children to say with you: *No, go away! Woof, woof,* etc.

Mini-dialogues – role play

- Say to one child: *You're the dog.* Now imitate the voice of the mouse and say: *Hello dog. Squeak, squeak. Let's play.* If necessary whisper to prompt the child: *No, go away. Woof, woof.*
- Say to another child: *You're the cat.,* etc.

Option: The story can also be acted out as a role play. (See Teacher's Book pp. 172–174 for the photocopiable master for masks.)

L E S S O N   7

Vocabulary, phrases and structures:

Receptive language: *The rabbit's sad; The duck goes away; Hello, dog, quack, quack. Let's play; No, go away, duck! Woof, woof!; Abracadabra, one, two, three!*

Linguistic skills:

Understanding sentences on the CD and matching to the pictures in the book.

Cognitive, motor and social skills:

Understanding sentences on the CD and ticking the corresponding pictures in the book.

Cross-curricular integration:

Topic: Speaking motivation 'Social behaviour'.
General knowledge: Speaking motivation 'How to behave (in a fair way)'.

Materials:

DVD (*The mouse*); (optional) masks for the story *The mouse* (in the appendix to the *Teacher's Book* p. 172–174)
CD 2/6; *Activity Book*, p. 25, ex. 5; (optional) answer key for self-checking

Revision

- Have the children perform the role play *The mouse* from Lesson 6. Give out the masks for the individual roles (optional). Show the DVD for revision before the children perform the story. Remember to give them applause (*Let's give them a big hand!*).

❺ Listen and tick (✓).
Listening exercise CD 2/6

- The children open their Activity Books on p. 25 and look at the pictures. Hold up your book and point at one picture after the other while speaking: *The mouse is sad./The rabbit's sad./The duck goes away/...* The children listen to you and point at the appropriate pictures in their books.
- Then say all the sentences in random order once again and the children point to the pictures.
- Tell the children that they are to listen to the CD and to tick the correct box in each of the pairs of pictures indicated by the coloured frames.

- Demonstrate one example. Stop the CD after the first example *Pink. The rabbit's sad.* Repeat the sentence and pretend to tick the right box of the first (pink) pair of pictures.
- Then play the whole recording again (CD 2/6). The children listen and tick the boxes.

Tapescript:

Speaker 1:	Pink. The rabbit's sad. Pink. The rabbit's sad.
Speaker 2:	Red. The duck goes away. Red. The duck goes away.
Speaker 1: Duck: Speaker 1: Duck:	Blue. Hello, Dog, quack, quack. Let's play. Blue. Hello, Dog, quack, quack. Let's play.
Speaker 2: Dog: Speaker 2: Dog:	Yellow. No, go away, Duck! Woof, woof! Yellow. No, go away, Duck! Woof, woof!
Speaker 1: Duck: Speaker 1: Duck:	Green. Hello, Cat. Hello, hamster. Let's play. Quack. Quack! Green. Hello, Cat. Hello, hamster. Let's play. Quack. Quack!
Speaker 2:	Purple. The cat's sad. Purple. The cat's sad.
Speaker 1: Dog: Speaker 1: Dog:	Orange. Abacadabra. One, two, three. Orange. Abacadabra. One, two, three.
Speaker 2: Dog: Speaker 2: Dog:	Black. A rabbit! Woof, woof! Black. A rabbit! Woof, woof!

Teacher's Book • Playway to English 1 Second edition   **81**

- The children listen again and check. Go around the class and help if necessary. Ask: *What about pink? Left or right?* Children: *Right.*
- Check the children's work.

Option: In high-ability classes you can put out an answer key for self-checking. On a sheet of paper draw eight pairs of boxes that represent the page in the Activity Book. Tick the correct box in each pair. The children go to the key and check their own work themselves.

Alternative: Draw eight pairs of boxes (in the corresponding colours) on the board that represent the page in the Activity Book. Have the children tell you the answers. Tick the corresponding boxes.

L E S S O N   8

Vocabulary, phrases and structures:

ghost; Kick the ball; Run!
Receptive language: *Let's play; Great; What's this?; Wonderful!; Abracadabra; A ghost; Stop!*

Linguistic skills:

Learning the meaning and pronunciation of the new word/phrases.
Understanding a story from the CD.
Understanding sentences from the story.

Cognitive, motor and social skills:

Understanding sentences from the CD and matching them to the pictures in the book.

Putting pictures in the correct order by numbering them.
Miming a role play in a group.
Following numbered pictures to create a mime sequence.

Cross-curricular integration:

Topic: Speaking motivation 'Community building'.

Materials:

Story Cards 22–33
CD 2/7; *Pupil's Book,* p. 28, ex. 5; CD 2/8;
Activity Book, p. 26, ex. 6

Revision

- Together with the children reconstruct the story *The mouse* with the story cards.

Vocabulary extension

ghost

- Introduce the new word with the aid of the illustration in the Pupil's Book on p. 28 or the flashcard.
- Say the word *ghost* several times and make an appropriate action with your arms to suggest a ghost. Get the children to imitate your action and to repeat after you.

❺ Listen and write the numbers.
Listening exercise: Story CD 2/7

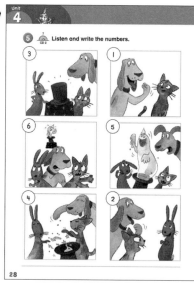

- As a warm-up exercise ask the children to look at the pictures on p. 28 in the Pupil's Book. Tell them that the pictures make up a story but that they are printed in the wrong order.
- Ask the children to tell you in L1 what they think the story is about.
- Play the story twice (CD 2/7). The children listen and put the pictures in order by numbering them from one to six.

Tapescript:

Dog:	Hello, Cat. Woof, woof. Let's play.
Cat:	OK, great. Miaow.
Dog:	Hello, Rabbit. Woof, woof.
Cat:	Hello, Rabbit. Miaow. Let's play.
Rabbit:	OK. Great.
Rabbit:	Oh, what's this?
Cat, Rabbit, Dog:	Wonderful!
Rabbit:	Abracadabra.
Cat, Rabbit, Dog:	One, two, three.
Ghost:	Ooooooooooh!
Cat, Rabbit, Dog:	A ghost, oh no!
Ghost:	Oh, stop. Let's play.
	Ooooooooooooh!

- Have the children call out words or phrases that they remember from the story.
- Play the CD again. The children check their work.
- Then check the answers as a whole class by saying: *What number is 'Hello, cat. Woof, woof. Let's play'?/…* Children: *(Number) one/…*

Vocabulary extension

Kick the ball; Run!

- Make the meaning of the new words/phrase clear through appropriate actions.

❻ Listen and write the numbers.
Listening exercise CD 2/8

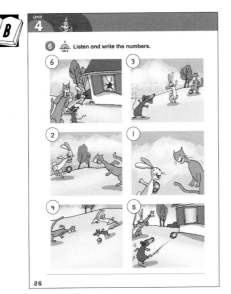

- Ask the children to open their Activity Books on p. 26 and look at the pictures in ex. 6. Tell them that they are to number the pictures according to what they hear on CD.
- Play CD 2/8 twice and get the children to order the pictures by numbering them from one to six.
- Play the CD again. The children listen and check.
- Finally, check the children's work by asking, e.g.: *What number is 'Hello, Cat. Let's play. – OK, Rabbit. Miaow.'?*

Tapescript:

Rabbit:	Hello, Cat. Let's play.
Cat:	OK, Rabbit. Miaow.
Cat:	Kick the ball, Rabbit.
Rabbit:	OK!
Mouse:	Hello, Rabbit. Hello, Cat. Let's play.
Rabbit and Cat:	OK. Great.
Rabbit and Cat:	Run, Mouse!
Mouse:	Yeaahhh!
Cat:	Kick the ball, Mouse!
Cat, Mouse, Rabbit:	Oh, no!

Role play

- Divide the class into groups of three. Tell each group to decide who is Rabbit, who is Mouse and who is Cat. The groups then use the numbered pictures in the Activity Book to create a mime of the story in ex. 6.
- Practice some possible mimes with the children before they begin, e.g. Say: *Run!* and run to the spot. Say: *Kick the ball!* and mime kicking a ball. Say: *Let's play!* and gesture for the children to come with you. Say: *Oh, no!* and look horrified.
- When they have had time to rehearse, invite groups to perform for the other children as you read out the tapescript or play the CD (2/8).

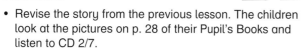

L E S S O N   9

Vocabulary, phrases and structures:

Abracadabra, one, two, three; a rabbit and a book; a plum and a banana; a mouse and a green pencil; a duck, a mouse, a little cat
Receptive language: *hat; What's number (two)?; What about number (three)?*

Linguistic skills:

Understanding the meaning and pronunciation of the new words.
Understanding magic spells from the CD.

Cognitive, motor and social skills:

Understanding magic spells from the CD and drawing accordingly.
Optional: Pair work: Reciting magic spells

Cross-curricular integration:

General knowledge: Speaking motivation 'Mystery'.

Materials:

CD 2/7; *Pupil's Book*, p. 28, ex. 5;
CD 2/9; *Activity Book*, p. 27, ex. 7; coloured pencils

Revision

- Revise the story from the previous lesson. The children look at the pictures on p. 28 of their Pupil's Books and listen to CD 2/7.

Vocabulary extension

little

- Explain the word *little* by indicating with your thumb and index finger that something is *little*.
- Say the new word several times and the children repeat after you.

❼ Listen and draw.

Listening exercise CD 2/9

- Ask the children to open their Activity Books at p. 27. Tell them that they are going to listen to four magic spells on the CD. They should listen very carefully and draw the appropriate objects or animals in the corresponding hats.

- Hold up your book and demonstrate the first magic spell. Point to the first picture. Say: *One.* Play the first magic trick from CD 2/9. Stop the CD. Look at the children questioningly. Ask: *What is it?* and prompt them to say: *A rabbit and a book.* Pretend to draw a rabbit and a book in the hat in picture 1 and say the spell as you do so.
- Play the next trick. Stop the CD and get the children to draw the appropriate fruit (*a plum and a banana*) in the hat in picture 2. Continue like this for the remaining pictures.

Tapescript:

Child 1:	*Abracadabra, one, two, three, a rabbit and a book, a rabbit and a book, a rabbit and a book for me! Heeheeheeheehee!*
Child 2:	*Abracadabra, eenie, meenie, moo, a plum and a banana, a plum and a banana, a plum and a banana for you!*
Cat:	*Abracadabra, miaow, miaow, miaow, A mouse and a green pencil, A mouse and a green pencil, Miaow, miaow, meeeeeeoooooooooow!*
Mouse:	*Abracadabra, here we go, a duck, a mouse, a little cat, a duck, a mouse, a little cat, are in my hat! Squeak, squeak.*

- Go around the class and check the children's work.
- Ask them: *What's number two?* Children: *A plum and a banana.* Say: *Yes./ Right. What about number three/ four?* The children answer accordingly.
- When you have checked their answers, the children can colour in the objects.

Step to creativity (optional)

- The children create their own spell and draw a picture of it on a piece of paper. Give the children sufficient time for this and go around the class to help if necessary.
- When the children have finished their work, get them to practise their spells together with a partner. Help with the language.

- Finally, ask volunteers to present their magic spells in front of the whole class. Remember to give applause. *(Let's give them a big hand!)*

C L I L:
Content and Language Integrated Learning

Vocabulary, phrases and structures:

Receptive language: *Cover the plates with plastic wrap; Put your fish on one plate; Put glue round the plate; Put the second plate on top; Glue string to the bowl; Hang your fish bowl in a window.*

Objective:

Training of fine motor skills.

Materials:

Pupil's Book, p. 29, ex. 6; for each child: coloured pencils, two paper plates, plastic wrap (cling film), a sheet of paper, scissors, glue, string, sellotape (optional)

Revision

- Revise the colours with the aid of coloured pencils. Show a red/blue/brown/, etc. pencil and ask the children to name the colour. *(Say the colours.)*

6 Make a fishbowl.

Make a window hanging

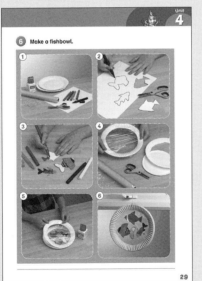

- Give the children time to look at the photos on p. 27 of the Pupil's Book.
- Make sure each child has two paper plates, some plastic wrap, a sheet of paper, glue, coloured pencils, string and scissors.
- Explain the instructions slowly. Repeat as often as necessary. Demonstrate what the children have to do. Say: *Cut out the centre of the plates.* The children cut out the insides of both plates so that the outside rings remain.
- Draw the outline of a fish on your sheet of paper, hold it up to show the children and ask: *What is it?* Accept answers in L1. Say: *Yes, that's right. (It's a) fish.* Encourage the children to repeat the word after you. Say: *Draw two or three fish.*
- When the children have finished drawing the outlines, hold up your scissors and start cutting out your fish. Say: *Cut out the fish.*
- When the children have cut out the fish, say: *Colour the fish.* Make sure the children colour both sides of the fish.
- When the children have finished colouring, demonstrate how to make the bowl. Demonstrate the process and give the instructions as follows:

Cover the plates with plastic wrap.
Put your fish on one plate.
Put glue round the plate.
Put the second plate on top.
Glue string to the bowl. (Or use sellotape.)
Hang your fish bowl in a window.

LESSON 1

Vocabulary, phrases and structures:
Checking of vocabulary acquisition.

Linguistic skills:
Understanding and saying the key vocabulary and phrases from Units 3–4 on the topic areas *Fruit* and *Pets*.

Cognitive, motor and social skills:
Matching words and phrases from the CD to the corresponding pictures in the book.
Numbering these words/phrases in the corresponding colours.
Checking the results in an answer key.
Self-evaluation

Materials:
CD 2/10–11; *Pupil's Book*, pp. 30–31, ex. 1–2; coloured pencils; (optional) answer key for self-checking

Self-evaluation

Option: Divide *Show what you can do* into two lessons.

Note: For notes on the basic methodology of this section, see *Show what you can do* on p. 18 of the introduction.

❶ Listen and write the numbers.
Listening exercise: Matching exercise CD 2/10

- Tell the children that they will now find out which words on Pupil's Book p. 30 they can already understand well and which words they can say.
- The children now check independently whether they can match the words they hear to the corresponding pictures. They have red, a blue and a green pencil in front of them on the desk.
- Play CD 2/10. The children write the numbers one to four in the appropriate colours in the circles for each picture. The first picture has already been numbered.
- Go around the class and help the children as necessary.
- Put out a completed sheet and let the children come out and check their results independently.

Tapescript:

Speaker 1: Take a red pencil. Write the numbers. Take a red pencil. OK? Here we go.

Number one: sad.
Number one: sad.

Number two: banana.
Number two: banana.

Number three: duck.
Number three: duck.

Number four: ghost.
Number four: ghost.

Speaker 2: Take a green pencil. Write the numbers. Take a green pencil. OK? Here we go.

Number one: rabbit.
Number one: rabbit.

Number two: pear.
Number two: pear.

Number three: dog.
Number three: dog.

Number four: apple.
Number four: apple.

Speaker 1: Take a blue pencil. Write the numbers. Take a blue pencil. OK? Here we go.

Number one: cat.
Number one: cat.

Number two: plum.
Number two: plum.

Number three: hamster.
Number three: hamster.

Number four: mouse.
Number four: mouse.

❶ Say and colour.
Speaking exercise

- Ask the children to look at the pictures again. Explain that if they can say the correct words for the pictures, they colour the frames in the corresponding colours.
- When the children have coloured the frames, give them an activity from Units 3 or 4 of the Teacher's Resource Pack to work on while you go around and check the individual answers to the colouring activity. Ask individual children to say the colours, e.g. Teacher: (*Tom*). (Tom): *banana – red.* Teacher: (*Daniel*). (Daniel): *dog – green.*
- Divide the class into groups of four or five to do this if it is easier to move from group to group to check their work.

❷ Listen and write the numbers.
Listening exercise: Matching exercise CD 2/11

- Tell the children that they will now find out which of the phrases on Pupil's Book p. 31 they can already understand well and which of them they can say.
- The children now check independently whether they can match the phrases they hear to the corresponding pictures. They have a red and a green pencil in front of them on the desk.
- Play CD 2/11. The children write the numbers one to four in the appropriate colours in the circles for each picture. The first picture has already been numbered.
- Go around the class and help the children as necessary.
- Put out a completed sheet and let the children come out and check their results independently.

Tapescript:

Speaker 1: *Take a red pencil. Write the numbers.*
Take a red pencil. OK? Here we go.

Number one: Help!
Number one: Help!

Number two: Say 'Hello' to your mum.
Number two: Say 'Hello' to your mum.

Number three: What's this?
Number three: What's this?

Number four: Show the picture to your mum.
Number four: Show the picture to your mum.

Speaker 2: *Take a green pencil. Write the numbers.*
Take a green pencil. OK? Here we go.

Number one: Cut open a plum.
Number one: Cut open a plum.

Number two: You're hungry.
Number two: You're hungry.

Number three: You're thirsty.
Number three: You're thirsty.

Number four: Go away!
Number four: Go away!

❷ Say and colour.
Speaking exercise

- Ask the children to look at the pictures again. Explain that if they can say the correct words for the pictures, they colour the frames in the corresponding colours.
- When the children have coloured the frames, give them an activity from Units 3 or 4 of the Teacher's Resource Pack to work on while you go round and check the individual answers to the colouring activity. Ask individual children to say the colours, e.g. Teacher: (*Ann*). (Ann): *What's this? – Red.* Teacher: (*Bastien*). (Bastien): *You're hungry – green.*
- Divide the class into groups of four or five to do this if it is easier to move from group to group to check their work.

L E S S O N   1

Vocabulary, phrases and structures:

teddy bear; train; plane; car; doll; computer game; ball; puzzle; seven; eight
Receptive language: *How many balls are there?; Three (balls).*

Linguistic skills:

Understanding the meaning and pronunciation of the new words.
Guessing toys.
Plural-*s*.

Cognitive, motor and social skills:

Finding toys hidden in a picture.
(Optional) Looking for toys hidden in a picture with a partner.
Counting the toys.

Cross-curricular integration:

Music
Topic: Speaking motivation 'The world of the child'.
Mathematics: Numbers one to eight

Materials:

Flashcards 35–44; 1–4; 23–24; Pupil's Book, p. 32, ex. 1; toys and a bag

Revision

- Revise the colours. Say, e.g.: *(Jacob), point to something (blue).* (Jacob) points to something (blue) in the classroom.

Introduction of vocabulary

teddy bear; train; plane; car; doll; computer game; ball; puzzle

- Show the flashcards one after the other. Say, e.g.: *Teddy bear.* and mime hugging a toy teddy bear. Say the word *teddy bear* again and ask the children to imitate your action.
- Introduce the rest of the new words in the same way.
- Say the new words in random order and ask the children to imitate your actions.
- Say all the words again and the children repeat after you.
- Practise the words with the following activities:
  – Say a word and ask the children to do the corresponding action.
  – Lip reading (Mouth the word but don't say it.)
  – Say: *Touch the … .*
  – Ask: *What's missing?* (See Unit 1, Lesson 9, Revision)
- Put the flashcards on the board. Point to the flashcards in order then point to them at random. The children say the corresponding words.

Note: Picture, sound and action reinforce the understanding and memorizing of the word. Repetition helps to store the sound pattern in the memory.

Pronunciation tip: Make the children aware of the difference between *plane* [p] and *ball* [b], *train* [t] and *doll* [d]. If the children hold a hand in front of their mouth, they can feel a burst of air when [p] and [t] are pronounced correctly. In the pronunciation of *puzzle*, a clearly voiced [z] similar to the buzzing of a bee can be heard.

Exercises for anchoring words in the children's productive memory

- Ask the children to close their eyes. Say the words one after the other in a variety of pitches and volumes. The children are to imitate them.
- Put toys into a bag and ask a child to put one hand in, feel a toy and guess what it is. Then the toy is pulled out and shown to the other children.
- Continue with different children until all the toys are on the table.

Note: The effect of the children closing their eyes is to remove visual distractions so they can concentrate fully and completely on the sound pattern. Accurately listening to and imitating different sound qualities helps to reinforce the correct pronunciation in the long-term memory.

Vocabulary extension

seven; eight

- Revise the numbers from one to six and introduce the new numbers with the flashcards.
- Show a flashcard and say the number several times. Get the children to repeat after you.

❶ Look and count. Say.

Hidden picture puzzle

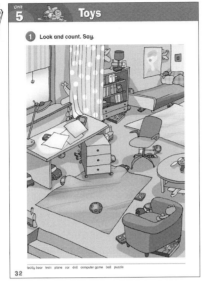

- Ask the children to open their Pupil's Books at p. 32. Look at the picture with the children.
- Tell them to find out how many dolls, balls, etc. are hidden in the picture. Option: They try to find the toys in pairs.
- Ask the children to look for one kind of toy together, e. g. the ball. Ask: *How many balls are there?* Children: *Three.* Say: *Yes, right. Three balls.*
- Check the number of the other toys in the same way. Help the children answer by whispering: *One puzzle. Two computer games.*, etc.

Answer key:

2 puzzles
6 computer games
8 balls
4 planes
5 trains
7 cars
1 teddy bear
3 dolls

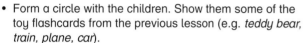

L E S S O N 2

Vocabulary, phrases and structures:
Listen; And there's a plane.

Linguistic skills:
Chanting rhythmically.

Cognitive, motor and social skills:
Paying attention to the correct rhythm.
Pointing to the right pictures while speaking rhythmically.
Chanting in two groups.

Cross-curricular integration:
Music
Topic: Speaking motivation 'The world of the child'.

Materials:
Flashcards 35–42
CD 2/12–13; *Pupil's Book*, p. 33, ex. 2

Revision

- Form a circle with the children. Show them some of the toy flashcards from the previous lesson (e.g. *teddy bear, train, plane, car*).
- Ask individual children to pick a card at random, look at it secretly and mime the toy. The others try to guess which toy is on the card.

**❷ Listen and point.
Say the chant.**

Chant: *Listen, listen!* CD 2/12–13

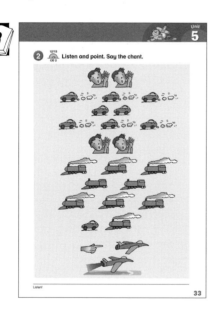

- Say: *Listen!* Hold your hand up to your ear and repeat *Listen!* several times. Make the sound of a car and say: *What's this?* The children answer: *(A) Car.* Respond: *Yes, a car.*
- Have them repeat: *A car.*
- Proceed in the same way with *train* and *plane*.
- Play the chant. (CD 2/12)

Tapescript:

Listen, listen!
Vroom, vroom, vroom.
A car, a car.
Vroom, vroom, vroom.
Listen, listen!
Shhh, shhh, shhh.
A train, a train.
Shhh, shhh, shhh.
A car, a train.
And there's a plane.
Zzzzzzzzzzzzzzzz...

- Play the chant again. The children point to the pictures on p. 33 in the Pupil's Book.
- Play the first part of CD 2/13 (*And now you!*) and say the chant with the children several times line by line. The children point to the corresponding pictures in the book as they say the chant.
- Play the karaoke section of CD 2/13 (*One more time!*) and ask the children to look at the page in the Pupil's Book and chant along in time.
- Get the class to say the chant in two groups:

  A: *Listen, listen!*
  B: *Vroom, vroom, vroom.*
  A: *A car, a car.*
  B: *Vroom, vroom, vroom.* etc.

- Ask the children to tap the rhythm on their desks.
- Divide the children into pairs or groups of three, or let them mill around the classroom individually, imitating a specific vehicle and its distinctive sound and calling out its name, e.g.; *Vroom, vroom, vroom. A car, a car*, etc.

L E S S O N 3

Vocabulary, phrases and structures:
Vocabulary revision: colours; toys; numbers one to eight
Receptive language: *What colour is your (train)?; How many … are there?*

Linguistic skills:
Understanding and saying colours and numbers.

Cognitive, motor and social skills:
Colouring in pictures of toys.
Counting toys and writing the numbers with a partner (optional).

Cross-curricular integration:
Art
Topic: Speaking motivation 'The world of the child'.
Mathematics: Numbers one to eight.

Materials:
Flashcards 35–42; pieces of coloured paper
Activity Book, p. 28, ex. 1; coloured pencils

Revision
- Get the class to say the chant *Listen, listen!* from the previous lesson in two groups.
- Revise the other toys with the flashcards.
- Give each child eight pieces of paper in the following colours: blue, red, green, yellow, orange, black, purple and pink.
- Call out the colours with the numbers one to eight that the children need to remember, say, e.g.: *Blue – one.* Practise this several times.
- Call out numbers one to eight and tell the children to shout out the corresponding colours while holding up the piece of coloured paper.
- Individual children hold up their pieces of paper and shout out the colour. The others respond by saying the corresponding number.

❶ Look and colour. Count and write the numbers.

Discovery picture

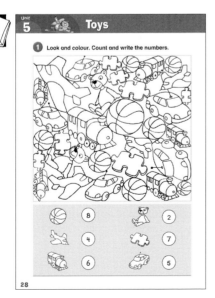

- Ask the children to open their Activity Books at p.28.
- Ask them to colour the toys in the box below the picture. Tell them to use the following colours: red, green, blue, yellow or pink.
- When they have finished, ask individual children: *What colour is your car/train/… Peter/Susan/…?*
- Explain that the children must colour the toys in the picture above accordingly and count how many toys there are. Option: They can do this step with a partner.
- The children write the appropriate numbers in the boxes next to the toys below the main picture. Go around the class and help if necessary.
- Check the children's work by asking, e.g.: *How many teddy bears are there?* Children: *Two teddy bears.* Help the children answer by whispering: *Two teddy bears.*, etc.

Answer key:
8 balls
7 puzzles
5 cars
2 teddy bears
6 trains
4 planes

L E S S O N 4

Vocabulary, phrases and structures:

Vocabulary revision: colours; toys; numbers one to eight

Receptive language: *What's number (four)?; What colour is the … / number …?*

Linguistic skills:

Reinforcing the meaning and pronunciation of the new numbers.

Understanding numbers and colours on the CD.

Cognitive, motor and social skills:

Understanding numbers and colours on the CD and colouring in shapes accordingly.

Cross-curricular integration:

Art

Topic: Speaking motivation 'The world of the child'.

Mathematics: Numbers one to eight.

Materials:

Flashcards 1–4, 23–24, 35–44

CD 2/14; *Activity Book*, p. 29, ex. 2; coloured pencils

Revision

- Revise the toys and the numbers from one to eight with the flashcards.

Vocabulary games for anchoring words in the children's productive memories

- Eight children stand in a row in front of the class. Tap one or more children on the back. These children sit down on the floor quickly. The rest of the class call out the number of children left standing.
- Ask two children to come to the board. Now call on individual children to call out numbers from one to eight. The children at the board clap the corresponding numbers.
- Ask the children to listen closely and call out the number that should follow in the sequence, e.g.:
  Three, four, five … Children: *Six.*
  Five, six, seven … Children: *Eight.*
  Four, five, six … Children: *Seven.*
  Eight, seven, six … Children: *Five.*
  Four, three, two … Children: *One.*

❷ **Listen and colour.**
Find, write the numbers and colour.

Matching exercise CD 2/14

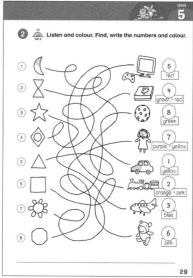

- Ask the children to open their Activity Books at p. 29. Hold up your book and point at the shapes on the left-hand side of the page. Count from one to eight and at the same time point at the corresponding shapes. The children point along in their books. Tell them that they are to listen to the CD and to colour the shapes.
- Play CD 2/14 twice and the children mark the shapes with the colour accordingly. They later colour them completely.

Tapescript:

Speaker 1: Number one – yellow.
           Number one – yellow.

Speaker 2: Number two – orange and pink.
           Number two – orange and pink.

Speaker 1: Number three – blue.
           Number three – blue.

Speaker 2: Number four – green and red.
           Number four – green and red.

Speaker 1: Number five – red.
           Number five – red.

Speaker 2: Number six – pink.
           Number six – pink.

Speaker 1: Number seven – purple and yellow.
           Number seven – purple and yellow.

Speaker 2: Number eight – green.
           Number eight – green.

- Check the children's work by asking: *What colour is number three?* etc.
- The children finish colouring the shapes.
- Demonstrate the next step. Hold up your book. Speak and point. Say: *Look. Number one. It's yellow.* Trace the line with your finger and point at the car which is already numbered and marked yellow. Say: *It's the car. Number one is the car.*
- Say: *Write the numbers.* The children trace each line and write the same number in the circles.
- Check the children's work by asking: *What's number four?* The children answer *The puzzle.*, etc.
- Hold up your book and point to the car. Ask: *What colour is the car?* Children: *Yellow.*
- The children colour the toys in the same colour as the shapes they are matched with on the left side of the page. Give the children sufficient time for this exercise. Go around the class and help if necessary.
- Ask what colour the toys are, e.g.: *What colour is the doll?*
- You can also ask: *What's number (seven)?* Children: *The doll.* Teacher: *What colour is it?* Children: *It's (purple and yellow).*, etc.

L E S S O N   5

Vocabulary, phrases and structures:

My (blue train); star

Linguistic skills:

Learning the meaning and pronunciation of the new word.
Understanding a rhyme from the CD.
Chanting a rhyme (*My blue train*) rhythmically in unison and individually with the support of pictures.
Reciting one's own rhyme.

Cognitive, motor and social skills:

Colouring in pictures of toys according to the CD.
Speaking rhythmically.
Composing, learning by heart and reciting fluently a self-composed rhyme.
Colouring in pictures of toys.

Cross-curricular integration:

Art
Topic: Speaking motivation 'The world of the child'.

Materials:

Flashcards 5–11, 20–22, 35–42
Flashcard 45; CD 2/15–16; *Pupil's Book*, p. 34, ex. 3–4; coloured pencils

Revision

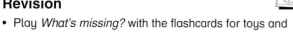

• Play *What's missing?* with the flashcards for toys and colours. (See Unit 1, Lesson 9, Revision.)
•

Vocabulary extension

star

• Hold up the toy flashcards and ask the children to say the words.
• Introduce the word *star* with the flashcard and encourage the children to repeat it several times.

❸ Listen and colour. Say.

Rhyme: *My blue train* CD 2/15

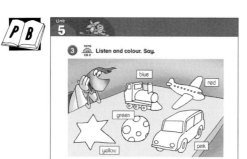

• The children look at ex. 3 on p. 34 of their Pupil's Books.
• Point to the toys in turn. Say: *A train... a plane...*, etc.
• Then point to individual toys in the picture. Have individual children name the corresponding toys.
• Make sure each child has a set of the following coloured pencils on their desk: *blue*, *red*, *green*, *pink* and *yellow*.
• Tell them to colour in the toys in the book according to what they hear on the CD.
• Play CD 2/15 once. The children just listen.

Tapescript:

My blue train.
My red plane.
My green ball.
My pink car.
My yellow star.

• Play the CD again. The children mark the toys in the corresponding colour as they listen (*Make one stroke only.*).
• Ask the children what colours the toys are: *What colour is the car/train/...?* The children answer accordingly.
• The children finish colouring the toys.
• Practise the rhyme thoroughly line by line with the children.

Option: The children can practise the rhyme in twos, and pairs of volunteers or individual children then recite the rhyme in front of the class.
High-ability groups can also try to recite the rhyme to the karaoke version (CD 2/16).

❹ Colour and say.

Speaking exercise:

Step to creativity (Word Play) CD 2/16

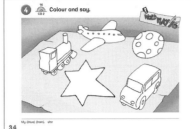

- Ask the children to open their Pupil's Books at p. 34 and look at ex. 4.
- Tell them that they are to colour in each toy in a different colour. Give the children sufficient time for this work. While they are doing this, circulate around the class and check that the children are only colouring each toy in one colour.
- When they have finished colouring, the children use their coloured toys to say the rhyme in ex. 3. They learn the text of their self-composed rhyme off by heart. Show the children the best way to do this. Hold up your book with coloured-in toys. Recite the rhyme in a low voice and point along in the book. Then go around the class and help if necessary.
- When they have practised their rhymes, individual children present their self-composed rhyme to the class. Remember to give them appropriate applause (*Let's give them a big hand!*).

Option: High-ability children can also recite their rhyme to the karaoke section of CD 2/16.

LESSON 6

Vocabulary, phrases and structures:

Receptive language: *You're in a car; There's a dog; Stop the car and get out; The dog jumps into your car; The dog drives off; Vroooooom!; You run after the car.*

Linguistic skills:

Understanding a chain of instructions in an Action Story (*A dog in your car*).
Understanding instructions from the CD and matching with the appropriate pictures.

Cognitive, motor and social skills:

Matching instructions with actions.
Understanding and miming actions with jumbled instructions.

Cross-curricular integration:

Sport
Topic: Road safety education

Materials:

CD 2/16
CD 2/17; *Pupil's Book*, p. 35, ex. 5

Revision

- Invite volunteers to recite their self-composed rhyme from the previous lesson to the karaoke section of CD 2/16.

Action Story: *A dog in your car*
Listen and imitate

- Ask the children to stand in a circle or stand up in their places.
- Say the lines of the Action Story (see tapescript below) and at the same time act them out in mimes/gestures.
- Keep repeating this until you see that the children have a good grasp of the lines in the story and the actions that go with them.

Carrying out instructions

- Tell the children that you are now going to give the same instructions but **not** carry them out yourself. Give the instructions as in the tapescript. The children mime the action. Do **not** do any of the actions yourself but give positive feedback (e.g. by nodding your head) when the children mime the action correctly.
- Keep repeating this until you see that the children can mime the instructions without difficulty. Gradually increase the tempo.

Carrying out the instructions in a different order

- Say that you are going to give the instructions jumbled up (*Now in jumbled order.*) and the children are to carry them out. Do **not** do any of the actions yourself.
- Now say the actions but in random order. Say, e.g.: *There's a dog.*, *You run after the car.*, etc.
- Keep repeating this until you see that the children can mime the actions without difficulty.
- Call on individual children and say the lines in random order for them to act out.

5 Listen and point.
Write the numbers. CD 2/17
Action Story: *A dog in your car*

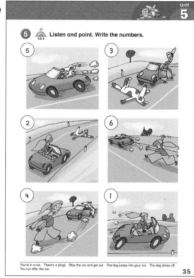

- The children open their Pupil's Books at p. 35. The six pictures are printed in random order. Give the children sufficient time to look at them.
- Play the Action Story (CD 2/17). The children point to the appropriate pictures in the book.

Tapescript:

You're in a car.
There's a dog.
Stop the car and get out.
The dog jumps into your car.
The dog drives off. Vroooooom!
You run after the car.

- Explain to the children that they should listen and number the pictures in the correct order. Number 1 is already done.

- Now play the Action Story again. The children look for the second picture and write the number in the corresponding box. Continue like this for the remaining pictures.
- Go around the class and check the children's work.

Option: Put out a completed Action Story for self-checking. The children go and check their own work themselves.

Alternative: Draw six boxes on the board that represent p. 35 in the Pupil's Book. Have the children tell you the numbers. (*What number is it?*) Write the numbers in the boxes.

L E S S O N   7

Vocabulary, phrases and structures:

I've got a cool, cool duck/dog/mouse/cat on a super bike/in a super car/train/plane.

Linguistic skills:

Singing a song (*My cool pets*).

Cognitive, motor and social skills:

Keeping to the rhythm and melody while speaking in unison and singing.
Pointing to the right pictures while speaking and singing.

Cross-curricular integration:

Music
Topic: Road safety education

Materials:

Flashcards 12–13, 29–34, 35–42
CD 2/18–19; *Pupil's Book*, p. 36, ex. 6

Revision

- Revise the words for pets and toys the children have learnt so far with the flashcards.
- Revise the instructions from the Action Story (*A dog in your car*) from the previous lesson and the children mime the actions.

❻ Listen and point.
   Sing the song.

Song: *My cool pets* **CD 2/18–19**

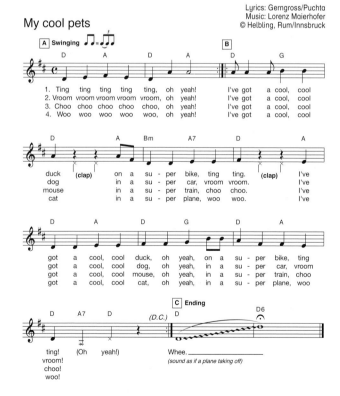

- Play the song (CD 2/18) and at the same time mime and make the corresponding sounds to facilitate understanding, e.g.: *I've got a cool, cool duck* – Imitate the quacking of a duck.
  on a super bike, ting ting – Ride an imaginary bike and ring an imaginary bicycle bell (*ting ting*).
  Wheeeeee! – Imitate the sound of a plane taking off and make a corresponding gesture, etc.

Unit 5 Toys

- Play the song again and the children point to the relevant pictures on p. 36 of the Pupil's Book.
- Say the words of the song with the children using the pictures in the book as prompts and point along again.
- The children stand in a circle. Go round the inside of the circle and hum the tune. The children you go past pick up the tune and begin to hum along. Go round in the circle several times until all the children are humming the tune with you.

- Play the CD again and sing the song with the children.
- Join the circle and do the corresponding mimes and gestures while singing. Use the karaoke section (CD 2/19). The children imitate your actions and sing along.

L E S S O N 8

Vocabulary, phrases and structures:

Please, give me my red train/…; Your red train/…; Here you are.
Receptive language: *What has Benny/Linda/he/she got?; Right, Benny's got a red train, an orange and green train…; You're on your bike; There's a cat; Stop and get off your bike; The cat jumps on your bike; The cat rides off! Ting ting ting; Shout, 'Stop!'.*

Linguistic skills:

Understanding short dialogues on the CD.
Understanding instructions from the CD and matching with the corresponding pictures.

Cognitive, motor and social skills:

Circling the pictures mentioned in dialogues on the CD.
Matching instructions with actions.
Understanding and carrying out jumbled instructions.
Pair work: Practising dialogues.

Cross-curricular integration:

Topic: Road safety education

Materials:

CD 2/19
CD 2/20–21; *Activity Book*, pp. 30–31, ex. 3–4

Revision

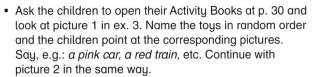

- Stand in a circle. Sing the song *My cool pets* from the previous lesson and do the corresponding mimes and gestures while singing. The children imitate your actions and sing along. Use the karaoke section (CD 2/19).

❸ Listen and circle.

Listening exercise CD 2/20

- Ask the children to open their Activity Books at p. 30 and look at picture 1 in ex. 3. Name the toys in random order and the children point at the corresponding pictures. Say, e.g.: *a pink car, a red train,* etc. Continue with picture 2 in the same way.
- Tell the children to listen to the CD and to circle the pictures of toys according to what they hear.
- Play the first part of CD 2/20 (*Number one, Max.*). The children listen.

Tapescript:

Speaker: Number one, Max.
Max: OK, Benny. Please give me my red train, my orange and green train and my red car.
Benny: OK, Max. Your red train, your orange and green train and your red car. Here you are.
Max: Thanks, Benny.

Speaker: Number two, Linda.
Linda: OK, Max, please give me my pink ball, my yellow and red computer game and my pink star.
Max: OK, Linda. Your pink ball, your yellow and red computer game and your yellow star. Heeheeheeheehee!
Linda: No, Max. And my pink star.
Max: Hehehe! OK. Here you are.

- Play the first part of the CD again and the children circle the appropriate toys in picture 1.
- Check the children's work. Ask: *What about Benny? What has Benny/he got?* Children: *… red train… orange and green train… red car.* Repeat the answer and say: *Right. Benny's got a red train, an orange and green train and a red car.*
- Continue with picture 2 in the same way. Play the second part of the CD 2/20 (*Number 2, Linda*). The children listen and circle the toys accordingly.
- Check the children's work by asking: *Now, what about Linda? What has Linda/she got?*

Pair work: Mini-dialogues

- Act out a few dialogues with individual children in class. Pretend the child has the toys. Say, e.g.: *Please, give me my blue car.* Child: *(Your blue car.) Here you are.* Help the children by whispering prompts if necessary.
- Get the children to practise these mini-dialogues with a partner. Go around the class and help if necessary.

Pre-teaching key phrases
Listen and imitate

- Ask the children to stand in a circle or stand up in their places.
- Say the following sentences and at the same time mime them and make gestures:

  You're on your bike.
  There's a cat.
  Stop and get off your bike.
  The cat jumps on your bike.
  The cat rides off! Ting ting ting.
  Shout, 'Stop!'

- Tell the children that you are now going to give the same instructions but not do them yourself. Give the same instructions in the same order, then in random order. The children do the corresponding actions.

❹ Listen and tick (✓).
Listening exercise CD 2/21

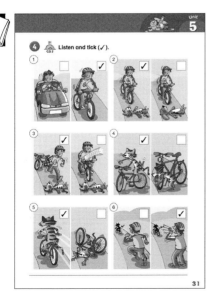

- The children open their Activity Books at p. 31 and look at the pictures in ex. 4. Hold up your book and point at one picture after the other in the correct order while speaking: *You're in your car./You're on your bike./ There's a cat./…* The children listen to you and point at the appropriate pictures in their books.
- Then say the sentences in random order and the children point along.
- Tell the children that they are to listen to the CD and to tick the correct box in each of the pairs of pictures numbered from one to six.
- Play CD 2/21 twice.

Tapescript:

One:	*You're on your bike.*
One:	*You're on your bike.*
Two:	*There's a cat.*
Two:	*There's a cat.*
Three:	*Stop and get off your bike.*
Three:	*Stop and get off your bike.*
Four:	*The cat jumps on your bike.*
Four:	*The cat jumps on your bike.*
Five:	*The cat rides off! Ting ting ting.*
Five:	*The cat rides off! Ting ting ting.*
Six:	*Shout, 'Stop!'.*
Six:	*Shout, 'Stop!'.*

- Play the CD again and the children check their work. Go around the class and help if necessary.
- Check the children's work. Ask: *What about number one? Left or right?* Children: *Right.*

Option: In high-ability classes you can put out an answer key for self-checking. The children go to the key and check their own work themselves.

Alternative: Draw six pairs of boxes numbered one to six on the board that represent the page in the Activity Book. Have the children tell you the answers. Tick the corresponding boxes.

Toys

L E S S O N   9

Vocabulary, phrases and structures:
Is your (plane) red?; No, it isn't; Yes, it is.

Linguistic skills:
Asking for colours of toys and answering accordingly.

Cognitive, motor and social skills:
Colouring in pictures.
Pair work: Doing an information gap activity.
Playing a game (Bingo!).

Cross-curricular integration:
Art

Materials:
Flashcards 5–13; 20–22, 35–42
Activity Book, p. 32, ex. 5–6; coloured pencils

Revision

- Hand out the flashcards for colours and toys to individual children. Say, e.g.: *Give me the red ball.* The two children with the appropriate flashcards come out to the board. They hold up the cards (for *red* and *ball*) and say: *Here you are.*

❺ Colour and say.
Pair work: Speaking exercise

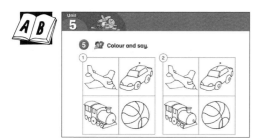

- Ask the children to open their Activity Books at p. 32 and look at ex. 5. They work with a partner. Tell them that they should put up a schoolbag or a book on the desk between each other's Activity Books so that they cannot see each other's work.
- Tell them to colour each of the four objects in the grid on the left (number 1) in one of the following colours: red, green, blue, yellow or pink. They should not let their partner see their colouring.
- Child A asks for the colour of the first object in child B's grid, e. g.: *Is your plane red?* Child B answers with: *No, it isn't.* or *Yes, it is.*
- When child A has guessed the colour, he/she colours the plane on the right in his/her own book (number 2) in the same colour.
- Then they swap roles and continue in the same way with the other toys in the grids.
- Go around the class and help if necessary.
- When they have finished colouring all the objects, the children compare results with their partner.

❻ Colour. Play bingo.
Game: Bingo!

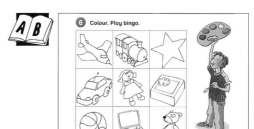

- Get the children to colour the toys in ex. 6 in one of the following colours: red, green, blue, yellow or pink.
- Explain that you will tell them what toys they should cross out in their Bingo grid. The child who has crossed out three pictures in a row (across or down) calls out *Bingo!*
- Slowly tell them what to cross out, e.g. *a pink car, a yellow teddy bear, a red train,* …etc. Keep a note of the colours of the items you say.
- To check, tell the winner to say the toys and the corresponding colours in their row.

L E S S O N 10

Vocabulary, phrases and structures:

I've got three/four/... cars/planes/...
Receptive language: *How many cars/... has (Anna) got?; How many cars/... have you got?*

Linguistic skills:

Learning the meaning and pronunciation of the new phrases.
Understanding statements from the CD.
Saying how many toys the children in the listening exercise have got.

Cognitive, motor and social skills:

Understanding words from the CD and matching them to pictures in the book.
Drawing oneself and making statements about oneself.
Pair work: Saying which and how many toys they have.

Cross-curricular integration:

Topic: Speaking motivation 'My toys'.
Mathematics: Counting from one to eight

Materials:

CD 2/19; *Flashcards* 1–4, 23–24, 36–38, 41, 43–44
CD 2/22; *Pupil's Book*, p. 37, ex. 7–8

Revision

- Sing the song *My cool pets* with the children using the karaoke section (CD 2/19).
- Revise the words *train*, *plane*, *car* and *ball* and the numbers one to eight with the flashcards.

❼ Listen and write the numbers.

Listening exercise CD 2/22

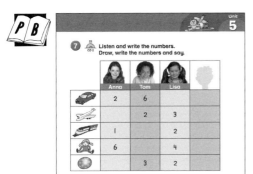

- Ask the children to open their Pupil's Books at p. 37 and look at the first column of the grid in ex. 7. Name the toys first in order, then jumbled up. The children point to the appropriate pictures in the book.
- Hold up your book, point to the photos of the children and give their names.
- Tell the children that they are going to hear which toys and how many of them Anna, Tom and Lisa have. They should listen and write the corresponding numbers in the boxes in the grid.
- Play CD 2/22. Stop after the first child (Anna). Ask: *How many cars has Anna got?* Child: *Two.* You: *Yes, right. / No, sorry.* etc.

Tapescript:

Anna: Hi, I'm Anna. I've got two cars, one train and six dolls. Again. I've got two cars, one train and six dolls.

Tom: Hi, I'm Tom. I've got six cars, two planes and three balls. One more time. I've got six cars, two planes and three balls.

Lisa: Hi, I'm Lisa. I've got three planes, two trains, four dolls and two balls. Again. I've got three planes, two trains, four dolls and two balls.

- Play the CD several times.
- Check the children's answers by asking: *How many cars has (Tom) got?* Child: *Six.* Teacher: *Yes, right./No, sorry.* etc.

❼ Draw, write the numbers and say.

Speaking exercise

- The children draw their own face in the silhouette in the top right of the grid in the Pupil's Book on p. 37. Then they fill in the last column for themselves so that they can say later, e.g.: *I've got three cars, four planes and three dolls.*
- Ask individual children: *(Monica), how many cars have you got?*. (Monica): *Six.*
- Say, e.g.: *Wow, that's a lot!*, etc.

❽ Say.

Pair work: Talking about toys

- The children work in pairs. Child A talks about his/her toys (*I've got …*), child B listens.
- Then child B says which and how many toys s/he has. When both partners have exchanged information about their toys, they swap partners. The new pairs talk about their toys.

Alternative: The children go around the classroom. When you clap your hands, the children form a pair with the person standing nearest to them. They talk about their toys. When you clap again, the children go around the classroom again.

L E S S O N   11

Vocabulary, phrases and structures:

What have you got?; I've got (three) red cars/…
Receptive language: What has (James) got?

Linguistic skills:

Understanding statements from the CD.
Asking and make statements about the number of toys.

Cognitive, motor and social skills:

Understanding words from the CD and matching them to pictures in the book.

Drawing one's own toys and making statements about oneself.
Pair work: Asking about each other's toys.

Cross-curricular integration:

Topic: Speaking motivation 'My toys'.
Mathematics: Counting from one to six

Materials:

a soft ball or the glove puppet Max
CD 2/23; *Activity Book*, p. 33, ex. 7–8; coloured pencils

Revision

- Stand in a circle. Say one of the toy words, e.g.: *train* and throw a soft ball or the glove puppet to a child. The child says another word that belongs to this word field and throws the ball to another child, and so on. Revise the word fields for pets, school and fruit in the same way.

❼ Listen and circle.
Listening exercise CD 2/23

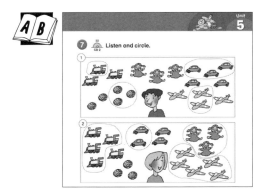

- Ask the children to open their Activity Books at p. 33 and look at ex. 7.
- Tell them to listen to the CD and circle the number of toys the two children (James and Ruby) have.
- Play the first part of CD 2/23 (James) twice. The children listen and circle the number of toys accordingly.

Tapescript:

Speaker: James.
James: I've got a train, three cars, two planes and three balls. Once more. I've got a train, three cars, two planes and three balls.

Speaker: Ruby.
Ruby: I've got three dolls, four trains, five planes and two cars. Once more. I've got three dolls, four trains, five planes and two cars.

- Play the second part of CD 2/23 (Ruby) twice. The children continue in the same way as above.
- Check the answers as a class. Ask: *What has James got?* The children answer: *Three cars, two planes and three balls.* Repeat for Ruby.

❽ Draw, colour and say.
Speaking exercise

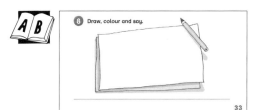

- Ask the children to open their Activity Books at p. 33 and look at ex. 8.
- Tell them to draw what toys they've got and to colour their toys accordingly.
- When the children have finished their work, they present to the class what they've got and say, e.g.: *I've got two red trains and three blue cars.* Help by whispering: *I've got…* if necessary.

Pair work

- The children work with a partner. Child A asks child B: *What have you got?* Child B answers accordingly. Then they swap roles.

Alternative: The children go around the classroom. When you clap your hands, the children form a pair with the person standing nearest to them. They talk about their toys. When you clap again, the children go around the classroom again.

Teacher's Book • Playway to English 1 Second edition

L E S S O N 1

Vocabulary, phrases and structures:

rain; sun; wind; cloud(s); snow; It's raining/ snowing; It's /sunny/windy/cloudy; a cap on a frog; Caps are always fun;
Receptive language: *What's the weather like?*

Linguistic skills:

Learning the meaning and pronunciation of the new words and phrases.
Reciting a chant (*A cap on a cat*) in unison and in groups.
Answering questions about the weather conditions.

Cognitive, motor and social skills:

Associating sounds with pictures in the book.
Pair work: Understanding/Saying words in pairs.
Associating sounds and words from the CD.

Listening to a chant on the CD and pointing along in the book.
Speaking in the rhythm of a group.
Distinguishing weather conditions and completing pictures by drawing the appropriate weather symbols.

Cross-curricular integration:

Topic: Speaking motivation 'Weather'.

Materials:

Flashcards 29, 31, 33
Flashcards 46–51; CD 2/24–25; *Pupil's Book,* p. 38, ex. 1–2; baseball cap or a drawn and cut out picture of a cap; *Activity Book,* p. 34, ex. 1; coloured pencils

Revision

- Revise the words *cat*, *dog*, and *rabbit* with the flashcards.

Introduction of vocabulary

rain; sun; wind; cloud(s); snow; It's raining/snowing; It's sunny/windy/cloudy.

- Show the *rain* flashcard and say: *Rain – It's raining.*
- At the same time make a gesture that symbolizes rain, for example, holding an umbrella or drumming with your fingers on the table. Say the word/phrase several times and ask the children to do the corresponding action.
- Introduce the other words and phrases in the same way.

❶ **Listen and point.**
Listening exercise CD 2/24

- Play CD 2/24. The children just listen to the weather sounds and phrases.
- Ask the children to open their Pupil's Books at p. 38. Play the CD again. The children point to the corresponding pictures in ex. 1.

Tapescript:

Rain – It's raining.
Wind – It's windy.
Snow – It's snowing.
Sun – It's sunny.
Cloud – It's cloudy.

Exercises for anchoring the vocabulary in the recognition memory

- Ask the children to close their eyes. Say the words at different volumes and pitches several times. The children just listen.
- Call individual children out to the board. Say, e.g.: *(Sandro), touch rain.* (Sandro) touches the corresponding flashcard on the board, etc.

❶ **Work in pairs.**
Pair work

- The children work in pairs with one Pupil's Book.
- Child A says a weather word, child B points to the appropriate picture in ex. 1. Then they swap roles.

Note: Pair work gives the children the possibility of practising the new words in a stress-free atmosphere. In addition it increases the time each individual child spends speaking.

Pronunciation tip: Take care with the pronunciation of *wind*. The [w] is spoken with rounded lips.

Vocabulary extension

cap; frog

- Introduce the word *cap* by showing the cap you have brought to class. Alternatively, use the picture of a cap you have drawn and cut out.
- Introduce the word *frog* with the flashcard.

❷ Listen and point.
Say the chant.

Chant: *A cap on a cat* CD 2/25–26

- Stick the flashcards of the animals (*cat, dog, rabbit, frog*) on the board. Take a cap and hold it briefly over each picture to give the impression that the animals are wearing the cap. At the same time, say and point along: *A cap on a cat, a cap on a dog, a cap on a rabbit, a cap on a frog.*
- Ask the children to look at ex. 2 on p. 38 of their Pupil's Books. Play the chant a few times (CD 2/25) and ask the children to point along in their books.
- Encourage the children to say the chant. Practise it line by line and point along with it on the board by using the flashcards and the cap as above.

Tapescript:

A cap on a cat.
A cap on a dog.
A cap on a rabbit.
A cap on a frog.
Rain, snow or sun.
Caps are always fun.

- Play the first part of CD 2/26 (*And now you!*) and say the chant with the children several times line by line. The children point to the corresponding pictures in the book and say the chant.
- Play the karaoke section of CD 2/26 (*One more time!*) and ask the children to look at the page in the Pupil's Book and chant rhythmically.
- Play the karaoke section again (*One more time!*). The children recite the chant in two groups A and B:

A: A cap on a cat.
A: A cap on a dog.
A: A cap on a rabbit.
A: A cap on a frog.
B: Rain, snow or sun.
B: Caps are always fun.

Note: Explain the line of text *Caps are always fun.* in L1.

Pronunciation tip: Take care with the pronunciation of *cap* and *cat.* Say the [æ] as open as possible.

❶ Draw to complete the pictures. Say.
Speaking exercise

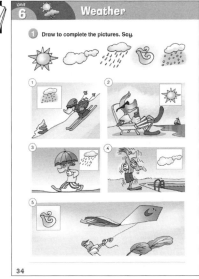

- Ask the children to look at the weather symbols at the top of p. 34 in their Activity Books. Hold up your book. Point to the weather symbols one after the other and ask the children to repeat the word or phrase, e.g. *Sun./It's sunny. Clouds/It's cloudy. Rain/It's raining. Wind./It's windy. Snow./It's snowing.*
- Tell the children to look at the five main pictures. Ask them to complete the pictures by drawing the appropriate weather symbols.
- Go around the class and help if necessary.
- To check the children's work ask, e.g.: *Number one. What's the weather like?* Prompt the children to answer: *It's snowing.* Continue with the other pictures in the same way.
- Alternatively, you can check the children's answers as follows:
  Teacher: *It's sunny. What picture is it?*
  Child: *Two.*, etc.

Background information:

If you teach in a country where children have never experienced snow, it might be useful to show the class photographs of snow-covered landscapes.

In the UK, some places have more snow than others. Parts of Scotland and North Wales can have a lot of snow but in England it snows most winters for a few days. For children, this is usually a magical time with everything covered in snow and traffic sometimes coming to a standstill. When there is snow, children like going sledging or having snowball fights.

Many children also make a snowman. They roll a ball of snow until it is so big that they cannot move it any more. They put a second, smaller ball on top of it for the head. Children stick a carrot in the snowman's head as his nose, and they use two pieces of coal or stones for his eyes and a twig for his mouth. Sometimes they dress the snowman in a hat and scarf.

L E S S O N   2

Vocabulary, phrases and structures:

snowman; grow; run
Receptive language: *Cap number one is orange;
How many (dogs) are there?*

Linguistic skills:

Reciting a rhyme (*Snowman grow*) and pointing to
the relevant pictures.
Reciting a rhyme with actions.
Recognising tracks in the snow.
Understanding instructions from the CD.

Cognitive, motor and social skills:

Listening to a rhyme on the CD and pointing to the
corresponding pictures in the book.
Saying a rhyme to the karaoke section of the CD.

Catching a ball and at the same time responding
with a word.
Colouring in pictures according to the instructions
from the CD.
Counting and naming the number of animals and
caps in a picture.

Cross-curricular integration:

Sport: Ball game with animal names.
Topic: Animal tracks in the snow.

Materials:

Flashcards 1–4, 23–24, 31–33, 46–50; CD 2/26
Flashcard 52; *Pupil's Book*, p. 39, ex. 3–4;
CD 2/27–28; a ball; CD 2/29; *Activity Book*, p. 35,
ex. 2; coloured pencils

Revision

- Revise the weather words, the numbers one to six, *cat*,
  duck and *rabbit* with the aid of the flashcards.
- Stand in a circle. Chant with the children *A cap on a cat.*
  from the previous lesson. Use the karaoke section of
  CD 2/26.

Introduction of vocabulary

snowman; grow; run

- Introduce the word *snowman* with the flashcard.
- Make clear the meaning of the words *grow* and *run*
  through appropriate actions. Say the words several
  times and get the children to imitate your actions and
  repeat after you.

❸ Listen and point. Say.

Rhyme: *Snowman grow*
CD 2/27–28

Tapescript:

Snow, snow.
Snowman grow.
Oh, the sun.
Snowman run.

- Play the rhyme (CD 2/27). Use gesture and mime to
  help convey meaning.
- Play the rhyme a second time (CD 2/27). The children
  open their Pupil's Books at p. 39 and point along in
  ex. 3.
- The children stand in a circle. Say the rhyme with mimes
  and gesture. The children imitate your actions.
- Ask the children to join in saying the rhyme and doing
  the actions.
- Use the karaoke section (CD 2/28). Say the rhyme again
  but stop doing the actions. The children recite and do the
  actions.

Vocabulary revision

dog; mouse; rabbit; duck; cat; hamster

- Revise the animals with the children sitting in a circle
  on the floor and rolling a ball to each other. The child to
  whom the ball is rolled names an animal and rolls the
  ball to another child, etc. The individual animal names
  may be used several times.

Note: This game can also be played in the gymnasium. The
children throw the ball to each other.

❹ Look and write the numbers. Say.
Discovery picture

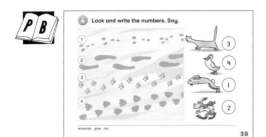

- The children open their Pupil's Books at p. 39 and look at ex. 4.
- Name the animals and Max in the right-hand column in order and the children point to them in the book.
- The children try to recognise the tracks in the snow and match them to the animals or to Max.
- Check the answers. Ask: *What's number one?* Child: *A rabbit. / A cat.* Teacher: *Yes, right. / No, sorry.*, etc.

Answer key:
1 rabbit
2 Max
3 cat
4 duck

❶ Listen and colour. Count and write the numbers.
Listening exercise CD 2/29

Tapescript:

Speaker 1: Cap number one is orange.
Speaker 2: Cap number two is black.
Speaker 1: Cap number three is green.
Speaker 2: Cap number four is brown.

- Ask the children to look at p. 35 in their Activity Books. Say, e.g.: *Point at a frog/a dog/a cap/a rabbit/a cat.* The children point to appropriate pictures in their book.
- Make sure that the children have coloured pencils ready: orange, black, green and brown.
- Tell the children to colour the caps at the top of the page according to the instructions they hear on the CD.
- Play CD 2/29. The children listen and only mark the caps in the corresponding colour.
- The children listen again and check their work. They then complete colouring all the caps on the page accordingly. E.g.: all the caps showing number one are coloured orange.
- Finally, they count the animals and the caps in the picture and write the appropriate numbers in the grid at the top.
- Ask, e.g.: *How many dogs are there? How many orange caps are there? How many frogs are there?* The children answer, e.g.: *Four (dogs).*, etc.

Answer key:
4 orange caps
6 black caps
5 green caps
2 brown caps
6 cats
4 dogs
2 rabbits
5 frogs

Teacher's Book • Playway to English 1 Second edition

Weather

L E S S O N 3

Vocabulary, phrases and structures:

bee; butterfly; flower; umbrella
Receptive language: *A little seed; The little seed is asleep; Hello, Bee; Hi, Butterfly; Look at the clouds; I've got an umbrella; Come with me; Aah! This is good; The little seed grows and grows; The rain stops; Thanks for the umbrella; That's OK. Careful!; Oh, dear!; Look. Here comes the sun; Fantastic!; A week later. The seed grows and grows. Look at the wonderful flower; Mmmmh, what a sweet smell; Bless you!*

Linguistic skills:

Understanding a story (*The little seed*) from the DVD and the CD and from narration by the teacher.
Gradually joining in with the story-telling.
(Optional) Acting out a role play.

Cognitive, motor and social skills:

Following the narrative structure of a story.
Representing a time sequence visually.
Completing a picture story with picture stickers.
(Optional) Presenting the story in scenes and to music.

Cross-curricular integration:

Topic: Speaking motivation 'A flower growing' and 'Cycles in nature'.

Materials:

CD 2/28; soft ball
Flashcards 46–47, 49; 53–56; DVD (*The little seed*); CD 2/30; *Pupil's Book*, pp. 40–41, ex. 5; *Story Cards* 34–45; picture stickers from the appendix of the *Pupil's Book*; (optional) a completed picture story for self-checking

Revision

- Use the karaoke section (CD 2/28) and say the rhyme *Snowman grow* from the previous lesson with the children.
- Stand in a circle. Revise the words for weather, colours and animals by playing a ball game. (See the Vocabulary revision activity in Lesson 2.)

Introduction of vocabulary and preliminary preparation of phrases

bee; butterfly; flower; umbrella; a little seed; grows; What a sweet smell!; Bless you!

- Introduce the words *bee*, *butterfly*, *flower* and *umbrella* with the flashcards.
- Draw the picture of a seed under the ground on the board. Point to the drawing and say: *Look. A little seed.* With your thumb and index finger make a sign for *little*. Say: *It's asleep.* To make it clearer mime asleep.
- Revise the words *rain*, *clouds* and *sun* with the flashcards. Make sure the children can recognise and say them.
- Draw several pictures of a seed at various stages of growth into a flower. Say: *Look at the seed. It grows and grows.* Point to the pictures and to make it clearer make a movement for growth. Finally, point to the flower and say: *Look! A flower!*
- Say the words *seed*, *flower*, and *grows* several times and encourage the children to repeat after you.
- Call one child for each word to the board and have each child point to the corresponding picture: *rain, sun, seed, flower, grows (and grows)*.
- Introduce the phrase *What a sweet smell!* by miming, e.g. sniffing a flower and smiling.

- Explain the meaning of *Bless you!* with the story card 45 or by pretending to sneeze and eliciting the response from the children in L1.
- Say the two phrases. The children do the corresponding actions.

❺ Watch the story.

Cartoon Story: *The little seed*

- Show the children the DVD sequence *The little seed* twice.

DVD script: *The little seed*

Storyteller:	The little seed is asleep.
Butterfly:	Hello, Bee.
Bee:	Hi, Butterfly.
	Oh. Look at the clouds.
Butterfly:	I've got an umbrella. Come with me.
Bee:	Aah! This is good!
Storyteller:	It's raining.
	The little seed grows and grows.
	The rain stops.
Bee:	Thanks for the umbrella.
Butterfly:	That's OK.
	Careful!
Bee:	Oh, dear!
Butterfly:	Look. Here comes the sun!
Bee:	Fantastic!
Storyteller:	A week later. The seed grows and grows.
Bee:	Hi, Butterfly.
Butterfly:	Hi, Bee. Look at the wonderful flower.
Bee:	Mmmh, what a sweet smell!
	A... A... Atishoo!
Butterfly:	Bless you!

---

❺ Listen and stick.

Listening exercise:
Sticker activity CD 2/30

- The children look at pp. 40 and 41 of their Pupil's Books.
- Play the audio version of the story twice (CD 2/30). The children follow the story in their books and complete the spaces with the picture stickers while they are listening.
- Go around the class and check the children's work.

Option: Place a completed picture story in the classroom. The children go and check their own work themselves.

Telling the story

- Put the story cards jumbled on the board. Tell the story and ask two children to put the pictures in the right order while you are telling the story.

Role play – Act it out

- In high-ability classes the story can also be performed as a role play after appropriate intensive practice. Proceed as follows:
- Play the CD. The children close their eyes and see the story in their mind's eye (*TV in the head*).
- Act the story. You play the part of the speaker and two children play the bee and the butterfly. Help the children by whispering cues. Option: a third child can also play the part of the little seed or the flower.

Option: Play classical music in the background, e.g. *Spring* from Vivaldi's *Four Seasons*. This has the advantage that there are no silent gaps in the pauses in speaking that might inhibit the presentation phases. The children stay in their pose until the next sentence.

C L I L: Content and Language Integrated Learning
Seeds – a mini-project

Receptive language:

sunflower seeds; cress seeds; orange pips; apple pips; beans; peas; lentils

Objective:

Promoting the creativity of the children.
Finding out about the growth of a plant in an experiment.
Finding out whether plants flourish better in light or dark places.

Materials:

Various sorts of seeds (sunflower, cress, orange pips, apple pips, beans, lentils); cardboard for each child, glue, two bowls or small pots; cotton wool; cress seeds

---

Art: Making a seed pattern

- Ask the children to bring different sorts of seeds (sunflower, cress, orange pips, apple pips, beans, lentils, etc.) to the lesson.
- Give each child a piece of cardboard.
- Show how the seeds can be laid out on the cardboard to make a pattern. While you are showing this, keep saying the appropriate words or accompany your actions with a commentary in English.
- Stick the seeds on the cardboard with glue.

Expressions:

Look, an orange pip / a sunflower seed / …
Give me a sunflower seed / a cress seed / an apple pip / a lentil / a bean.
(Let's) put it on the cardboard like this.
It looks nice!
Give me some glue, please.
(Let's) stick the seeds on the cardboard.

Science: Growing cress

- Take two bowls or small pots together with cotton wool and cress seeds to the lesson. Ask the children to put the cotton wool into the pots, moisten it and spread the cress seeds evenly over it. Then put one pot on the window sill and the other in a dark place. Accompany your actions with instructions in English.
- Ask the children to keep the cotton wool in both pots moist and to watch the cress grow.
- In which pot does it grow better? Why?

Expressions:

Let's grow some cress.
Put some cotton wool in the pots.
Pour a little water over it.
Put the cress seeds onto the wet cotton wool.
Put one pot in the light.
Put one pot in the dark.

L E S S O N 4

Vocabulary, phrases and structures:
It's raining; Come out; Oh, what a rainy day.

Linguistic skills:
Understanding a story on the CD.
Singing a song (*It's raining*).

Cognitive, motor and social skills:
Understanding sentences on the CD and ticking pictures accordingly.
Listening to a song on the CD and pointing along in the book.
Paying attention to the right rhythm while speaking in unison, singing and walking.
Setting the song to movements.

Cross-curricular integration:
Topic: Speaking motivation 'Weather'.
Music

Materials:
DVD (The little seed); *Story Cards* 34–45
CD 2/31; *Activity Book*, p. 36, ex. 3; CD 2/32–33;
Pupil's Book, p. 41, ex. 6

Revision
- Revise the story *The little seed* with the support of the DVD and the story cards.

❸ Listen and tick (✓).
Listening exercise CD 2/31

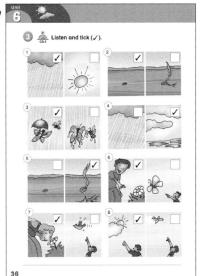

Tapescript:

Speaker 1:	*One. It's raining.*
	One. It's raining.
Speaker 2:	*Two. The little seed is asleep.*
Speaker 2:	*Two. The little seed is asleep.*
Speaker 1:	*Three.*
Butterfly:	*Come here, Bee. I've got an umbrella.*
Bee:	*This is good.*
Speaker 1:	*Three.*
Butterfly:	*Come here, Bee. I've got an umbrella.*
Bee:	*This is good.*

Speaker 2:	*Four. The rain stops.*
Speaker 2:	*Four. The rain stops.*
Speaker 1:	*Five. The little seed grows and grows.*
Speaker 1:	*Five. The little seed grows and grows.*
Speaker 2:	*Six. Look at the wonderful flower.*
Speaker 2:	*Six. Look at the wonderful flower.*
Speaker 1:	*Seven.*
Child:	*Mmmmh, what a sweet smell!*
Speaker 1:	*Seven.*
Child:	*Mmmmh, what a sweet smell!*
Speaker 2:	*Eight. Look, here comes the sun.*
Speaker 2:	*Eight. Look, here comes the sun.*

- The children open their Activity Books at p. 36 and look at the pictures for about ten seconds. Tell them to close their books and ask them to say any words or phrases they associate with the pictures.
- The children open their books again. Play CD 2/31. The children look at each pair of pictures and tick the one that matches what they hear.
- The children listen again and check.
- Check the children's work. Ask: *What about number one? Left or right?* Children: *Left.*

Option: In high-ability classes you can put out an answer key for self-checking. The children go to the key and check their own work themselves.

Alternative: Draw four pairs of boxes numbered one to eight on the board that represent the page in the Activity Book. Have the children tell you the answers. Tick the corresponding boxes

❻ **Listen and point.
Sing the song.**

Song: *It's raining* CD 2/32–33

Lyrics: Gerngross/Puchta
Music: Lorenz Maierhofer
© Helbling, Rum/Innsbruck

It's raining

It's rain - ing, it's rain - ing, come out and let's play,

run and jump, oh what a rai - ny day,

run and jump, oh what a rai - ny day!

- Play the song (CD 2/32) and do actions to facilitate the understanding of the text.
- Ask the children to join in. Say, e.g.: *It's raining.* Hold an imaginary umbrella or drum the fingers of both hands on a table top, etc.
- Play the song again. The children point along with it on p. 41 (ex. 6) in the Pupil's Book.
- Say the words of the song and encourage the children to join in. They use the pictures in the book as prompts and point along again.

- Use the karaoke section (CD 2/33). Sing the song with the children. Make the sound of rain by rapidly tapping your finger tips on the table top. At the line *Run and jump*, clap your hands three times.
- Play the karaoke section again. (CD 2/33). This time the children stand in a circle and do the actions. They turn right and follow each other round in a circle singing and doing the actions.
- At *It's raining*, hold an imaginary umbrella.
- At *Come out and let's play*, beckon the children to turn to the centre of the circle.
- At *Run and jump*, run and jump on the spot.
- At *Oh, what a rainy day*, crouch down and drum your fingers on the floor.

L E S S O N   5

Vocabulary, phrases and structures:

Vocabulary revision: *rain; sun; wind; cloud(s); snow; It's raining/snowing; It's sunny/windy/cloudy.* Receptive language: *What's the weather like today?; It's very (cloudy).*

Linguistic skills:

Understanding short weather reports from the CD. Understanding geographical information about the weather in Great Britain through photos.

Cognitive, motor and social skills:

Understanding weather reports from the CD and putting pictures in the correct order by numbering them.
Pair work: Playing a mime game with weather vocabulary.

Cross-curricular integration:

Curriculum content: Speaking motivation 'Weather and climate'.

Materials:

CD 2/33
Pupil's Book, p. 42, ex. 7–8; CD 2/34

Revision

- Use the karaoke section (CD 2/33) and sing the song *It's raining* with the children.

Preliminary preparation of phrases

What's the weather like today?; It's sunny/raining

- Ask the children: *What's the weather like today?* Look out of the window and elicit *It's sunny/raining/...* Help the children by whispering to them.

Tapescript:

Number one. It's very cloudy.
Number one. It's very cloudy.

Number two. It's very windy.
Number two. It's very windy.

Number three. It's very sunny.
Number three. It's very sunny.

Number four. It's raining.
Number four. It's raining.

❼ Listen and point.
Write the numbers.

Listening exercise: *Weather reports* CD 2/34

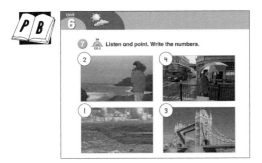

- The children open their Pupil's Books at p. 42 and look at the photos in ex. 7. They call out any relevant weather words that occur to them.
- Tell the children that they are going to hear short weather reports on the CD and are to number the pictures to match what they hear.
- Play CD 2/34. Stop the CD after the first weather report and do the first example with the children.
- Play the remaining three weather reports. The children number the photos in the book.
- Check the children's answers by asking: *There's a strong wind./It's windy. What number is it?* etc.

❽ Say.

Pair work

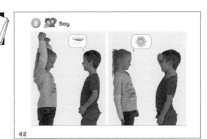

- Demonstrate the pair work with a child in front of the class. Make a gesture that symbolizes e.g.: *rain.* (Elicit the word *rain* or *It's raining.*)
- The children work in pairs. Child A mimes the weather and child B says the word or the phrase. Then they swap roles. Go around the class and help if necessary.

Option: The children walk round the classroom. When you clap your hands they form pairs with the person standing nearest to them. They do the pair work. When you clap again the children walk round the classroom again.

L E S S O N 6

Vocabulary, phrases and structures:

Receptive language: *The little caterpillar is asleep; It's windy; It's snowing/raining; Here comes the sun. The caterpillar is happy; The caterpillar grows and grows; Look at the wonderful butterfly. It's blue, red and orange.* weather; fruit; toys

Linguistic skills:

Understanding sentences from the CD and matching them with the corresponding pictures.

Cognitive, motor and social skills:

Associating illustrations with what they hear on the CD and numbering them accordingly.
Categorizing pictures and copying them.

Cross-curricular integration:

Topic: Speaking motivation 'Weather'.
Art

Material:

Flashcards 46–50, 54
CD 2/35; *Activity Book*, pp. 37–38, ex. 4–5; coloured pencils; (optional) answer key for self-checking

Revision

• Revise the words for weather and *butterfly* with the flashcards.

❹ **Listen and write the numbers.**
Listening exercise CD 2/35

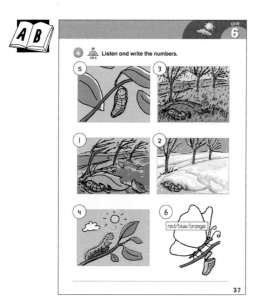

Tapescript:

The little caterpillar is asleep. It's windy.
It's snowing.
It's raining.
Here comes the sun. The caterpillar is happy.
The caterpillar grows and grows.
Look at the wonderful butterfly. It's blue, red and orange.

• Play the CD again. The children listen and number the pictures from one to six. Go around the class and help if necessary.
• Check the answers. Ask, e.g.: *What number's 'Here comes the sun.'*?
• Say a number and the children say the corresponding sentence/s. Help through whispering cues. Repeat the sentence/s and get the children to repeat after you.

Option: In high-ability classes you can put out an answer key for self-checking. The children go to the key and check their own work themselves.

Alternative: Draw six boxes on the board that represent the page in the Activity Book. Have the children tell you the answers. Write the numbers in the boxes.

• Ask the children to look at the pictures on p. 37 in the Activity Book. Introduce the word *caterpillar* by pointing at it in one of the pictures. Let the children repeat the word several times. Tell them that they are to number the pictures according to what they hear on CD.
• Play the CD (CD 2/35). The children only listen and look at the pictures in the book.

❺ Look and draw. Say.
Forming categories

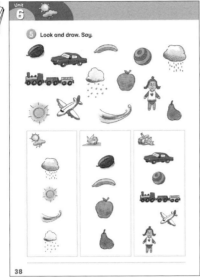

- Ask the children to look at the pictures in ex. 5 on p. 38 in the Activity Book for about ten seconds. Then have the children close their books and name words that they can remember (*Close your books.*). Say: *Give me words.* The children call out the words.
- The children open their books again. They put the pictures into categories by drawing them in the appropriate column.
- Ask the children to look at the pictures at the top of each column and say which category they think each picture represents (weather, fruit, toys). Tell the children they are all topics they have studied so far and they can flick through their books for help.
- Check the answers. Ask: *What goes with weather? Tell me the words.*, etc. Child: *Rain, wind, sun, snow.*

Answer key:
(weather): rain, wind, sun, snow
(fruit): apple, pear, plum, banana
(toys): car, plane, train, doll, ball

L E S S O N 7

Vocabulary, phrases and structures:
Vocabulary revision: school things; pets; toys; fruit

Linguistic skills:
Understanding vocabulary on the CD and matching it to pictures in the book.

Cognitive, motor and social skills:
Understanding vocabulary on the CD and ticking the corresponding pictures in the book.
Pair work: Drawing pictures and playing a vocabulary game.

Cross-curricular integration:
Art

Material:
Flashcards 14–19, 25–42
CD 2/36; *Activity Book*, p. 39, ex. 6–7; coloured pencils; (optional) answer key for self-checking

Revision

- Sit in a circle with the children. Revise school things, pets, toys and fruit using the flashcards.
- Ask the children to stand and clap with you as you repeat the words rhythmically.
- The children sit down. Say a number of words from one category, including a word that does not belong to this category, e. g. *car, plane, apple, train, doll.* Instruct the children to put their hands up when they hear the odd word out.

❻ Listen and tick (✓). Say.
Listening exercise CD 2/36

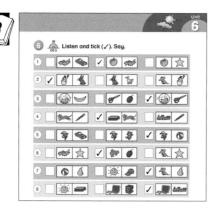

Tapescript:

One:	*an apple and a plane*
Two:	*a snowman and a rabbit*
Three:	*a hamster and scissors*
Four:	*a pencil case and a cat*
Five:	*a doll and a ball*
Six:	*a puzzle and a plum*
Seven:	*a mouse and a pear*
Eight:	*a computer game and a train*

- The children open their Activity Books at p. 39 and look at the pictures in ex. 6. Hold up your book and point at each pair of pictures one after the other while saying: *A plane and a car, an apple and a plane...* The children listen to you and point along in their books.
- Tell them that they are to listen to the CD and to tick the appropriate picture in each line indicated by numbers (one to eight).
- Demonstrate the first one. Stop the CD after the first example *One. An apple and a plane.* Repeat the words and pretend to tick the box in the second pair of pictures in the book.
- Then play the whole exercise (CD 2/36). The children listen and tick the appropriate pair of pictures.
- Play the CD again. The children listen and check their work. Go around the class and help if necessary.
- Check the answers, e.g.: *What about number one?* Children: *Apple and plane!*

Option: In high-ability classes you can put out an answer key for self-checking. The children go to the key and check their own work themselves.

❼ Draw and say.
Pair work: Step to creativity

- Tell the children to draw two pictures of their own choice into the first frame in ex. 7 on p. 39 in their Activity Books. Then they continue with the other three frames in the same way.
- Ask the children to work in pairs. Child A says the words in one of his/her frames to child B. Child B points at the appropriate picture in child A's Activity Book.
- They then swap roles and continue in this way. Go around the class to help if necessary.

C L I L:
Content and Language Integrated Learning

Objective:
Doing an experiment to find out about the formation of a rainbow.
Naming the colours of the spectrum.

Materials:
Flashcards 5–11, 20–22
Pupil's Book, p. 43, ex. 9; glass container; a large sheet of white paper; torch; a jug of water; coloured pencils; photocopiable master (appendix p. 175 of the Teacher's Book)

Revision
• Revise the colours with the aid of the flashcards.

❾ Look and draw.
Experiment

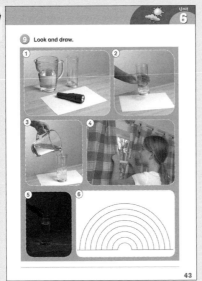

• Explain to the children that you are going to show them an experiment to find out about the colours of the rainbow. Say that first you will mime the stages of the experiment together to learn them. Use L1 where necessary to help with understanding the presentation.

• Show the children the glass container and the sheet of paper. Say:

Put the paper on the desk. (Do this.)
Put the container on the paper. (Do this.)
Fill the container with water. (Mime this.)
Draw the curtains. (Mime or do this.)
Take a torch. (Do this.)
Shine the light into the water. (Shine the torch into the empty container.)
Look at the paper. (Do this.)

• Say: *Now let's do the actions.* Repeat the process and encourage the children to mime with you. Let them stand in their places to mime doing the actions if you prefer.

• Practise this sequence of actions several times until the children are confident.

• Repeat the process one more time. At the end, look at the paper and say: *What can you see on the paper?* Translate the question if necessary. If the children cannot guess the answer (colours of the rainbow) do not tell them yet.

• Ask the children to open their Pupil's Books at p. 43.

• Say the instructions several times, also in the wrong order. The children point to the appropriate pictures.

• Finally, do the experiment, this time putting the water into the container. Invite the children to come and look at the paper. Ask: *What can you see on the paper?* Children: *Colours (of the rainbow).* Say: *Tell me the colours.*

• Give a photocopiable worksheet to each child. Ask the children to colour the colour sequence correspondingly.

Note: If necessary introduce the new colours *indigo* and *violet* in L1.

Answers:

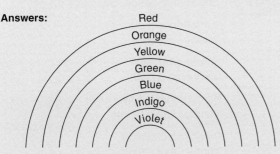

Red
Orange
Yellow
Green
Blue
Indigo
Violet

L E S S O N 1

Vocabulary, phrases and structures:
Checking of vocabulary acquisition.

Linguistic skills:
Understanding and saying key vocabulary and phrases from Units 5–6 on the topic areas *Toys* and *Weather*.

Cognitive, motor and social skills:
Matching words and phrases from the CD to the corresponding pictures in the book.

Numbering these words/phrases in the corresponding colours.
Checking the results in an answer key.
Self-evaluation

Materials:
CD 2/37–38; *Pupil's Book*, pp. 44–45, ex. 1–2; coloured pencils; (optional) answer key for self-checking

Self-evaluation

Option: Divide *Show what you can do* into two lessons.

Note: For notes on the basic methodology of this section, see *Show what you can do* on p. 18 of the introduction.

❶ **Listen and write the numbers.**
Listening exercise: Matching exercise CD 2/37

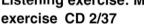

- Tell the children that they will now find out which words on Pupil's Book p. 44 they can already understand well and which words they can say.
- The children now check independently whether they can match the words to the corresponding pictures. They have a red, a green and a blue pencil in front of them on the desk.
- Play CD 2/37. The children write the numbers one to four in the appropriate colours in the circles for each picture. The first picture has already been numbered.
- Go around the class and help the children as necessary.
- Put out a completed sheet and let the children come out and check their results independently.

Tapescript:

Speaker 1: Take a red pencil. Write the numbers. Take a red pencil. OK? Here we go.

Number one: umbrella
Number one: umbrella

Number two: butterfly
Number two: butterfly

Number three: train
Number three: train

Number four: snow
Number four: snow

Speaker 2: Take a green pencil. Write the numbers. Take a green pencil. OK? Here we go.

Number one: sun
Number one: sun

Number two: plane
Number two: plane

Number three: ball
Number three: ball

Number four: wind
Number four: wind

Speaker 1: Take a blue pencil. Write the numbers. Take a blue pencil. OK? Here we go.

Number one: car
Number one: car

Number two: star
Number two: star

Number three: flower
Number three: flower

Number four: cloud
Number four: cloud

❶ Say and colour.
Speaking exercise

- Ask the children to look at the pictures again. Explain that if they can say the correct words for the pictures, they colour the frames in the corresponding colours.
- When the children have coloured the frames, give them an activity from Units 5 or 6 of the Teacher's Resource Pack to work on while you go around and check the individual answers to the colouring activity. Ask individual children to say the colours, e.g. Teacher: (*Mona*). (Mona): *plane – green.* Teacher: (*John*). (John): *car – blue.*
- Divide the class into groups of four or five to do this if it is easier to move from group to group to check their work.

❷ Listen and write the numbers.
Listening exercise: Matching exercise CD 2/38

- Tell the children that they will now find out which phrases on Pupil's Book p. 45 they can already understand well and which phrases they can say.
- The children now check independently whether they can match the phrases to the corresponding pictures. They have a red and a green pencil in front of them on the desk.
- Play CD 2/38. The children write the numbers one to four in the appropriate colours in the circles for each picture. The first picture has already been numbered.
- Go around the class and help the children as necessary.
- Put out a completed sheet and let the children come out and check their results independently.

Tapescript:

Speaker 1:   Take a red pencil. Write the numbers. Take a red pencil. OK? Here we go.

Number one: The dog is asleep.
Number one: the dog is asleep.

Number two: It's raining.
Number two: It's raining.

Number three: Jump!
Number three: Jump!

Number four: Get into the car.
Number four: Get into the car.

Speaker 2:   Take a green pencil. Write the numbers. Take a green pencil. OK? Here we go.

Number one: Drive off!
Number one: Drive off!

Number two: Come with me.
Number two: Come with me.

Number three: What a sweet smell.
Number three: What a sweet smell.

Number four: Run after the dog!
Number four: Run after the dog!

❷ Say and colour.
Speaking exercise

- Ask the children to look at the pictures again. Explain that if they can say the correct words or phrases for the pictures, they colour the frames in the corresponding colours.
- When the children have coloured the frames, give them an activity from Units 5 or 6 of the Teacher's Resource Pack to work on while you go round and check the individual answers to the colouring activity. Ask individual children to say the colours, e.g. Teacher: (*Ann*). (Ann): *It's raining. – Red.* Teacher: (*Lucas*). (Lucas): *Come with me. – Green.*
- Divide the class into groups of four or five to do this if it is easier to move from group to group to check their work.

L E S S O N 1

Vocabulary, phrases and structures:

sheriff; princess; bear, ghost; clown; monster; nine; ten
Receptive language: What's missing? *Close your books. How many (bears) are there? What is there?*

Linguistic skills:

Learning the meaning and pronunciation of the new words and numbers.
Finding and saying the number of costumes hidden in a picture.

Cognitive, motor and social skills:

Understanding new words on the CD and pointing to the corresponding pictures in the book.
Discovering costumes hidden in a picture.

Cross-curricular integration:

Mathematics: Numbers one to ten
Topics: Speaking motivation 'Fancy dress party'.
Art

Materials:

Flashcards 1–4, 23–24, 43–44; 29, 33, 51
Flashcards 57–64; Pupil's Book, p. 46, ex. 1;
CD 3/1; *Activity Book, p. 40, ex. 1*

Revision

- Revise the words for *cat, dog* and *frog* with the flashcards.
- Revise the numbers one to eight with the flashcards.

Introduction of vocabulary

sheriff; princess; bear; ghost; clown; monster; nine; ten

- Introduce the new words *sheriff, princess, bear, ghost, clown* and *monster* and the new numbers *nine* and *ten* with the flashcards. Say all the words and get the children to repeat after you. Put the flashcards on the board one by one. Call out individual children and say: *(Jan), come out. Touch the sheriff.*, etc.
- Play *What's missing?* (See Unit 1, Lesson 9, Revision)

❶ Look and count. Say.
Discovery picture

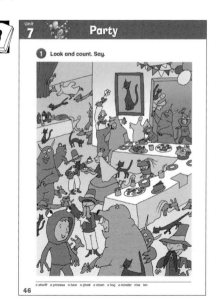

- Tell the children to look at the picture of a fancy dress party on p. 46 in their Pupil's Books for about 20 seconds. Then tell them to close their books.
- Ask the children to tell you the English words for the animals and costumes they can remember: *princess, sheriff, clown, ghost, bear, cat, dog, frog.*
- Recite the following counting rhyme aloud, and count on your fingers so that all the children can see you.

One cat.
Two cats.
Three cats.
Four.
Five cats.
Six cats.
Seven cats.
More.

Note: This rhyme makes the children aware of the use of the plural *-s*. The rhyme can be easily varied. *Cat* can be replaced by other nouns. However, avoid *mouse* or *princess* as they are irregular plurals.

- Say the rhyme again and encourage the children to join in saying it and counting on their fingers.
- The children look at the picture again. Ask them to look for one kind of animal or costume. Say, e.g.: *How many (sheriffs) are there?* The children count and give you the appropriate answer: *Three (sheriffs).* Say: *Right, there are three sheriffs.*
- Continue with the other costumes/animals in the same way.

Answer key:
six frogs
five ghosts
four monsters
one princess
three sheriffs
nine cats
ten dogs
two bears
one clown

❶ Look and colour.
Vocabulary revision with discovery picture

- Ask the children to open their Activity Books at p. 40 and look at the party picture for 20 seconds. The object is to find as many costumes as possible in this time. After 20 seconds say: *Stop. Close your books. What is there?* Children: *Ghosts.* Teacher: *OK.*
- The children say the costumes that they have found in the picture: *a princess, sheriffs, ghosts, clowns, bears.* If the children say the singular, e.g.: *sheriff*, then say: *OK, there are sheriffs.*
- Tell the children that they are now to find out how many princesses, clowns, etc. are hidden in the picture. At first have the children look for one costume, e.g.: bears. Say: *How many bears are there?*
- When the children have found the (six) hidden bears, tell them that they are to colour the six bears yellow in the rows below the party picture.
- The children look for the other hidden costumes and colour the number of pictures in the row as indicated by the coloured pencil.

Note: The children check their answers in the 'Listen and check' activity that follows.

❶ Listen and check.
Listening exercise CD 3/1

Tapescript:

Eight ghosts,
one princess,
two clowns,
three sheriffs,
six bears.

- Tell the children that they will now hear the correct answers to the picture puzzle on the CD. They are to listen carefully and check their answers.
- Play CD 3/1 twice. Pause it after each item in the list to give the children time to count the coloured pictures along the rows in their book.
- Check the answers. Ask: *How many (princesses) are there?* Children: *One (princess).*

L E S S O N 2

Vocabulary:
A party for a princess

Linguistic skills:
Understanding a chant (*A party for a princess*) from the CD.

Cognitive, motor and social skills:
Hearing a chant on the CD, pointing along in the book and chanting it rhythmically in unison. Completing logical number sequences. (Option) Pair work: Completing number sequences.

Cross-curricular integration:
Music
Mathematics: Numbers one to ten
Topic: Speaking motivation 'Fancy dress party'.

Materials:
*Flashcards 1–4, 23–24, 43–44, 63–64; 29, 30, 31, 33, 51; 57–62
CD 3/2–3; Pupil's Book*, p. 47, ex. 2–3; glove puppet Max; (optional) answer key for self-checking

Revision

- With the flashcards revise the words for *frog*, *cat*, *dog*, *rabbit*, *mouse* and the costumes.
- Put the flashcards on the board and number them by putting the number flashcards next to each animal/costume. Say, e.g.: *Princess – one, sheriff – two, bear – three*, etc. Tell the children to learn the costumes and the corresponding numbers by heart. Give them about 30 seconds time for this. Then close the board.
- Say a number and the children name the corresponding costume/animal that goes with it.

❷ **Listen and point.
   Say the chant.**

Chant: *A party for a princess* CD 3/2–3

- Ask the children to open their Pupil's Books at p. 47 and look at the picture in ex. 2. Say the costumes several times and the children point to the corresponding pictures.
- Put on the glove puppet. Present the chant with the glove puppet as dialogue partner.

  Glove puppet: *A party for a princess.*
  Teacher: *...a sheriff and a dog.*
  Glove puppet: *...a bear, a cat, a monster,*
  Teacher: *...a ghost and a frog!*

- Play the chant (CD 3/2). The children listen.

Tapescript:

*A party for a princess,
a sheriff and a dog,
a bear, a cat, a monster,
a ghost and a frog!*

- Play the chant again (CD 3/2). The children point to the costumes as they hear them in the chant.
- Practise the chant line by line with the children. Mime each costume character and encourage the children to copy you. Use the appropriate flashcards (*princess/ sheriff/bear/ghost/frog/cat/monster/dog*) as visual support.
- Recite the chant several times with the children miming the costume character as they say the word.
- Play the first part of CD 3/3 (*And now you!*) and say the chant with the children several times line by line. The children mime the corresponding costume character as they say the chant.
- Play the karaoke section of CD 3/3 (*One more time!*) and ask the children to look at the page in the Pupil's Book and chant rhythmically.
- Divide the class into two groups to recite the chant. One group is lead by you, one group by the glove puppet. The pictures in the book act as support.

❸ **Think and write the numbers.**

Logical sequences

- Demonstrate a few logical sequences. Write, e.g. the sequence 2 _ 4 on the board. Say: *Two.* Point to the blank space, then to 4 and say: *Four.* Ask the children: *What's missing?* When the children say: *Three.* write the number in the space. Read out the sequence: *Two, three, four.*
- The children open their Pupil's Books at p. 47 (ex. 3). Say the numbers one to ten in random order. The children point to the corresponding numbers in the book.

- The children now work individually and put the missing numbers into the logical sequences in the book.
- Check the answers. Ask individual children to read out the sequences of numbers.

Options: Put out a completed answer key for self-checking. The children go to the key and check their work.
This exercise can also be carried out as pair work.

L E S S O N   3

Vocabulary, phrases and structures:
What colour is number (one)?; Is number six (blue)?; Yes, it is./No, it isn't.

Linguistic skills:
Understanding sentences on the CD.
Asking about colours and giving the appropriate answers.

Cognitive, motor and social skills:
Understanding sentences on the CD and ticking the corresponding pictures in the book.
Colouring numbers from one to ten in one's own choice.
Pair work: A colour and number game.

Cross-curricular integration:
Topics: Speaking motivation 'Fancy dress party'.
Mathematics: Numbers from one to ten.
Art

Materials:
Flashcards 57–62
CD 3/4; *Activity Book*, p. 41, ex. 2–3; coloured pencils

Revision
- Revise the words for costumes with the flashcards. Hand out the flashcards to individual children. Give simple instructions, e.g.: *(Simon), give the sheriff to (Sarah). (Thomas), put the clown on the board. (Hannah), touch the clown.*, etc.

❷ **Listen and tick (✓).**
Listening exercise CD 3/4

Tapescript:

One. A party for a princess, a sheriff, a bear, a cat and a frog.
One. A party for a princess, a sheriff, a bear, a cat and a frog.

Two. 'Hooray!' 'Hooray!' A party for a monster, a sheriff, a bear, a dog and a ghost.
Two. 'Hooray!' 'Hooray!' A party for a monster, a sheriff, a bear, a dog and a ghost.

- The children open their Activity Books on p. 41 and look at the pictures in ex. 2. Hold up your book and say, e.g.: *Look. A party for a princess, a cat, a frog, a bear and a sheriff.* The children listen to you and point at the appropriate pictures in their book.
- Tell the children that they are to listen to the CD and to tick the correct box in each of the pairs of pictures.
- Play CD 3/4 twice.
- The children listen and tick the appropriate pictures.
- Check the children's work. Draw two pairs of boxes on the board that represent the exercise in the Activity Book. Ask *Left or right?* Have the children tell you the answer. Tick the boxes.

❸ **Colour and say.**

Step to creativity: Pair work

- Tell the children to look at the numbers from one to ten in ex. 3. Say the numbers in the cloud in random order. The children point along in their books.
- Then tell them to colour the numbers as they choose, each number in one colour only.
- The children then work in pairs. Child A shows his/her numbers to child B for about ten seconds. Get child A to count up to ten and then close their book. While A is counting, B tries to remember the colours of the numbers in A's book.

- Child A asks child B: *What colour is number one?* Child B tries to remember and if he/she gives the correct answer, child A puts a tick in the box below number one. Child A continues asking child B for the colours of all the numbers. Then A counts how many ticks B has and writes the number in the circle next to the cloud. They then swap roles.
- The children now take three colours of their own choice. They then individually colour the numbers in the houses, each number in one of the three colours. Child B tells child A which three colours he/she has selected. Child A starts by asking child B: *Is number six (blue)?* B answers: *Yes, it is./No, it isn't.* B puts a tick in the box below number six if A has guessed correctly. Child A continues by asking child B about the colours of all the numbers. Child B counts how many ticks child A has and writes the number in the circle above the number ten. They then swap roles.

L E S S O N 4

Vocabulary, phrases and structures:

Receptive language: *You're a magician; Get a piece of cake; A clown grabs your plate; Turn the clown into a bird; The bird flies away; Eat your piece of cake; The clown eats the cake*

Linguistic skills:

Understanding instructions in an Action Story (*You're a magician*).
Understanding instructions from the CD and matching with the corresponding pictures.

Cognitive, motor and social skills:

Matching instructions with actions.
Understanding and carrying out jumbled instructions.
Understanding sentences from the CD and ticking the corresponding pictures in the book.

Cross-curricular integration:

Sport

Materials:

CD 3/3
Flashcards 65–68; CD 3/5; *Pupil's Book*, p. 48, ex. 4; (optional) answer key for self-checking; CD 3/6; *Activity Book*, p. 42, ex. 4

Revision

- Say the chant *A party for a princess* with the children to the karaoke section of CD 3/3.

Introduction of vocabulary

cake; plate; bird; magician

- Introduce the new words with the flashcards.

4 Listen and point.
   Write the numbers.
Action Story: *You're a magician* **CD 3/5**

- Work on the Action Story by carrying out the following steps as in previous units. (See introduction p. 16.)
  - Listen and imitate
    The children stand up in a circle or in their places. Give the instructions and mime the actions. The children imitate you. Repeat until the children are confident.
  - Carrying out instructions
    Give the instructions again but do not do them yourself. Repeat until the children are confident. Gradually increase the tempo.
  - Carrying out the instructions in a jumbled order
    Give the instructions in jumbled order. Do not do the actions yourself. Repeat until the children are confident. Give random instructions to individual children.
- The children open their Pupil's Books at p. 48. The six pictures are printed in random order. Give the children sufficient time to look at the pictures.
- Play the Action Story (CD 3/5). The children point to the appropriate pictures.

Tapescript

You're a magician.
Get a piece of cake.
A clown grabs your plate.
Turn the clown into a bird.
The bird flies away.
Eat your piece of cake.

- Tell the children to put the pictures in the correct order by numbering them. Number 1 is already done.

- Now play the Action Story again. The children listen and number the pictures in the book.
- Go around the class and check the children's work.

Option: In high-ability classes you can put out an answer key for self-checking. The children go to the key and check their own work themselves.

Alternative: Draw six boxes on the board that represent the page in the Activity Book. Have the children tell you the answers. Write the numbers in the boxes.

4 Listen and tick (✓).
Listening exercise CD 3/6

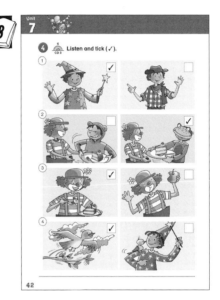

Tapescript

Speaker 1:   *One. You're a magician.*
             One. You're a magician.

Speaker 2:   *Two. A frog grabs the clown's plate.*
             Two. A frog grabs the clown's plate.

Speaker 1:   *Three. The clown eats the cake.*
             Three. The clown eats the cake.

Speaker 2:   *Four. The bird flies away.*
             Four. The bird flies away.

- The children open their Activity Books at p. 42 and look at the pictures in ex. 4.
- Tell the children that they are to listen to the CD and to tick the correct picture in each of the pairs of pictures according to what they hear on the CD.
- Play CD 3/6 twice.
- The children listen and tick the appropriate pictures.
- Check the children's work. Draw eight boxes on the board that represent the page in the Activity Book. Have the children tell you the answers. Tick the boxes.
- Check the children's work. Ask: *What about number 1? Left or right?* Children: *Left.*

L E S S O N 5

Vocabulary, phrases and structures:
Receptive language: *What a lovely cake; Lovely pears; Here you are; Thank you; Is this your dog/cat?; Yes, it is; Watch out!; Oh, no!; Stop. Look at the cat.*

Linguistic skills:
Understanding dialogues from the CD.
Understanding dialogues from the CD and matching with pictures in the book.

Cognitive, motor and social skills:
Understanding dialogues from the CD and numbering pictures in the book accordingly.
Acting out a dialogue.

Cross-curricular integration:
General knowledge: Speaking motivation 'Fancy dress party'.
Sport

Materials:
CD 3/7; *Pupil's Book*, p. 49, ex. 5; CD 3/8;
Activity Book, p. 43, ex. 5

Revision
- Say the instructions from the Action Story *You're a magician* from the previous lesson. The children do the corresponding actions.

❺ Listen and point. Act out.
Role play CD 3/7

- Present the role play. Speak as a boy. Say: *What a lovely cake.* Answer as the girl with: *Here you are.* and swap places. Develop the dialogue in this way and act it out several times in front of the class.
- Then encourage one child to take on the role of the girl and act out the dialogue. Whisper cues to help. Ask another child to take on the role of the boy and you take the part of the girl. In this way act out the dialogue in front of the class with several children.
- Ask the children to open their Pupil's Books at p. 49 and look at the picture story.
- Tell the children to listen to the dialogue (CD 3/7) and to point at the pictures in the book.
- Play CD 3/7 twice. The children listen and point to the pictures.
- The children practise the dialogue in pairs.
- Finally, volunteers act out the dialogue as a role play in front of the whole class. Ask the class to applaud the actors. (*Let's give them a big hand!*)

Tapescript:

Boy:	What a lovely cake.
Girl:	Here you are.
Boy:	Thank you.
	Is this your dog?
Girl:	Yes, it is.
	Watch out!
Boy:	Oh, no!

❺ Listen and write the numbers.
Listening exercise CD 3/8

- Ask the children to look at the pictures on p. 43 in their Activity Books. The pictures are in jumbled order. Tell the children that they are to listen to the dialogue on the CD and number the pictures accordingly.
- Play CD 3/8 twice. The children listen and number the pictures in the book.
- Check the children's work. Ask: *What number is 'Here you are.'?*
- Alternatively you can ask: *What's number two?* Children: *Here you are*, etc.

L E S S O N   6

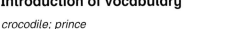

Vocabulary, phrases and structures:

Abracadabra; One, two, three; I'm a magician; Look at me!; A ghost into a sheriff; a bear into a car; a prince into a crocodile; Oh, I'm a superstar!

Linguistic skills:

Singing a song (*I'm a magician*).
Learning self-composed lyrics by heart and singing them.

Cognitive, motor and social skills:

Keeping to the rhythm and melody while speaking in unison and singing.
Pointing to the right pictures while speaking and singing.
Composing their own lyrics.
Speaking rhythmically.

Cross-curricular integration:

Music
Topic: Speaking motivation 'Magic and wizardry'.

Materials:

Flashcards 57–62, 68
Flashcards 69–70; CD 3/9–10; Pupil's Book,
pp. 50–51, ex. 6–7;

Revision

- Revise the words for costumes and *magician* with the flashcards.

Introduction of vocabulary

crocodile; prince

- Introduce the new words with the flashcards. Say them several times with the children repeating after you.

❻ Listen and point.
Sing the song.

Song: *I'm a magician* CD 3/9–10

I'm a magician

Lyrics: Gerngross/Puchta
Music: Lorenz Maierhofer
© Helbling, Rum/Innsbruck

- Play the song (CD 3/9) and at the same time do the corresponding actions and make any sound effects to facilitate the understanding of the text.
- Play the song again and the children point along with it on p. 50 (ex. 6) of the Pupil's Book.
- Say the words of the song together with the children. They use the pictures in the book as prompts and point along again.

- The children make a circle. Go around the inside of the circle and hum the tune. The children you go past pick up the tune and begin to hum along. Go around in the circle several times until all the children are humming the tune with you.
- Start to sing the words.
- Join the circle and do the corresponding actions as you sing. Use the karaoke version (CD 3/10). The children imitate your actions and sing along.

❼ Draw and say.

Step to creativity (Word Play)
CD 3/10

- The children look at the pictures on p. 51 (ex. 7) of their Pupil's Books.
- Explain to the children that they are to compose their own lyrics by filling in the empty frames with their own drawings.
- Do an example with the children. Hold up your book. Point to the pictures and say: *Abracadabra, one, two, three. I'm a magician. Look at me! A …*
- Now point to the first blank space in the book. Look questioningly at the children and collect a few ideas, e.g.: *a dog and a rabbit.*
- The children work on their own to complete the other frames. When they have finished drawing, they learn the lyrics of their song by heart by saying the lyrics in a low voice and pointing along in the Pupil's Book. Go around the class and help if necessary.
- Finally, individual children can read out their lyrics in front of the class. Volunteers can also sing their songs. Remember to applaud them! (*Let's give them a big hand!*)

Option: For advanced classes the children can also sing their own compositions to the karaoke section (CD 3/10).

L E S S O N 7

Vocabulary, phrases and structures:

Receptive language: *Draw a line from number ... to number ...*
Vocabulary revision: Numbers and colours

Linguistic skills:

Formulating simple addition sums in English.
Following instructions from the CD.

Cognitive, motor and social skills:

Doing simple addition.
(Option) Checking sums with a partner.
Following instructions given on the CD to complete a dot-to-dot picture.
Colouring numbers according to the CD and solving a discovery picture.

Cross-curricular integration:

Art
Mathematics: Addition range one to ten

Materials:

CD 3/10; *Pupil's Book*, pp. 50–51, ex. 6–7
CD 3/11–12; *Activity Book*, pp. 44–45, ex. 6–8; coloured pencils

---

Revision

- Sing the song *I'm a magician* with the children to the karaoke section (CD 3/10). Use p. 50 in the Pupil's Book as visual support. Ask the children whether some of them want to present their own compositions to the karaoke version (CD 3/10).

❻ Do the sums. Say.
Addition

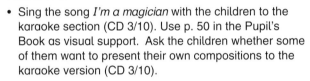

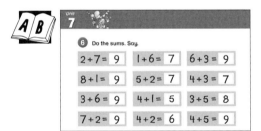

- Demonstrate several simple additions on the board, e.g.: 4 + 1 = ...
- Say: *Four plus one is ...* Children: *Five.* Say: *Yes, that's right.* Complete the addition on the board and say: *Four plus one is five.* The children repeat after you.
- The children open their Activity Books at p. 44 and do the sums in ex. 6 on their own. Say: *Now do the sums.*
- Give the children sufficient time for this work. Go around the class and help if necessary.
- Check the sums by writing them on the board in figures. As you do this, say the sums together with the children.
- Alternatively, the children take turns to read out one of the sums to one another.

❼ Listen and complete the picture.

Listening exercise CD 3/11

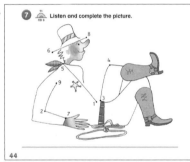

Tapescript:

Draw a line from number six to number eight.
Number six to number eight.

Draw a line from number four to number three.
Number four to number three.

Draw a line from number two to number nine.
Two to number nine.

Draw a line from number five to number one.
Number five to number one.

Draw a line from number two to number seven.
Number two to number seven.

What is it?

A sheriff!

- Ask the children to look at ex. 7 on Activity Book p. 44.
- Tell the children to listen and draw lines from one number to the other according to what they hear on the CD.
- Play CD 3/11 twice. The children listen and draw lines accordingly.
- If necessary ask them: *What is it?* Children: *(A) sheriff.* Pause the CD after the question: *What is it?*
- Play the last line of the tapescript to confirm the children's answer.

Option: The children colour the picture.

❽ Listen and colour.

Discovery picture CD 3/12

Tapescript:

Speaker 1: Five – red. Five – red.

Speaker 2: Six – blue. Six – blue.

Speaker 1: Seven – green. Seven – green.

Speaker 2: Eight – yellow. Eight – yellow.

Speaker 1: Nine – pink. Nine – pink.

- Ask the children to open their Activity Books at p. 45 and look at the picture. Get them to guess what is hidden in there. Say: *What is it? Guess.*
- Ask the children to have the following coloured pencils ready: green, red, blue, yellow and pink. Play CD 3/12 and get the children to mark the numbers with the appropriate colour as they listen. They then listen again and check.
- Afterwards, give them time to colour the numbers accordingly, e.g.: all spaces marked with a five in red.
- When they have finished, ask: *What is it?* Children: *(A) clown.*

L E S S O N 1

Vocabulary, phrases and structures:

bed; tooth/teeth; knees; (a glass of) milk
Receptive language: *Get out of bed; Wash your face; Clean your teeth; Bend your knees; Jump; Have a glass of milk; Sing a song; Have an apple; Run to school.*

Linguistic skills:

Understanding instructions in an Action Story (*Bend your knees*).
Understanding instructions on the CD and matching with the corresponding pictures.

Cognitive, motor and social skills:

Matching instructions with actions.
Understanding and carrying out jumbled instructions.
Understanding instructions from the CD and numbering pictures accordingly.

Cross-curricular integration:

Topic: Speaking motivation 'Health'.
Sport

Materials:

CD 3/10
Flashcards 71–74; CD 3/13; *Pupil's Book*, p. 52, ex. 1; (optional) answer key for self-checking; CD 3/14; *Activity Book*, p. 46, ex. 1;

Revision

* Sing the song *I'm a magician* from Unit 7 to the karaoke version (CD 3/10). Then invite volunteers to recite their own compositions or sing them to the karaoke version.

Introduction of vocabulary

bed; tooth/teeth; knees; (a glass of) milk

* Introduce the new words with the flashcards. Say the words as you show the card and the children repeat after you.

❶ Listen and point. Write the numbers.

Action Story: *Bend your knees* CD 3/13

* Work on the Action Story by carrying out the following steps as in previous units. (See introduction p. 16.)

  – Listen and imitate

    The children stand up in a circle or in their places. Give the instructions and mime the actions. The children imitate you. Repeat until the children are confident.

  – Carrying out instructions

    Give the instructions again but do not do them yourself. Repeat until the children are confident. Gradually increase the tempo.

  – Carrying out the instructions in a jumbled order

    Give the instructions in jumbled order. Do not do the actions yourself. Repeat until the children are confident. Give random instructions to individual children.

* The children open their Pupil's Books at p. 52. The six pictures are printed in random order. Give the children sufficient time to look at the pictures.
* Play the Action Story (CD 3/13). The children point to the appropriate pictures.

Tapescript:

Get out of bed.
Wash your face.
Clean your teeth.
Bend your knees – one, two, three.
Jump – one, two, three.
Have a glass of milk.

---

* Tell the children to put the pictures in the correct order by numbering them. Number 1 is already done.
* Now play the Action Story again. The children listen and number the pictures.
* Go around the class and check the children's work.

Option: In high-ability classes you can put out an answer key for self-checking. The children go to the key and check their own work themselves.

Alternative: Draw six boxes on the board that represent the page in the Pupil's Book. Have the children tell you the answers. Write the numbers on the board.

Pronunciation tips: The lips must be rounded for the formation of the [w] in *wash*.
For the pronunciation of the word *teeth* [ti:θ] the children should be able to feel the tip of their tongue against their teeth. Avoid using an [s]. Note that the 'j' in *jump* is soft and voiced [dʒ]. Use the following sentence for practice: *Jump, Charley, jump.* The [tʃ] in *Charley* is spoken unvoiced and 'hard'.

❶ **Listen and write the numbers.**
Listening exercise CD 3/14

- Ask the children to open their Activity Books at p. 46 and look at the pictures in ex. 1. They are shown in random order.
- Tell the children that they are to listen to the CD and number the pictures according to what they hear. Number 1 is already done.
- Play CD 3/14 twice. The children listen and number the pictures.

Tapescript:

Get out of bed.
Wash your face.
Clean your teeth.
Sing a song.
Have an apple.
Run to school.

- Check the children's work by asking, e.g.: *Wash your face. What number is it?*

L E S S O N   2

Vocabulary, phrases and structures:

Get out of bed; Wash your face; Clean your teeth; Bend your knees; Jump; Let's keep fit.

Linguistic skills:

Singing a song (*Get out of bed*).
Matching instructions from the CD to pictures in the book.

Cognitive, motor and social skills:

Singing while imitating actions, clapping or dancing.
Learning the words of a song by pointing along to lines of pictures and by movements.
Keeping to the right rhythm while speaking in unison and singing.

Cross-curricular integration:

Topic: Speaking motivation 'Health'.
Music

Materials:

CD 3/15–16; *Pupil's Book*, p. 53, ex. 2;
CD 3/17; *Activity Book*, p. 47, ex. 2;
(optional) answer key for self-checking

Revision

• Give the instructions from the Action Story (*Bend your knees*) from the previous lesson. The children do the actions.

❷ Listen and point.
   Sing the song.

Song: *Get out of bed* CD 3/15–16

Lyrics: Gerngross/Puchta
Music: Lorenz Maierhofer
© Helbling, Rum/Innsbruck

Get out of bed

1. Get out of bed, wash your face, wash your face,
2. Get out of bed, clean your teeth, clean your teeth,
3. Get out of bed, bend your knees, bend your knees,

wash your face. wash your face. And Ref.: jump, jump,
clean your teeth. clean your teeth. And
bend your knees. bend your knees. And

let's keep fit, and jump, jump, let's keep fit, and let's keep fit!

• Play the song (CD 3/15).
• Say the words of the song line by line and indicate meaning by doing the actions.
• Play the song again. The children point along with it on p. 53 in the Pupil's Book.
• Now say the words with the children. They use the pictures in the book as prompts and point along again.
• The children make a circle. Go around the inside of the circle and hum the tune. The children you go past pick up the tune and begin to hum along. Go around in the circle several times until in the end all the children are humming the tune with you.
• Play the karaoke version (CD 3/16). Start to sing the song. Join the circle and do the actions with the children. At *Let's keep fit!* Clap your hands three times.
• The children imitate your actions and sing along.

❷ **Listen and tick (✓).**
Listening exercise CD 3/17

- Ask the children to look at the pictures on p. 47 of their Activity Books.
- Say: *One. Smile. Wash your face. Two. Get out of bed. Clean your teeth,* etc. Get the children to point to the corresponding pictures in the book.
- Tell the children that they are to listen to the CD and tick the corresponding picture of each pair.

- Play CD 3/17 twice. Now the children tick the appropriate pictures in the book.
- The children then listen again and check. Go around the class and check the children's work.

Tapescript:

Speaker 1: One. Wash your face.
             One. Wash your face.

Speaker 2: Two. Get out of bed.
             Two. Get out of bed.

Speaker 1: Three. Bend your knees.
             Three. Bend your knees.

Speaker 2: Four. Drink a glass of milk.
             Four. Drink a glass of milk.

Speaker 1: Five: Jump.
             Five: Jump.

Speaker 1: Six: Clean your teeth.
             Six: Clean your teeth.

Option: In high-ability classes you can put out an answer key for self-checking. The children go to the key and check their own work themselves.

Alternative: Draw six pairs of boxes on the board that represent the page in the Activity Book. Point at the first pair of boxes. Say: *Left or right?* The children tell you the answers. Tick the corresponding boxes on the board.

L E S S O N   3

Vocabulary, phrases and structures:
lemon; orange; chocolate; ice cream
Receptive language: *I win, I think; No, Dad; I win!; Have an apple / a banana, Dad; I love chocolate / ice cream / lollies; Bananas, oranges; Look! Mr Fruit Face; What?; I'm hungry; Oh dear … I know … a good walk; A big ice cream, please; What's the matter, Dad?; My tooth hurts; Go to the dentist; The dentist … No … not the dentist; Don't worry; Come on; Next; Come in; Take a seat; The other way; Relax; Nice chair; Some music?; Oh. Lovely; Where's the dentist?; Oh … It's her; Open your mouth; Don't worry; Come on, Dad; Not today; An apple for me!*

Linguistic skills:
Understanding a sketch (*At the dentist*) from the DVD and the CD.

Understanding mini-dialogues (scenes from the sketch) from the CD.

Cognitive, motor and social skills:
Understanding mini-dialogues from the CD and numbering the pictures in the book in the correct order.

Cross-curricular integration:
Topic: Speaking motivation 'A healthy snack'.

Materials:
CD 3/16
Flashcards 75–76; DVD (*At the dentist*); CD 3/18; *Pupil's Book*, p. 54, ex. 3; CD 3/19; *Activity Book*, p. 48, ex. 3

Revision
- Sing the song *Get out of bed* from the previous lesson with the children to the karaoke version (CD 3/16). Do the corresponding actions.

Introduction of vocabulary

orange; ice cream; lemon; chocolate

• Introduce the words *orange* and *ice cream* with the flashcards. Explain the meaning of *lemon* and *chocolate* with simple drawings on the board.

Preliminary preparation of phrases

My tooth hurts; Go to the dentist.

• Say: *My tooth hurts* and explain the meaning by a corresponding gesture/mime.
• Say: *Go to the dentist* and look questioningly at the children. Ask: *What's dentist?* in L1. If the children cannot guess the meaning, translate the word.

❸ Watch the story.

Mr Matt sketch: *At the dentist*

• Show the children the Mr Matt sketch (*At the dentist*) twice.

DVD script: *At the dentist*

Mr Matt:	I win, I think.
Danny:	No, Dad! I win!
	Have an apple, Dad!
Mr Matt:	No, thanks.
Mr Matt:	I love chocolate!
Daisy:	Bananas, oranges, a lemon, banana …
	Look! Mr Fruit Face!!!
Mr Matt:	What?
Daisy:	Mr Fruit Face!
Mr Matt:	Oh. Hello, Mr Fruit Face! I'm hungry!
Daisy:	Have a banana, Dad!
Mr Matt:	No, thanks!
	I love lollies!!!
	Oh dear … I know … a good walk!
Mr Matt:	Ice cream!
	A big ice cream, please!
Van man:	Here you are.
Mr Matt:	Thank you. Here you are.
Van Man:	Thank you.
Mr Matt:	I love ice cream!
Mr Matt:	Awwwww!
Daisy:	What's the matter, Dad?
Mr Matt:	My tooth hurts!
Danny and Daisy:	Go to the dentist!
Mr Matt:	The dentist … the dentist …
	No … no … not the dentist!
Daisy:	Dad … Dad … Don't worry.
Danny:	Come on!!!
Mr Matt:	OK …
Dentist:	Next!
Dentist:	Come in!
Mr Matt:	Thank you. Hello.
	Goodbye!

Dentist:	Take a seat!
	The other way!
Mr Matt:	Oh … Yes.
Dentist:	Relax!
Mr Matt:	Ooooh! Nice chair!
Dentist:	Some music?
Mr Matt:	Yes please!
	Oh. Lovely!
Mr Matt:	Where's the dentist?
Dentist:	It's me!
Mr Matt:	Oh … It's her!
Dentist:	Open your mouth.
Mr Matt:	Ooohh.
Dentist:	Don't worry. Open your mouth!
Danny:	Look! Ice cream!
Daisy:	Come on, Dad!
Danny:	A big ice cream, Dad?
Mr Matt:	Not today. An apple for me!

---

❸ Listen and write the numbers.

Listening exercise CD 3/18

• The children open their Pupil's Books at p. 54 and look at the pictures. Explain to the children that they will now hear individual sentences or short dialogues on the CD and are to match them to the corresponding pictures in the book. Picture 1 has already been numbered.
• Play the listening exercise twice (CD 3/18). The children listen and write the corresponding numbers in the circles in the book.

Tapescript:

Announcer:	Picture one.
Mr Matt:	My tooth hurts.
Announcer:	Once again.
	Picture one.
Mr Matt:	My tooth hurts.

Announcer:	Picture two.
Mr Matt:	A big ice cream, please.
Man:	Here you are.
Announcer:	Once again.
	Picture two.
Mr Matt:	A big ice cream, please.
Man:	Here you are.

Announcer:	Picture three.
Danny:	Have an apple, Dad.
Mr Matt:	No, thanks.
Announcer:	Once again.
	Picture three.
Danny:	Have an apple, Dad.
Mr Matt:	No, thanks.

Announcer:	Picture four.
Dentist:	Open your mouth.
Announcer:	Once again.
	Picture four.
Dentist:	Open your mouth.

- Hold your book up. Point to the first picture and ask: *What number is it?* Children: *Three.*, etc.

Note: You can also check the children's answers by saying, e.g.: *Have an apple, Dad.* Children: *(It's number) Three.*

❸ Listen and write the numbers.
Listening exercise CD 3/19

- Ask the children to open their Activity Books at p. 48 and look at the pictures in ex. 3. The six pictures are shown in random order.
- Tell them that they are to listen to the CD and number the pictures according to what they hear.
- Play CD 3/19 twice. The children listen and number the pictures.

Tapescript:

| Speaker: | One. |
| Boy: | I love chocolate. |

| Speaker: | Two. |
| Boy: | My tooth hurts. |

| Speaker: | Three. |
| Girl: | Have a banana. |

| Speaker: | Four. |
| Dentist: | Come in. |

| Speaker: | Five. |
| Dentist: | Take a seat. |

| Speaker: | Six. |
| Dentist: | Open your mouth. |

- Check the children's work by asking, e.g.: *My tooth hurts. What number is it?*

L E S S O N   4

Vocabulary, phrases and structures:

Three lollies, please; Yummy; Tea's ready; No,
thank you, Dad; What's the matter?; I feel sick.

Linguistic skills:

Understanding mini-dialogues on the CD.

Cognitive, motor and social skills:

Understanding mini-dialogues on the CD and
pointing along in the book.
Saying mini-dialogues or performing a role play in
front of the class.
Pair work: Practising a dialogue. (Option) Acting it
out.
Categorising food into healthy or unhealthy.
Drawing/Copying food items.

Cross-curricular integration:

Topic: Speaking motivation 'A healthy snack'.
Art

Materials:

a soft ball; *Flashcards* 25–28, 65, 74–76
CD 3/20; *Pupil's Book*, p. 55, ex. 4; glove puppet
Max; *Activity Book*, p. 49, ex. 4

Revision

- Stand in a circle with the children. Say a number and
throw the ball to a child. The child catches the ball, says
another number and throws the ball to another child, etc.
Revise colours, school things, pets and toys in this way.
- Revise the food items the children have learnt so far. Put
the flashcards on the board and play *What's missing?*
(See Unit 1, Lesson 9, Revision)

Preliminary preparation of phrases

Tea's ready; I feel sick

- Translate the phrases *Tea's ready.* and *I feel sick.*
- Tell the children that in the UK the afternoon snack is
called tea without tea necessarily being served. Children
ask for example: *What's for tea, mum?* Mum: *A glass of*
milk and a sandwich.

❹ Listen and point.

Listening exercise CD 3/20

Tapescript:

Boy:	Three lollies please.
Man:	Here you are.
Boy:	Thank you. – Yummy.
Boy:	A big ice cream, please.
Woman:	Here you are.
Boy:	Thank you. – Yummy.
Dad:	Tea's ready.
Boy:	No, thank you, Dad.
Dad:	What's the matter?
Boy:	I feel sick.

- The children look at the pictures on p. 55 in the Pupil's
Book. Play the listening exercise several times
(CD 3/20). The children listen and point along in the book.

Mini-dialogues

- Take the glove puppet and act out the first part
of the dialogue.

  Max: Hello. Three lollies, please.
  Assistant: Here you are.
  Max: Thank you. – Yummy!

- Act out the dialogue with the glove puppet again. This
time encourage the children to repeat the lines. Repeat
until the children are confident.
- Act out the dialogue with a child. Play the part of Max.
Repeat the dialogue several times with different children.
Then invite volunteers to come and play the part of Max
and you play the Assistant. Continue with the next parts
of the dialogue in the same way until the children are
able to say the whole sketch.
- Now the children work in pairs and choose one sequence
of the dialogue. Then they mime it in front of the class.
The others have to guess what they are acting out. Ask:
What is it? Children answer e.g.: *What's the matter? – I*
feel sick.

Shopping List Memory Game.

- Divide children into small groups where possible. Alternatively have high-ability children together in one group.
- Sit the children in a circle. The child to start asks the child to their left for something on an imaginary shopping list, e.g.: *Four bananas, please.* The child then responds with: *Here you are* before turning to the next child in the circle. They repeat the order and add an item of their own, e.g.: *Four bananas and three pears, please.* Play moves to the left, and each child adds a new item to the list. The children see how many items they can add to their list.

Pre-teaching key words

healthy; unhealthy

- Explain the words *healthy/unhealthy*. Get the children to repeat the new words several times after you. Put the food flashcards on the board and draw a lemon and some chocolate. Point at the *apple* flashcard. Ask, e.g.: *What about the apple? Is it healthy or unhealthy food?* Prompt them to answer *(It's) healthy (food)*. Say: *That's right/OK. The apple is healthy food. Let's put it here.* Put the flashcard underneath a drawing of a 'thumbs up' 👍 sign on the board. Continue with the other flashcards. Put the flashcards with food classified as unhealthy underneath the drawing of a 'thumbs down' 👎 sign.

❹ Think and draw. Say.
Catagorising food

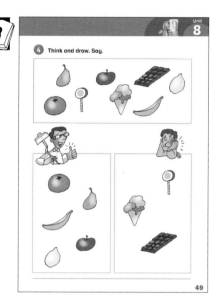

- Take the flashcards off the board.
- Ask the children to look at the food items at the top of p. 49 in the Activity Book. Name them and the children point at the corresponding pictures.
- Tell the children to draw the items in the appropriate boxes according to whether they are healthy or unhealthy food.
- Check the children's work by asking: *What about the (banana)?* The children answer: *It's healthy*, etc.

L E S S O N   5

Vocabulary, phrases and structures:

Go and clean your teeth, Ben; Yes, Dad; Let's sing a song; OK, sir; My tooth hurts; Open your mouth; Clean your teeth; I feel sick; Wash your face; I'm hungry.

Linguistic skills:

Understanding mini-dialogues/sentences from the CD.

Cognitive, motor and social skills:

Understanding mini-dialogues on the CD and pointing along in the book.
Saying mini-dialogues or performing a role play in front of the class.

Pair work: Practising a dialogue. (Option) Acting it out.
Understanding sentences from the CD and numbering pictures accordingly.
Pair work: Miming instructions.

Cross-curricular integration:

Topic: Speaking motivation 'A healthy snack'.

Materials:

CD 3/21; *Pupil's Book*, p. 56, ex. 5; CD 3/22; *Activity Book*, p. 50, ex. 5–6;

Revision

- Ask volunteers to act out their dialogues from the previous lesson.

❺ Listen and point. Act out.
Role play CD 3/21

Tapescript:

Dad: Go and clean your teeth, Ben.
Ben: Yes, Dad.
Teacher: Let's sing a song.
Students: Yes!
Teacher: Ben, here you are. Go and clean your teeth.
Ben: OK, sir.
Students: Yeaaahh!

- Ask the children to open their Pupil's Books at p. 56 and look at the picture story.
- Tell the children to listen to the dialogue (CD 3/21) and to point at the pictures in the book.
- Play CD 3/21 twice. The children listen and point.
- Present the content of the dialogue as a role play. Say: *Go and clean your teeth, Ben.* In another voice answer: *Yes, Dad.* As Ben, pretend to clean your teeth and, instead, clean an imaginary mirror with an imaginary toothbrush. Hum a song while doing this.
- In this way develop the whole dialogue and act it out several times in front of the class.
- Then encourage a child to take on the role of Ben. Play the parts of dad and the teacher yourself. Four or five children (or the rest of the class) take the part of the students and sing the song *Get out of bed* together with you.
- Divide the class in four groups and get them to practise the dialogue. Any additional students in each group play the students. Go around the class and help if necessary.
- Finally, volunteers act out the role play in front of the class. Ask the class to applaud. (*Let's give them a big hand!*)

❺ Listen and write the numbers.
Listening exercise CD 3/22

- Ask the children to look at the pictures in ex. 5, on p. 50 in their Activity Books. Say the sentences illustrated by the pictures in random order. The children point to the corresponding pictures. Clarify the meaning of *I feel sick.* through gesture and mime.
- Tell the children to number the pictures according to what they hear on the CD.
- Play CD 3/22. The children write the numbers.

Tapescript:

Speaker 1: One.
Speaker 2: Open your mouth.

Speaker 1: Two.
Speaker 2: Wash your face.

Speaker 1: Three.
Speaker 2: Clean your teeth.

Speaker 1: Four.
Speaker 2: My tooth hurts.

Speaker 1: Five.
Speaker 2: I'm hungry.

Speaker 1: Six.
Speaker 2: I feel sick.

❻ Say and mime.
Pair work

- Say the six sentences from ex. 5 one by one and mime the action. The children repeat after you and do the action.
- When the children are confident, demonstrate the pair work with a child in front of the class.

- Say one of the six sentences. Get the child to mime the sentence. Then the child says a sentence and you try to mime it. Continue with two or three other sentences in the same way.
- The children work in pairs. Child A says three sentences and child B mimes them.
- Then they swap roles. Circulate around the class and help if necessary.

L E S S O N 6

Vocabulary, phrases and structures:
Vocabulary revision

Linguistic skills:
Reading out logical sequences.

Cognitive, motor and social skills:
Completing logical sequences and reading them out.
Creating one's own logical sequence and reading it out.
Pair work: Completing a logical sequence and reading it out.

Cross-curricular integration:
Art

Materials:
Activity Book, p. 51, exs. 7–8; coloured pencils; (optional) answer key for self-checking

Revision

- Ask the children to stand in two rows facing each other. Assign roles A and B to each row.
- Start by calling out each action the children have learnt so far in this unit, e.g.: *Get out of bed. Wash your face. Clean your teeth.*, etc. Child A mimes the first action and child B mirrors their action. Then child B mimes the second action and child A mirrors their action.

Note: This leads to instant recall and comprehension.

❼ Complete and say.
Logical sequences

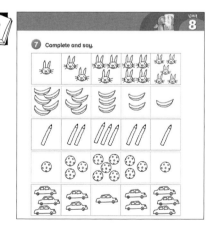

- Ask the children to open their Activity Books at p. 51 and look at the pictures in ex. 7 for about five seconds. Get them to close their books and give you words they can remember. Say: *Give me words.*
- Then the children open their books again. Tell them to complete the number sequences.
- Give the children enough time to do this. Go around the class and help if necessary.
- To check the children's work, get them to read out the sequences.

Option: Put out an answer key for self-checking. The children go to the key and check their own work themselves.

❽ Draw and say.
Step to creativity: Pair work

- Tell the children to create their own logical sequence individually by drawing items of their own choice in the blank row in ex. 8 on p. 51 in the Activity Book. Tell them to leave the last box in the row blank.
- They then work with a partner, complete each other's sequence and read it out to one another.

C L I L:
Content and Language Integrated Learning

Objective:
Making the children aware of what they can do for their own health.

Materials:
CD 3/23; *Pupil's Book*, p. 57, ex. 6

Revision

- Stand in a circle. Play the game *Max says...* Give instructions, e.g.: *Wash your face/hands., Clean your teeth., Have a banana., Stretch., Sit down., Stand up., Walk around., Jump., Smile.,* etc.
  The children follow your instructions, but only when you begin them with *Max says...* If you give an instruction without saying *Max says...* first, the children must not carry it out. The children who make a mistake are 'out'.

Pre-teaching vocabulary

before/after meals; Don't eat too many sweets; toilet; lots of

- Make the meaning of the vocabulary phrases clear. Translate if necessary.
- Tell the children that there is the saying in the UK *An apple a day keeps the doctor away.* Ask them in L1 what it could mean.

❻ Listen and write the numbers.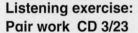
Listening exercise:
Pair work CD 3/23

Tapescript:

Speaker 1: *Number one: Wash your hands before meals.*

Speaker 2: *Number two: Wash your hands after you go to the toilet.*

Speaker 1: *Number three: Don't eat too many sweets.*

Speaker 2: *Number four: Clean your teeth after meals.*

Speaker 1: *Number five: Eat lots of fruit.*

Speaker 2: *Number six: Keep fit.*

- Ask the children to look at the pictures on p. 57 in their Pupil's Books.
- Tell them to listen to a radio programme about health and look at the pictures. Play CD 3/23. The children listen and look at the pictures in the book.
- Play the CD again and now the children number the pictures accordingly.
- Check the children's work by asking: *Clean your teeth after meals. What number is it?*
- The children choose a partner. Get them to think about one rule they'd like their partner to stick to in the following week. The children draw a picture of their partner engaged in the activity to illustrate this, e.g.: washing hands before/after meals, eating lots of fruit, keeping fit, etc.
- When the children have finished their drawings, sit in a circle. They show their pictures to the others, give it to their partner and say, e.g.: *Wash your hands/Clean your teeth/Keep fit/Eat lots of fruit...*
- When all the children have presented their rules, they stick the pictures on the wall in the classroom.

Show what you can do

L E S S O N 1

Vocabulary, phrases and structures:
Checking of vocabulary acquisition

Linguistic skills:
Understanding and saying the important words and phrases from Units 7–8 on the topic areas *Party* and *Health*.

Cognitive, motor and social skills:
Matching words and phrases from the CD to the corresponding pictures in the book.
Numbering these words and phrases in the corresponding colours.
Checking the results in an answer key.
Self-evaluation

Materials:
CD 3/24–25; *Pupil's Book*, pp. 58–59, ex. 1–2; coloured pencils; answer key for self-checking

Self-evaluation

Option: Divide *Show what you can do* into two lessons.

Note: For notes on the basic methodology of this section, see *Show what you can do* on p. 18 of the introduction.

❶ Listen and write the numbers.
Listening exercise: Matching exercise CD 3/24

- Tell the children that they will now find out which words on Pupil's Book p. 58 they can already understand well and which words they can say.
- The children now check independently whether they can match the words to the corresponding pictures. They have a red, a green and a blue pencil in front of them on the desk.
- Play CD 3/24. The children write the numbers one to four in the appropriate colours in the circles for each picture. The first picture has already been numbered.
- Go around the class and help the children as necessary.
- Put out a completed sheet and let the children come out and check their results independently.

Tapescript:

Speaker 1: Take a red pencil. Write the numbers. Take a red pencil. OK? Here we go.

Number one: dentist.
Number one: dentist.

Number two: face.
Number two: face.

Number three: milk.
Number three: milk.

Number four: glass.
Number four: glass.

Speaker 2: Take a green pencil. Write the numbers. Take a green pencil. OK? Here we go.

Number one: bed.
Number one: bed.

Number two: ice cream.
Number two: ice cream.

Number three: crocodile.
Number three: crocodile.

Number four: plate.
Number four: plate.

Speaker 1: Take a blue pencil. Write the numbers. Take a blue pencil. OK? Here we go.

Number one: knee.
Number one: knee.

Number two: a piece of cake.
Number two: a piece of cake.

Number three: frog.
Number three: frog.

Number four: bear.
Number four: bear.

❶ **Say and colour.**

Speaking exercise

- Ask the children to look at the pictures again. Explain that if they can say the correct words for the pictures, they colour the frames in the corresponding colours.
- When the children have coloured the frames, give them an activity from Units 7 or 8 of the Teacher's Resource Pack to work on while you go around and check the individual answers to the colouring activity. Ask individual children to say the colours, e.g. Teacher: (*Steve*). (Steve): *face – red.* Teacher: (*Mona*). (Mona): *crocodile – green.*
- Divide the class into groups of four or five to do this if it is easier to move from group to group to check their work.

❷ **Listen and write the numbers.**

Listening exercise: Matching exercise CD 3/25

- Tell the children that they will now find out which phrases on Pupil's Book p. 59 they can already understand well and which phrases they can say.
- The children now check independently whether they can match the words to the corresponding pictures. They have a red, a green and a blue pencil in front of them on the desk.
- Play CD 3/25. The children write the numbers one to four in the appropriate colours in the circles for each picture. The first picture has already been numbered.
- Go around the class and help the children as necessary.
- Put out a completed sheet and let the children come out and check their results independently.

Tapescript:

Speaker 1:   *Take a red pencil. Write the numbers.*
             Take a red pencil. OK? Here we go.

             Number one: Open your mouth.
             Number one: Open your mouth.

             Number two: Look at the dog.
             Number two: Look at the dog.

             Number three: Clean your teeth!
             Number three: Clean your teeth!

             Number four: Have a banana.
             Number four: Have a banana.

Speaker 2:   *Take a green pencil. Write the numbers.*
             Take a green pencil. OK? Here we go.

             Number one: Have an apple.
             Number one: Have an apple.

             Number two: The bird flies away.
             Number two: The bird flies away.

             Number three: No thanks!
             Number three: No thanks!

             Number four: Wash your face.
             Number four: Wash your face.

❷ **Say and colour.**

Speaking exercise

- Ask the children to look at the pictures again. Explain that if they can say the correct words or phrases for the pictures, they colour the frames in the corresponding colours.
- When the children have coloured the frames, give them an activity from Units 7 or 8 of the Teacher's Resource Pack to work on while you go round and check the individual answers to the colouring activity. Ask individual children to say the colours, e.g. Teacher: (*Peter*). (Peter): *Clean your teeth. – Red.* Teacher: (*Ann*). (Ann): *Have an apple. – Green.*
- Divide the class into groups of four or five to do this if it is easier to move from group to group to check their work.

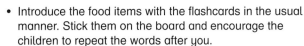
L E S S O N   1

Vocabulary, phrases and structures:

butter; Lots of spaghetti / chicken on a big, big plate; with butter and cheese / ketchup and chips; spaghetti / chicken is great; pizza

Linguistic skills:

Understanding the meaning and pronunciation of new words.
Saying a chant (*Lots of spaghetti*).
Understanding sentences from the CD.

Cognitive, motor and social skills:

Keeping the rhythm of a chant in the group.
Pointing to pictures while speaking rhythmically.

Saying a chant in two groups.
Understanding sentences on the CD and numbering the corresponding pictures.

Cross-curricular integration:

Music
Curriculum content: Speaking motivation 'Food'.

Materials:

Flashcards 66; 77–81; CD 3/26–27; *Pupil's Book*, p. 60, ex. 1; Glove puppet Max; CD 3/28; *Activity Book*, p. 52, ex. 1

Revision

- Ask the children to give you some ideas of what you can do to keep fit and healthy, e.g.: *Eat fruit., Bend your knees.; Run to school.*, etc.
- Ask them about their ideas and whether they are easy or difficult to follow. Discuss in L1.

Introduction of vocabulary

butter; spaghetti; chicken; cheese; chips

- Introduce the food items with the flashcards in the usual manner. Stick them on the board and encourage the children to repeat the words after you.
- Revise the word *plate* with the flashcard.

Exercises for anchoring words in the children's recognition and productive memory

- Give the instruction: *Touch the butter.* Invite a child to come to the board and touch the corresponding flashcard.
- Ask the children to close their eyes. Say the words aloud. The children listen closely. Then say each word individually, changing your voice. Say the words in a loud, soft, high-pitched, deep, happy, sad, angry and lively way. Ask the children to repeat the words exactly as you say them.

Note: Shutting off the visual channel allows the child to concentrate completely on the pronunciation. Listening closely to and imitating different modes of sound is good practice in listening and phonetics, and helps store the pronunciation of the words in long-term memory.

- Hold a flashcard with its back towards the children and ask: *What is it?* The children try to guess which item it is: *Cheese? Butter?*, etc.
  Answer: *Yes, it is.* or *No, it isn't.* When a child has guessed correctly, show the picture on the card.

Note: *chips* = British English; *French fries* = American English

❶ Listen and point. Say the chant.

Chant: *Lots of spaghetti*
CD 3/26–27

Tapescript:

*Lots of spaghetti
on a big, big plate.
With butter and cheese.
Spaghetti is great.*

*Lots of chicken
on a big, big plate.
With ketchup and chips.
Chicken is great.*

- Play the chant (CD 3/26). Present the chant with appropriate gesture and mime, e.g.: *on a big, big plate* – use both hand to mime a big plate, etc.
- Ask the children to open their Pupil's Books at p. 60. Play the chant again. Hold your book up and point along at the pictures. The children listen and do the same in their books.
- Practise the chant with the children by saying it out loud line by line and showing the corresponding flashcards (*spaghetti, plate, butter, cheese, chicken, chips*) as visual support. The children repeat after you.
- Play the first part of CD 3/27 (*And now you!*) and say the chant with the children several times line by line. The children point to the corresponding pictures in the book as they say the chant.
- Play the karaoke section of CD 3/27 (*One more time!*) and ask the children to look at the page in the Pupil's Book and chant rhythmically.
- Divide the class into two groups. One group is lead by you; one group by the glove puppet. For example, one group chants the first verse and the other the second. Alternatively, one group could chant the first three lines of each verse and the other the final lines: *Spaghetti is great! Chicken is great!* The pictures in the book act as support.

Vocabulary extension

pizza

- Introduce the new word *pizza* with the flashcard in the usual manner. Practise the word by saying it and the children repeating several times.

Pronunciation tip: Take care that the *i* in *pizza* is pronounced long ['piːtsə].

❶ Listen and write the numbers.
Listening exercise CD 3/28

- Ask the children to open their Activity Books on p. 52 and look at the pictures. The six pictures are shown in random order.
- Tell the children that they are to listen to the CD and number the pictures according to what they hear.
- Play CD 3/28 twice. The children listen and number the pictures.

Tapescript:

One. Milk is great.
One. Milk is great.

Two. Apples are great.
Two. Apples are great.

Three. Cheese is great.
Three. Cheese is great.

Four. Chicken is great.
Four. Chicken is great.

Five: Pizza is great.
Five: Pizza is great.

Six: Spaghetti is great.
Six: Spaghetti is great.

- Check the children's work by asking, e.g.: *Chicken is great. What number is it?*
- Alternatively, check by asking, e.g.: *What's number four?* Children: *Chicken is great.*

L E S S O N 2

Vocabulary, phrases and structures:

Vocabulary revision: food
Receptive language: *What do the children like?;*
What does Linda/Benny like?; I like...

Linguistic skills:

Guessing food items in a game.
Understanding statements on the CD.
Making statements about one's own preferences.
Option: Asking other people about their
preferences.

Cognitive, motor and social skills:

Matching flashcards to the corresponding words.
Understanding statements on the CD and marking
the corresponding pictures in the book.
Understanding statements on the CD and
matching pictures by drawing lines.

Cross-curricular integration:

Curriculum content: Speaking motivation 'Healthy
eating'.
Art

Materials:

CD 3/27; *Flashcards 25–28; 65; 74–82*
Flashcard 83; CD 3/29; *Pupil's Book*, p. 61, ex. 2;
a red pencil; *Activity Book*, p. 53, ex. 2; CD 3/30;
glove puppet Max

Revision

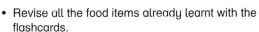

- Revise all the food items already learnt with the flashcards.
- Have the children say the chant *Lots of spaghetti* from the previous lesson in two groups. Option: Use the karaoke section (CD 3/27) for rhythmic support.

Pre-teaching a key phrase

I like...

- Put the food flashcards on the board. Say: *I like spaghetti.* and draw a heart on the board next to the *spaghetti* flashcard. Then take the glove puppet and ask, e.g.: *Max, what about you?* Answer as Max, e.g.: *I like (cheese). Yummy!* Draw a heart next to the appropriate flashcard on the board.

Vocabulary extension

cornflakes

- Introduce the word *cornflakes* with the flashcard.

❷ Listen and colour. Say.

Listening exercise CD 3/29

- Tell the children that they will hear what Linda and Benny like to eat and drink.
- Tell them to look at the pictures on p. 61 of the Pupil's Book. As they listen they are to use a red pencil to mark the hearts next to those items of food that Linda and Benny like.
- Play the listening exercise several times (CD 3/29). The children first mark the hearts in red.

Tapescript:

Speaker: *Linda*
Linda: *I like spaghetti, cornflakes, pears, apples and milk.*

Speaker: *Benny*
Benny: *I like chips, bananas, apples, pizza and spaghetti.*

• Play the listening exercise again. The children listen again and check their answers independently. They then finish colouring the hearts.
• To check the answers ask: *What does Linda like?* Children: *Spaghetti, cornflakes, pears, apples, milk.* Check Benny in the same way.

Mini-dialogues

• Ask the children what they like.

   Teacher: *Laura, what do you like?*
   Laura: *I like spaghetti*, etc.

• In high-ability groups the children can also ask each other.

❷ Listen and match.

Listening exercise CD 3/30

• Ask the children to look at ex. 2 on p. 53 in their Activity Books. Then hold up your book. Point to the children and read out their names: *Look, here are Lily, Harry, Ruby and Danny.*
• Get the children to close their books and tell you the names of the four children. Then they open their books again. Name some of the food items on the tables and the children point at them.
• Say: *What do the children like?* Listen.
• Play CD 3/30 once. The children just listen and look at the pictures.

Tapescript:

Hi, I'm Lily.
I like pizza, milk, chips, apples, pears and bananas.
I like pizza, milk, chips, apples, pears and bananas.

Hi, I'm Harry.
I like cornflakes, milk, chips, cheese, pears and bananas.
I like cornflakes, milk, chips, cheese, pears and bananas.

Hi, I'm Ruby.
I like pizza, milk, chicken, apples, pears and plums.
I like pizza, milk, chicken, apples, pears and plums.

Hi, I'm Danny.
I like cornflakes, milk, chips, apples, pears, plums and bananas.
I like cornflakes, milk, chips, apples, pears, plums and bananas.

• Demonstrate with an example. Play the CD for Lily again and repeat her words. Say: *Let's look.* Point to the tables and repeat the things Lily likes, showing the children you are looking for the right one. When you find the correct table, say: *This one! Now draw a line.* Show the children. Draw a pencil line from Lily to the table.
• Play the CD twice more. The children listen and draw lines accordingly.
• To check the children's work, draw the four children and outlines of the four tables on the board. Ask children to come out and match the drawings of the children with the tables.

LESSON 3

Vocabulary, phrases and structures:

Receptive language: *You're hungry/thirsty; Go into the kitchen; Take a plate of cheese; There's a big spider on the cheese; Drop the plate; Run out of the kitchen; I like pizza; Have some cheese.*

Linguistic skills:

Understanding instructions in an Action Story (*The spider*).
Understanding instructions on the CD and matching with the pictures in the book.

Cognitive, motor and social skills:

Matching instructions with actions.
Understanding and carrying out jumbled instructions.

Cross-curricular integration:

Curriculum content: Speaking motivation 'A healthy snack'.

Materials:

Flashcards 25–28; 65; 74–83
Flashcard 84; CD 3/31; *Pupil's Book*, p. 62, ex. 3; CD 3/32; *Activity Book*, p. 54, ex. 3; (optional) answer key for self-checking

Revision

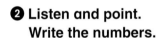

- Use the flashcards to revise all the food items the children have learnt.

Introduction of vocabulary

kitchen; spider

- Introduce the word *spider* with the flashcard.
- Explain the meaning of the word *kitchen* in L1.

❷ Listen and point.
  Write the numbers.

Action Story: *The spider* CD 3/31

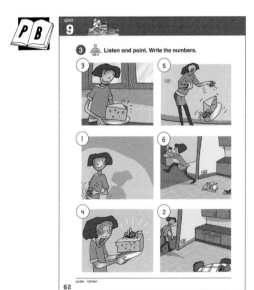

- Work on the Action Story by carrying out the following steps as in previous units. (See introduction p. 16.)

  – Listen and imitate

    The children stand up in a circle or in their places. Give the instructions and mime the actions. The children imitate you. Repeat until the children are confident.

  – Carrying out instructions

    Give the instructions again but do not do them yourself. Repeat until the children are confident. Gradually increase the tempo.

  – Carrying out the instructions in a jumbled order

    Give the instructions in jumbled order. Do not do the actions yourself. Repeat until the children are confident. Give random instructions to individual children.

- The children open their Pupil's Book at p. 62. The six pictures are printed in random order. Give the children sufficient time to look at the pictures.
- Play the Action Story (CD 3/31). The children point to the appropriate pictures.

Tapescript:

You're hungry.
Go into the kitchen.
Take a plate of cheese.
There's a big spider on the cheese.
Drop the plate.
Run out of the kitchen.

- Tell the children that the pictures are to be put in the correct order by numbering them. Number 1 is already done.
- Now play the Action Story again. The children number the pictures in the book.
- Go around the class and check the children's work.

Option: In high-ability classes you can put out an answer key for self-checking. The children go to the key and check their own work themselves.

Alternative: Draw six boxes on the board that represent the page in the Pupil's Book. Have the children tell you the numbers. Write the numbers in the boxes.

❸ **Listen and tick (✓).**
Listening exercise CD 3/32

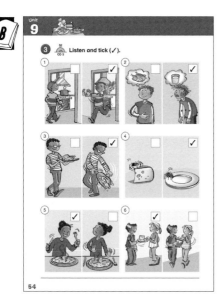

- Tell the children to open their Activity Books at p. 54 and look at the pictures.
- Tell the children that they are to listen to the CD and tick the correct picture in each of the pairs of pictures according to what they hear on the CD.
- Play CD 3/32 twice. The children listen and tick the appropriate pictures.

Tapescript:

Speaker 1:   *One. Run out of the kitchen.*
         One. Run out of the kitchen.

Speaker 2:   *Two. You're thirsty.*
         Two. You're thirsty.

Speaker 1:   *Three. Oh, no! You drop the plate.*
         Three. Oh, no! You drop the plate.

Speaker 2:   *Four. There's a spider on the plate.*
         Four. There's a spider on the plate.

Speaker 1:   *Five. I like pizza.*
         Five. I like pizza.

Speaker 2:   *Six. Have some cheese.*
         Six. Have some cheese.

- The children then listen again and check. Go around the class and check the children's work.

Option: Put out an answer key for self-checking. The children go to the key and check their own work themselves.

Alternative: Draw six pairs of boxes on the board that represent the page in the Activity Book. Point at the first pair of boxes. Say: *Left or right?* The children answer: *Right.* Tick the corresponding boxes on the board.

L E S S O N   4

Vocabulary, phrases and structures:

Orange or banana?; Sorry, no toast; We're hungry; What's for breakfast, Dad?; Watch this!
Receptive language: *We're hungry; What's for breakfast, Dad?; Tea and toast?; Where's our toast?; Just a minute; Sorry, no toast; But, Dad; A smoothie?; Yes. Yoghurt. Milk; Orange or banana?; Sorry, no smoothie; But, Dad, we're hungry!; Eggs? Hey; Watch this!; Don't worry; There are two more eggs.*

Linguistic skills:

Understanding a sketch (*What's for breakfast?*) from the DVD.
Understanding mini-dialogues (scenes from the sketch) from the CD.
Reading out logical sequences.

Cognitive, motor and social skills:

Understanding mini-dialogues/sentences from the CD and numbering pictures in the book.
Completing logical sequences and reading them out.
Pair work: Creating one's own logical sequences for a partner to complete and 'read' out.

Cross-curricular integration:

Curriculum content: Speaking motivation 'Healthy eating'.

Materials:

Flashcards 25–28; 65; 74–83
Flashcard 85; DVD (What's for breakfast?);
CD 3/33; *Pupil's Book*, p. 63, ex. 4; *Activity Book*, p. 55, ex. 4–5; (optional) answer key for self-checking

Revision

• Play the game *What's missing?* with the food flashcards. Give out the flashcards to individual children. Then name one food item after another. The child with the corresponding flashcard comes out and puts it on the board. When all the flashcards are on the board, ask the children to close their eyes. Say: *Close your eyes.* Take away one flashcard and say: *Open your eyes. What's missing?* The children open their eyes and name the missing food item. Continue in this way until there are no more flashcards on the board.

Preliminary preparation of vocabulary

eggs; toast; yoghurt; smoothie; breakfast

• Introduce the meaning of *eggs* with the flashcard.
• Draw some toast in a toaster on the board to elicit and teach the word *toast*. Introduce *yoghurt* in a similar way.
• Explain to the children that a *smoothie* is a popular mixed drink made from yoghurt or milk and fruit.
• Explain the meaning of the word *breakfast*.

❹ Watch the story.

Mr Matt sketch: *What's for breakfast?*

• Show the children the Mr Matt sketch (*What's for breakfast?*) twice.

DVD script: *What's for breakfast?*

Danny and Daisy:	We're hungry.
	What's for breakfast, Dad?
Mr Matt:	Tea and toast?
Danny and Daisy:	OK.
	Dad, where's our toast?
Mr Matt:	Just a minute.
Danny and Daisy:	Dad, where's our toast?
Mr Matt:	Just a minute.
Danny and Daisy:	Dad, where's our toast?
Mr Matt:	Just a minute.
	Sorry. No toast.
Danny and Daisy:	But, Dad! We're hungry!
Mr Matt:	A smoothie?
Danny and Daisy:	Yes!
Mr Matt:	Yoghurt. Milk.
	Orange or banana?
Danny and Daisy:	Banana.
Mr Matt:	OK. Banana.
	Sorry. No smoothie.
Danny and Daisy:	But Dad, we're hungry!
Mr Matt:	Eggs?
Danny and Daisy:	Yes, please.
Mr Matt:	Hey. Watch this!
Danny and Daisy:	No, Dad, please!
Mr Matt:	Don't worry.
	Watch this!
Danny and Daisy:	Oh, no!
Mr Matt:	No problem. There are two more eggs.
	Sorry. No eggs.

❹ Listen and write the numbers.

Listening exercise CD 3/33

- The children open their Pupil's Books at p. 63 and look at the pictures. Tell them that they will now hear individual sentences or short dialogues on the CD and are to match them to the corresponding pictures in the book. Picture 1 has already been numbered.
- Play CD 3/33 (optionally) twice. The children listen and write the corresponding numbers in the circles.

Tapescript:

Announcer:	*Picture one.*
Mr Matt:	*Orange or banana?*
Announcer:	*Once again.*
	Picture one.
Mr Matt:	*Orange or banana?*
Announcer:	*Picture two.*
Mr Matt:	*Sorry, no toast.*
Announcer:	*Once again.*
	Picture two.
Mr Matt:	*Sorry, no toast.*
Announcer:	*Picture three.*
Danny and Daisy:	*We're hungry.*
	What's for breakfast, Dad?
Announcer:	*Once again.*
	Picture three.
Danny and Daisy:	*We're hungry.*
	What's for breakfast, Dad?
Announcer:	*Picture four.*
Mr Matt:	*Watch this!*
Announcer:	*Once again.*
	Picture four.
Mr Matt:	*Watch this!*

- Check the answers. Hold up your book. Point to the first picture and ask: *What number is it?* Children: *Three.*

Option: Check the children's answers by saying, e.g.: *We're hungry. What's for breakfast, Dad?* Children: *(It's number) Three.*

❹ Complete and say.

Logical sequences

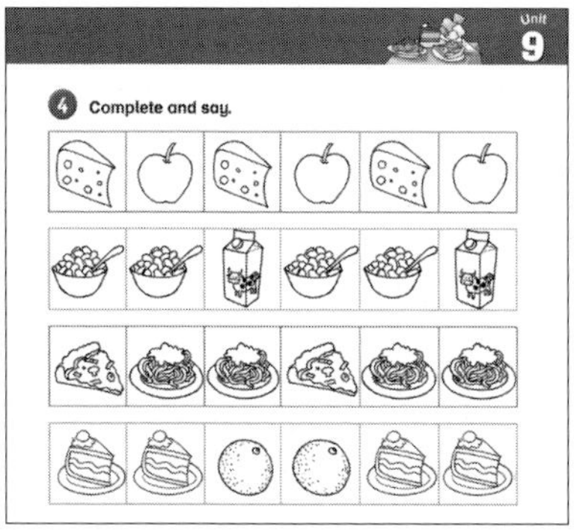

- Ask the children to open their Activity Books at p. 55 and look at ex. 4. Tell them to complete the sequences.
- Give the children enough time to do this. Go around the class and help if necessary.
- To check the children's work, get them to read out the sequences.

Option: Put out an answer key for self-checking. The children go to the key and check their own work themselves.

❺ Draw and say.

Pair work: Step to creativity

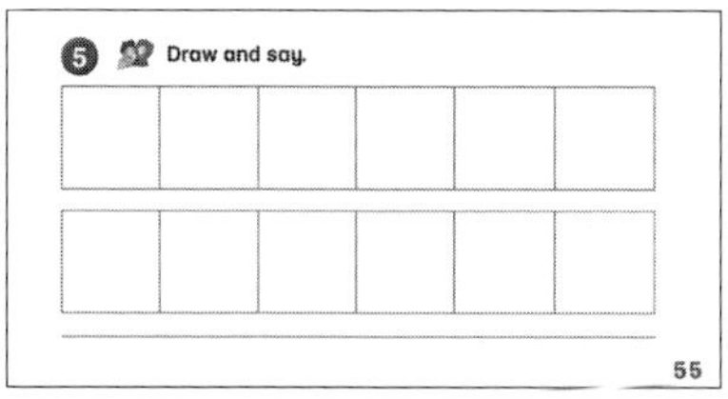

- Tell the children to create their own logical sequence by drawing items of their own choice in the blank rows. Tell them to leave blank the last box in the row.
- They then work with a partner, complete each other's row and read the sequence out to one another.

L E S S O N 5

Vocabulary, phrases and structures:

I like (pizza).

Linguistic skills:

Saying a chant (*Pizza, pizza*) in groups or with the support of percussion instruments.
Understanding the chant from the CD.
Learning by heart and reciting fluently a self-composed rhyme (Word Play).

Cognitive, motor and social skills:

Keeping to a rhythm.
Pointing to the correct pictures while saying a chant.
Chanting in two groups.
(Option) Accompanying a chant with percussion instruments.
Drawing the food one likes and composing one's own chant.
Reciting one's own chant rhythmically.

Cross-curricular integration:

Music
Curriculum content: Speaking motivation 'Healthy eating'.
Art.

Materials:

Flashcards 25–28; 65; 74–83; 85; DVD (*What's for breakfast?*)
CD 3/34–35; *Pupil's Book*, p. 64–65, ex. 5–6; glove puppet Max; (optional) percussion instruments

Revision

- Revise the food items with the flashcards.
- Revise the Mr Matt sketch *What's for breakfast?* from the previous lesson. Use the DVD.

**❺ Listen and point.
  Say the chant.**

Chant: *Pizza, pizza* CD 3/34–35

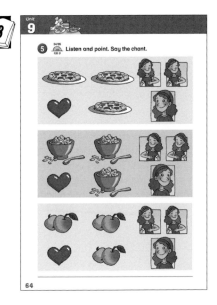

Tapescript:

A: *Pizza, pizza.*
   Yummy, yummy.
B: *I like pizza.*
   Mmmmmmmmh.

A: *Cornflakes, cornflakes.*
   Yummy, yummy.
B: *I like cornflakes.*
   Mmmmmmmmh.

A: *Apples, apples.*
   Yummy, yummy.
B: *I like apples.*
   Mmmmmmmmh.

- Play the chant once as a model (CD 3/34). The children just listen.
- Ask the children to open their Pupil's Books at p. 64. Play the chant again. Practise the chant with the children by saying it out loud line by line and making the appropriate gestures. The children imitate your actions and say it after you. Use the illustrations in the book as visual support.
- Play the karaoke section of CD 3/35 and ask the children to look at the page in the Pupil's Book and chant rhythmically.
- Divide the class into two groups. One group is lead by you; one group by the glove puppet. For example, one group chants verses one and three and the other chants verse two. Or, the groups chant alternate lines, A and B. The rows of pictures in the book act as support.

Option: Use various percussion instruments. The rhythm of the chant is supported by two different instruments, e.g. the tambourine and xylophone, to stress the dialogue character of the chant.

❻ Draw and say.

Step to creativity (Word Play)
CD 3/35

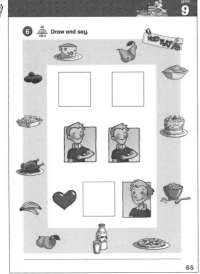

- Ask the children to look at p. 65 of their Pupil's Books and name the food items that are illustrated around the page.
- Tell the children that they are going to compose their own chant. Hold your book up and point along in the book as you demonstrate. The children choose items that they like to eat or drink from the pictures and draw one item each in the three blank spaces. E.g.:

Chicken, chicken. – Yummy, yummy!
I like chicken. – Mmmmmmmmmmmh.

Plums, plums – Yummy, yummy!
I like plums – Mmmmmmmmmmh.

Cake, cake – Yummy, yummy!
I like cake – Mmmmmmmmmmh.

- Give the children sufficient time for this work. When they have finished the drawings, the children learn their self-composed chant off by heart. Show the children the best way to do this. Hold up your book. Recite your chant several times in a low voice and point along in the book. Then go around the class and help if necessary.
- Finally, individual children present their chants to the class. Remember to give them appropriate applause. (*Let's give them a big hand!*)
- In large classes the children can also present their chant to a partner or in a small group.

Option: Give the children the option of presenting their chant just to you on their own first so that if necessary you can help with the pronunciation.

High-ability children can also recite their chant to the karaoke section (CD 3/35).

L E S S O N   6

Vocabulary, phrases and structures:

Vocabulary revision: food
I like ...; What do you like?; What is it?

Linguistic skills:

Saying mini-dialogues.
Formulating categories.

Cognitive, motor and social skills:

Pair work: playing a guessing game.
Colouring hearts in the book and saying what one likes.
Finding the odd one out and formulating categories.

Cross-curricular integration:

Curriculum content: Speaking motivation 'My favourite food'.

Materials:

CD 3/35; *Flashcards* 25–28; 65; 74–83; 85 glove puppet Max; *Activity Book*, pp. 56–57, ex. 6–7; coloured pencils

---

Revision

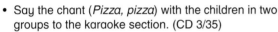

- Say the chant (*Pizza, pizza*) with the children in two groups to the karaoke section. (CD 3/35)
- Revise the food items already learned with the flashcards. Play *What's missing?* (See Lesson 4, Revision)

Mini-dialogues

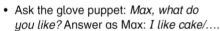

- Ask the glove puppet: *Max, what do you like?* Answer as Max: *I like cake/....*
- Practise the expressions: *What do you like?* and *I like ...* by saying and repeating them several times. Use the flashcards as prompts. The children repeat after you.
- Now the children take over the roles and ask each other, e.g.: *(Sally), what do you like?* (Sally): *I like ....*

❻ Colour and say.

Pair work

- Ask the children to open their Activity Books at p. 56. Tell them to mark the food items they like by colouring the heart next to the relevant drawings.
- When the children have finished, ask, e.g.: *(Julian), what about you?/What do you like?* (Julian): *I like pears, cake and pizza.*, etc.
- Ask the children to walk around the classroom. Play some music (CD or tambourine/xylophone). When you stop the music, the children stop walking and tell the child nearest to them what they like. When you start the music again, the children walk on, etc.

---

❼ Odd one out.
Pair work: Guessing game

- Give the children about ten seconds to look at the pictures in ex. 7 on p. 57 of their Activity Books. Ask them to close their books and give you words they remember. Say: *Give me words*.
- Explain the pair work guessing game. Child A takes a rubber (or sharpener), covers one of the pictures in row one, and asks: *What is it?*
- Child B has three chances to guess what the object is. They then swap roles and child B covers a picture in the second row.
- The children continue like this, swapping roles after each row. Go around the class and help where necessary.
- When the children have finished playing the game, look at the first row with them again. Say: *Look at the pictures in row number one. Which picture is the odd one out?* Children: *Train*. Tell the children to cross it out. Point to the example to clarify. Explain the task in L1 and do the second row with the children if necessary.
- Now the children work individually (optionally in pairs) to look for the odd pictures out in the remaining rows and cross them out.
- Go around the class and check their answers and ask: *What about row (three)?* Children: *(Rain)*.

Option: Individual children 'read' out the words in each row that belong to one category.

L E S S O N   1

Vocabulary, phrases and structures:

lion; elephant; monkey; snake; hippo; Is it the…?
Receptive language: *The lion is ill; The elephant/ hippo/monkey/snake wants to help; Listen to my music; Stop it, please; Thank you for the wonderful music.*

Linguistic skills:

Understanding the meaning and pronunciation of new words.
Understanding a story (*The lion is ill*) on the DVD and the CD and from narration by the teacher.
Gradually joining in with the story-telling.

Cognitive, motor and social skills:

Following the narrative structure of a story.
Completing a picture story with picture stickers
Representing a time sequence visually.

Comparing a variation of the story containing errors with the original version.
(Optional) Trying to get into the characters of the various roles.

Cross-curricular integration:

Curriculum content: Speaking motivation 'Animals, social cohesion, making someone happy'.

Materials:

Flashcards 86–90; DVD (*The lion is ill*); *Story Cards* 46–57; CD 3/36; *Pupil's Book*, pp. 66–67, ex. 1; picture stickers from the appendix of the *Pupil's Book*; (optional) a bag; toy animals; (optional) answer key for self-checking; props for the role play

Revision

- Form a circle with the children. Tell them that they are each a certain animal, e.g.: *(Lucy), you are a mouse. (David), you are a rabbit.*, etc. Then call out instructions rhythmically and invite individual children to perform the movements, e.g.: *Mouse, clean your teeth. Rabbit, jump.* Use the instructions learnt so far, e.g.: *Clean your teeth., Wash your face., Get out of bed., Stretch., Run*, etc.

Option: Encourage the children to come up with suggestions for other actions to be carried out by the various animals, e.g.: *Rabbit, rabbit, give me a banana./Open your schoolbag./Sit down./…*

Introduction of vocabulary

lion; elephant; hippo; monkey; snake

- Introduce the new words with the flashcards in the usual manner and stick them on the board.

Exercises for anchoring the vocabulary in the recognition memory

- Say each word several times and mime it with an action that symbolically represents the corresponding animal. The children imitate you, e.g.:

  lion – with both arms lifted make a wide gesture as if you were getting ready to pounce.

  elephant – wave your arm in front of your face like a trunk.

- Then just say the words and the children do the actions.
- Give the instruction: *Touch the snake/….* A child comes to the board and touches the appropriate flashcard.

Exercises for anchoring words in the productive memory

- The children close their eyes and listen. Say each word individually and change your voice, e.g.: try to express the characteristics of the animal in question with your voice. Then the children repeat the word exactly as you say it.
- Hold a flashcard with the reverse side to the children and have them guess what animal it is. Say: *What is it? What do you think?* Children: *Is it the lion/the monkey…?* Say: *Yes, it is. / No, it isn't.* When a child has guessed the animal, show the flashcard.
- You can also use toy animals you have put into a bag. Get individual children to feel them and guess which animal it is.

Note: Practise the question *Is it the …?* intensively beforehand by saying and having the children repeat it several times.

Preliminary preparation of key phrases

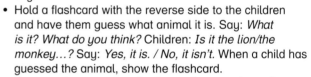

The lion is ill; The elephant wants to help.

- Stick story card 46 that illustrates the sentence *The lion is ill* on the board. Point to the lion in bed and say: *Look, the lion is ill.*
- Now take story card 47 that illustrates the sentence *The elephant wants to help.* and explain the phrase *wants to help* in L1.

❶ Watch the story.

Cartoon Story: *The lion is ill*

• Show the children the DVD sequence *The lion is ill* twice.

DVD script: *The lion is ill*

Storyteller:	The lion is ill.
	The elephant wants to help.
Elephant:	Lion, listen to my music.
Lion:	Stop it, please.

Storyteller:	The hippo wants to help.
Hippo:	Lion, listen to my music.
Lion:	Stop it, please.

Storyteller:	The monkey wants to help.
Monkey:	Lion, listen to my music.
Lion:	Stop it, please.

Storyteller:	The snake wants to help.
Snake:	Lion, listen to my music.
Lion:	Stop it, please.
	What's this?

Storyteller:	It's the elephant, the hippo,
	the monkey and the snake.
Lion:	Oh, thank you for the wonderful music.
	Thank you.

---

❶ Listen and stick.

Listening exercise:
Sticker activity CD 3/36

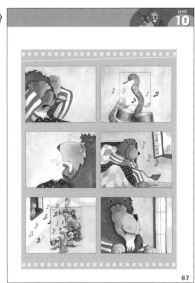

• The children open their Pupil's Books at pp. 66 and 67.
• Play the audio version of the story twice (CD 3/36). The children follow it in the book and complete the pictures with the stickers while they are listening.
• Go around the class and check the children's work.

Option: Place a completed picture story in the classroom. The children go and check their own work themselves.

Telling the story

• Now tell the story with the aid of the story cards.
• While you are telling the story, stick the corresponding cards on the board. Tell the whole story in this way.
• Later, try to encourage the children to join in telling parts of the story.
• Say, e.g.: *The lion is ill. The ...* Children: *elephant ...* Teacher: *... wants to help. Lion, listen to my music.* Children: *Stop it, please.*, etc.

Story-telling game

• Tell the children that you are tired and you may get some of the facts wrong while telling the story. The children are to listen carefully and correct the mistakes.
Say, e.g.: *The lion is ill. The dog wants to help.*
The children correct the mistake: *The elephant...*
Repeat the sentence with the right wording: *The elephant wants to help.*
Say, e.g.: *Lion, dance/sing/speak to my music.*
The children correct the mistake: *Lion, listen ... music.*
• Continue like this for the rest of the story.

Additional task for high-ability groups

Role play – Act it out.

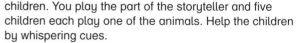

- Play the audio version of the story (CD 3/36). The children close their eyes and visualise the story in their mind's eye (*TV in their head*).
- Act out the story with the roles distributed among the children. You play the part of the storyteller and five children each play one of the animals. Help the children by whispering cues.
- After several presentations, one child can perhaps also take on the role of the storyteller.

Note: Give the children props that distinguish them as the animals in question.

L E S S O N   2

Vocabulary, phrases and structures:

Vocabulary revision: animals; colours; numbers
How many (red) elephants (are there)?
Listen to the animals; What a wonderful song; Come on, sing and dance with me.

Linguistic skills:

Asking about the number of animals in a certain colour.
Saying the number of animals of a certain colour.
Singing a song (*Listen to the animals*).
Understanding sentences from the CD and matching with pictures in the book.

Cognitive, motor and social skills:

Pair work: Finding out information from one another.
Keeping to the rhythm and melody while speaking in unison and singing.
Pointing to the right pictures while speaking and singing.

Following the rules of a game.
Learning a simple dance.
Understanding sentences on the CD and ticking the corresponding pictures.

Cross-curricular integration:

Curriculum content: Speaking 'Animals'.
Mathematics: Number range one to ten.
Art
Music
Sport

Materials:

Story Cards 46–57
Activity Book, p. 58, ex. 1; coloured pencils (red, green, blue, yellow); CD 3/37–38; *Pupil's Book*, p. 68, ex. 2; CD 3/39; *Activity Book*, p. 59, ex. 2; (optional) answer key for self-checking

Revision

- Use the story cards to elicit the story *The lion is ill*.

❶ Colour and say.

Speaking exercise: Pair work

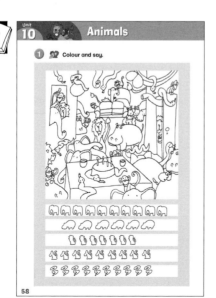

- Tell the children to get out red, green, blue and yellow coloured pencils and open their Activity Books at p. 58.
- Ask the children to colour the animal party scene as they choose using the four colours. Tell them to colour each type of animal in each of the colours at least once.
- When they have finished colouring, the children then work in pairs. They should not look at each other's pictures. Child A asks child B: *How many red elephants (are there)?* When child B answers, e.g.: *Three,* child A colours three of the elephants in the row below the picture red. Child A carries on asking: *How many green elephants (are there)?* This continues until child A has coloured all the animals.
- Then it's child B's turn. Child B now asks what colour the animals are in child A's drawing.
- Go around the class and help if necessary.

❷ **Listen and point.**
   Sing the song.

Song: *Listen to the animals* CD 3/37–38

Lyrics: Gerngross/Puchta
Music: Lorenz Maierhofer
© Helbling, Rum/Innsbruck

Listen to the animals

Lis- ten to the el- e- phant. (Doo doo doo!)   Lis- ten to the hip- po.

(Doo doo doo!)   Lis- ten to the mon- key.   (Doo doo doo doo!)

Lis- ten to the snake.   (Sssss!)   Ref.: What a won- der- ful song,

one, two, three,   come on,   sing and   dance with me!   dance with me!

- Play the song (CD 3/37), do the actions and make sounds to facilitate the understanding of the text, e.g.: *Listen to the elephant.* – cup your hand behind your ear. *Doo doo doo!* show a trumpeting elephant by using your arm as a trunk.
- Play the song again and the children point along with it on p. 68 of the Pupil's Book.
- Say the words of the song line by line with the children. Use the pictures in the book as prompts and point along as you do this.
- The children form a circle. Go around the inside of the circle and hum the tune. The children you go past pick up the tune and begin to hum along. Go around in the circle several times until in the end all the children are humming the tune with you.
- Then start to sing the words.

- Now join the circle and do the corresponding actions while singing. The children imitate your actions and sing along.
- At *One, two, three, come on* - everyone claps their hands, finds a partner and holds hands with them. At *Sing and dance with me* they spin round in a circle with their partners.
- Use the karaoke version (CD 3/38). The children sing and do the actions again.

❷ **Listen and tick (✓).**

Listening exercise CD 3/39

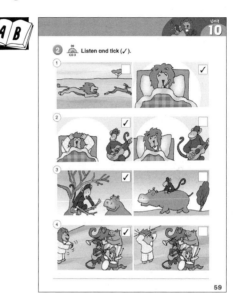

- The children open their Activity Books on p. 59 and look at the pictures for about ten seconds. Tell them to close their books. Get them to tell you words or phrases that they associate with the pictures.
- Then the children open their books again and check their ideas.
- Play CD 3/39. The children listen and tick the correct picture in each pair.

Tapescript:

Speaker:	*One. The lion is ill.*
	One. The lion is ill.
Speaker:	*Two.*
Lion:	*Stop it, please.*
Speaker:	*Two.*
Lion:	*Stop it, please.*
Speaker:	*Three.*
Monkey:	*Help me, please.*
Speaker:	*Three.*
Monkey:	*Help me, please.*
Speaker:	*Four.*
Lion:	*Thank you, my friends.*
	Thank you for the wonderful music.
Speaker:	*Four.*
Lion:	*Thank you, my friends.*
	Thank you for the wonderful music.

- Play the CD again. The children then listen again and check their answers.
- To check the answers, ask: *What about number one? Left or right?* Children: *Left.*

Option: In high-ability classes put out an answer key for self-checking. The children go to the key and check their own work themselves.

Alternative 1: Say, e.g.: *One.* The children reply: *The lion is ill.*

Alternative 2: Draw six pairs of boxes numbered one to six on the board that represent the page in the *Activity Book*. Ask a child to come to the board and tick the correct pictures.

L E S S O N   3

Vocabulary, phrases and structures:

Receptive language: *Dad, can I have a banana/an orange, please?; Just a minute; It's empty; That's (very) strange!; Can I have some popcorn, please?; Come on, Danny! Let's go! Go from (nine) to (three).*

Linguistic skills:

Understanding a sketch (*The thief*) from the DVD. Understanding mini-dialogues (scenes from the sketch) from the CD.

Cognitive, motor and social skills:

Understanding mini-dialogues from the CD and numbering the corresponding pictures in the book. Following instructions from the CD to connect numbers in a dot-to-dot picture.

Cross-curricular integration:

Curriculum content: Speaking motivation 'Animals'.

Materials:

CD 3/38
DVD (*The thief*); CD 3/40; *Pupil's Book*, p. 69, ex. 3; CD 3/41; *Activity Book*, p. 60, ex. 3

Revision

- In a circle, use the karaoke section (CD 3/38) and sing the song *Listen to the animals* while rocking left and right.
- Mime one of the animals. The child who has guessed what animal it is mimes the next animal.

Preliminary preparation of phrases

It's empty; That's very strange.

- Introduce *It's empty* by emptying out your pencil case and then showing it to the children and saying: *It's empty.*
- Translate the phrase *That's very strange.* into L1.

❸ Watch the story.

Mr Matt sketch: *The thief*

- Show the children the DVD sequence *The thief* twice.

DVD script: *The thief*

Danny:	Dad?
Mr Matt:	Yes?
Danny:	Can I have a banana, please?
Mr Matt:	Here you are.
Danny:	Just a minute. Dad!
Mr Matt:	Yes?
Danny:	It's empty!

Mr Matt:	That's strange!
Danny:	Dad?
Mr Matt:	Yes?
Danny:	Can I have an orange, please?
Mr Matt:	Here you are.
Danny:	Just a minute. Dad!
Mr Matt:	Yes?
Danny:	It's empty!
Mr Matt:	That's very strange!
Danny:	Dad?
Mr Matt::	Yes?
Danny:	Can I have some popcorn, please?
Mr Matt:	Here you are.
Danny:	Just a minute. Dad!
Mr Matt:	Yes?
Danny:	It's empty!
Mr Matt:	That's very, very strange! Mmh! Come on, Danny! Let's go!
Danny:	Come on, you. Back to the zoo!

- At the end of the story, a sentence appears as a subtitle on the DVD. (*Good. The food is much better there.*) Translate this sentence in L1 and ask the children: *Who thinks that? Is it Mr Matt, Danny or the gorilla?*

 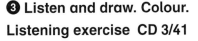

❸ Listen and write the numbers.
Listening exercise CD 3/40

❸ Listen and draw. Colour.
Listening exercise CD 3/41

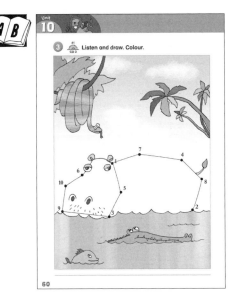

- The children open their Pupil's Book on p. 69 and look at the pictures. Explain to the children that they will now hear individual sentences on the CD and are to match them to the corresponding pictures in the book. Picture 1 has already been numbered.

- Ask the children to look at p. 60 in their Activity Books. Say: *What is it?* and get them to guess what animal is hidden in the picture. The children try to guess: *It's a lion/snake,* etc. Say: *OK. Listen carefully. Draw lines and find out.*
- Play CD 3/41. The children draw lines connecting the numbers in the picture.

Tapescript:

Announcer:	Picture one.
Danny:	Dad, can I have an orange, please?
Announcer:	Once again.
	Picture one.
Danny:	Dad, can I have an orange, please?
Announcer:	Picture two.
Mr Matt:	Come on, Danny! Let's go!
Announcer:	Once again.
	Picture two.
Mr Matt:	Come on, Danny! Let's go!
Announcer:	Picture three.
Danny:	Dad. It's empty.
Announcer:	Once again.
	Picture three.
Danny:	Dad. It's empty.
Announcer:	Picture four.
Mr Matt:	That's very strange.
Announcer:	Once again.
	Picture four.
Mr Matt:	That's very strange.

Tapescript:

OK? Here we go:
Start at number six.
Go from six to ten.
Go from ten to nine.
Go from nine to three.
Go from three to five.
Go from five to one.
Go from one to seven.
Go from seven to four.
Go from four to eight.
And go from eight to two.
What is it?

- Play the CD a second or third time if necessary. The children listen and check.
- Finally, ask: *What is it?* Children: *A hippo.*

- Play the audio version of the sketch twice (CD 3/40). The children listen and write the corresponding numbers in the circles in the book.
- Then hold your book up. Point to the first picture and ask: *What number is it?* Children: *Three.*

Option: Check the children's answers by saying, e.g.: *Dad, it's empty.* Children: *(It's number) Three.*

L E S S O N   4

Vocabulary, phrases and structures:

Receptive language: *Which animal is it?; Open your picnic basket; A monkey grabs it and climbs a tree; The monkey's mum comes; Come down!; The monkey comes down the tree; Have a picnic with your two friends, the monkeys; Row number (one)…*

Linguistic skills:

Naming animals.
Understanding sentences/a story from the CD and matching them with pictures.

Cognitive, motor and social skills:

Deciding which animals the tails belong to.
Understanding sentences/a story from the CD and numbering pictures.

Cross-curricular integration:

Topic: Speaking motivation 'Animals'.

Materials:

Flashcards 29–34, 51; 53, 54, 59, 67, 69, 86–90; DVD (*The thief*)
Activity Book, p. 61, ex. 4; CD 3/42; *Pupil's Book*, p. 70, ex. 4; (optional) answer key for self-checking

Revision

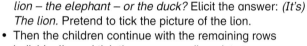

- Take a flashcard and the mime the animal shown on it. Don't show the card to the children. Say: *Which animal is it? Guess.* The children try to guess. The child who guesses correctly takes another card and mimes the next animal.
- Revise the Mr Matt sketch *The thief* from the previous lesson. (DVD)

❹ Look and tick (✓). Say.
Guessing game

- Ask the children to look at the pictures on p. 61 in their Activity Books.
- Tell the children to look at the tail at the beginning of each row and decide which animal it belongs to. They tick the corresponding picture.
- Do the first row together with the children. Hold up your book. Point to the tail. Say: *Which animal is it?* Then read out the animals on the right. Pause between each animal to give the children sufficient time to compare the animal with the tail: *Is it the snake – the mouse – the*

lion – the elephant – or the duck? Elicit the answer: *(It's) The lion.* Pretend to tick the picture of the lion.
- Then the children continue with the remaining rows individually and tick the corresponding pictures.
- Check the children's work by asking: *Row number two. Which animal is it?* Children: *(The) mouse.*, etc.

❹ Listen and point.
Write the numbers.

Listening exercise CD 3/42

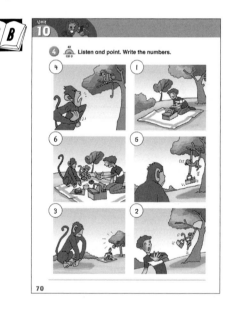

- The children open their Pupil's Book at p. 70. The six pictures are printed in random order. Give the children sufficient time to look at the pictures. Clarify the meaning of the words *picnic/basket* and *climb a tree* using the pictures in the book and through gesture and mime.
- Play CD 3/42. The children point to the appropriate pictures in the book.

Tapescript:

One: Open your picnic basket.
Two: A monkey grabs it and climbs a tree.
Three: The monkey's mum comes.
Four: She says: 'Come down!'
Five: The monkey comes down the tree.
Six: Have a picnic with your two friends,
        the monkeys.

- Tell the children that this time they should put the pictures in the correct order by numbering them.
- Play the CD again and the children number the pictures accordingly.
- Go around the class and check the children's work.

Option: Put out an answer key for self-checking. The children go to the key and check their work themselves.

Alternative: Draw a grid with six boxes on the board. This grid represents the Activity Book page. Ask the children to tell you the numbers of the pictures. (*What number is it?*) Write the numbers on the board.

L E S S O N   5

Vocabulary, phrases and structures:

Vocabulary revision: animals
Receptive language: *What's missing?; Open/Close your eyes; You're having a picnic; A gorilla comes; Drop the banana; Climb a tree; The gorilla is hungry and grabs the banana; The gorilla eats your apples and plums; The gorilla goes away; Your basket is empty; What number is it?; on the left; Which (picture) is the same?; Tell me the number.*

Linguistic skills:

Understanding sentences on the CD and matching the pictures.
Naming animals.

Cognitive, motor and social skills:

Understanding sentences from the CD and numbering the corresponding pictures in the book.
Recognising matching shapes.
Colouring in the matching frames of pictures.

Cross-curricular integration:

Topic: Speaking 'Animals'.

Materials:

Flashcards 29–34, 51; 53, 54, 59, 67, 69, 86–90
CD 3/43; *Activity Book*, pp. 64–65, ex. 5–6; coloured pencils; (optional) answer key for self-checking

Revision

- Play the game *What's missing?* with the animal flashcards. Give out the flashcards to individual children. Then name one animal after another. The child with the corresponding flashcard comes out and puts it on the board. When all the flashcards are on the board, ask the children to close their eyes. Say: *Close your eyes.* Take away one flashcard and say: *Open your eyes. What's missing?* The children open their eyes and name the missing animal. Continue in this way until there are no more flashcards on the board.
- Revise the animals also through, e.g.: lip reading, miming and guessing, etc.

Preliminary preparation of vocabulary

gorilla

- Introduce the word *gorilla* with the help of the illustration in the Activity Book p. 62.

❺ **Listen and point.**
   Write the numbers.
Listening exercise CD 3/43

- The children look at the eight pictures on p. 62 in their Activity Books. The pictures are in random order.
- Play CD 3/43 and the children point at the appropriate pictures.

Tapescript:

One: You're having a picnic.
One: You're having a picnic.

Two: A gorilla comes.
Two: A gorilla comes.

Three: Drop the banana.
Three: Drop the banana.

Four: Climb a tree.
Four: Climb a tree.

Five: The gorilla is hungry and grabs the banana.
Five: The gorilla is hungry and grabs the banana.

Six: The gorilla eats your apples and plums.
Six: The gorilla eats your apples and plums.

Seven: The gorilla goes away.
Seven: The gorilla goes away.

Eight: Your basket is empty.
Eight: Your basket is empty.

- Play the CD again. The children number the pictures accordingly. Number 1 is already done.
- Check the children's work by asking, e.g.: *Climb a tree. What number is it?*

Option: Put out an answer key for self-checking. The children go to the key and check their answers.

Pre-teaching a key phrase

Which is the same?

- Draw a shape on the board, e. g. a circle. Then draw four more shapes, among them another circle:

  e.g.: ○ ▢ ○ △ ◇ .

  Point to the first shape on the left and say: *Which is the same?* Ask a child to come to the board and point at the matching shape on the right.

❻ Look and colour.
Matching exercise

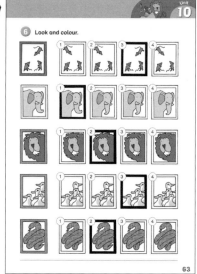

- Tell the children to look at the rows of pictures on p. 63 of their Activity Books.
- Do the first example together with the class. Say: *Look at the picture on the left.* Hold up your book and point to the picture. Say: *Which picture is the same? Tell me the number.* Elicit the correct answer: *Two.*
- Tell the children to colour in the matching frame in the same colour as the frame on the left.
- Get the children to continue like this individually or in pairs.
- Finally, check their answers in the same way as above.

C L I L:
Content and Language Integrated Learning

Vocabulary:

whale(s); turtle(s); penguin(s); lay eggs; have babies; mouse (mice)

Objective:

Finding out whether the animals/birds/reptiles lay eggs or have live births.

Materials:

Flashcards 29–34, 51; 53, 54, 59, 67, 69, 86–90
Flashcards 91–93; CD 3/44; Pupil's Book, p. 71, ex. 5

Revision

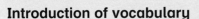

- Revise all the animals the children have learnt so far with the flashcards.
- Revise the plurals by holding up a flashcard and saying, e.g.: *One elephant. (Four) …?* Children: *Elephants.* Do not include *mouse* (irregular plural) in this practise.

Introduction of vocabulary

whale(s); turtle(s); penguin(s); lay eggs; have babies; mouse (mice)

- Introduce the new animals with the flashcards.
- Introduce *lay eggs* and *have babies* using L1 if necessary.
- Introduce the plural *mice* by holding up the *mouse* flashcard and saying: *One mouse. Six …?* The children will probably try to say *mouses*. Shake your head and say: *No, (it isn't). Listen. Mice.* Say the word several times and have the children repeat after you. If you wish, revise the new animals, and plurals of some of the others, with the flashcards as in the Revision activity above and include the mouse amongst them this time.

❺ Who lays eggs? Tick the correct pictures (✓). Listen and check.

Listening exercise CD 3/44

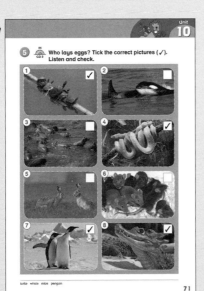

- Ask the children to look at the pictures on p. 71 of their Pupil's Books. Read out the picture numbers and ask the children to say the names of the animals: *Picture one. Which animal is it?* Children: *Turtles.* Teacher: *Picture six.* Children: *Rabbits.*
- The children work in pairs. Ask: *Who lays eggs?* Give the pairs time to look at the pictures and discuss the answers.
- Then tell the children that are going to listen to a radio programme and will find out whether the mammals/birds/ reptiles lay eggs or have babies.
- Play CD 3/44. The children work individually and tick the corresponding pictures.

Option: The pairs could tick the boxes, or just outside the boxes, before they listen and then compare their answers with those on the recording.

Tapescript:

Number one. Turtles lay eggs.
Number two. Whales have babies.
Number three. Hippos have babies.
Number four. Snakes lay eggs.
Number five. Rabbits have babies.
Number six. Mice have babies.
Number seven. Penguins lay eggs.
Number eight. Crocodiles lay eggs.

- Play the CD a second time. The children listen again and check. Give the children some time back in their pairs to discuss whether their predictions were correct.
- Finally, check the answers as a class. Say: *OK. What about (hippos)? Babies or eggs?* Children: *Babies!* Say: *Yes, right. (Hippos) have babies. (Snakes) lay eggs.*, etc.

L E S S O N 1

Vocabulary, phrases and structures:
Checking of vocabulary acquisition

Linguistic skills:
Understanding and saying key vocabulary and phrases from Units 9–10 on the topic areas *Food* and *Animals*.

Cognitive, motor and social skills:
Matching words and phrases from the CD to the corresponding pictures in the book.
Numbering these words/phrases in the corresponding colours.
Checking the results in an answer key.
Self-evaluation

Materials:
CD 3/45–46; *Pupil's Book*, pp. 72–73, ex. 1–2; coloured pencils; answer key for self-checking

---

Self-evaluation

Option: Divide *Show what you can do* into two lessons.

Note: For notes on the basic methodology of this section, see *Show what you can do* on p. 18 of the introduction.

❶ Listen and write the numbers.

Listening exercise: Matching exercise CD 3/45

- Tell the children that they will now find out which words on Pupil's Book p. 72 they can already understand well and which words they can say.
- The children now check independently whether they can match the words to the corresponding pictures. They have a red, a green and a blue pencil in front of them on the desk.
- Play CD 3/45. The children write the numbers one to four in the appropriate colours in the circles for each picture. The first picture has already been numbered.
- Go around the class and help the children as necessary.
- Put out a completed sheet and let the children come out and check their results independently.

Tapescript:

Speaker 1:   Take a red pencil. Write the numbers. Take a red pencil. OK? Here we go.

Number one: monkey.
Number one: monkey.

Number two: eggs.
Number two: eggs.

Number three: butter.
Number three: butter.

Number four: snake.
Number four: snake.

Speaker 2:   Take a green pencil. Write the numbers. Take a green pencil. OK? Here we go.

Number one: chicken.
Number one: chicken.

Number two: chips.
Number two: chips.

Number three: lion.
Number three: lion.

Number four: hippo.
Number four: hippo.

Speaker 1:   Take a blue pencil. Write the numbers. Take a blue pencil. OK? Here we go.

Number one: ill.
Number one: ill.

Number two: spider.
Number two: spider.

Number three: cheese.
Number three: cheese.

Number four: toast.
Number four: toast.

❶ Say and colour.
Speaking exercise

- Ask the children to look at the pictures again. Explain that if they can say the correct words for the pictures, they colour the frames in the corresponding colours.
- When the children have coloured the frames, give them an activity from Units 9 or 10 of the Teacher's Resource Pack to work on while you go around and check the individual answers to the colouring activity. Ask individual children to say the colours, e.g. Teacher: (*Tom*). (Tom): *spider – blue.* Teacher: (*Daniel*). (Daniel): *chips – green.*
- Divide the class into groups of four or five to do this if it is easier to move from group to group to check their work.

❷ Listen and write the numbers.

Listening exercise: Matching exercise CD 3/46

- Tell the children that they will now find out which phrases on Pupil's Book p. 73 they can already understand well and which phrases they can say.
- The children now check independently whether they can match the phrases to the corresponding pictures. They have a red, a green and a blue pencil in front of them on the desk.

- Play CD 3/46. The children write the numbers one to four in the appropriate colours in the circles for each picture. The first picture has already been numbered.
- Go around the class and help the children as necessary.
- Put out a completed sheet and let the children come out and check their results independently.

Tapescript:

Speaker 1: Take a red pencil. Write the numbers. Take a red pencil. OK? Here we go.

    Number one: Drop the ball.
    Number one: Drop the ball.

    Number two: Where's my toast?
    Number two: Where's my toast?

    Number three: Go into the kitchen.
    Number three: Go into the kitchen.

    Number four: Listen to my music.
    Number four: Listen to my music.

Speaker 2: Take a green pencil. Write the numbers. Take a green pencil. OK? Here we go.

    Number one: I like pizza.
    Number one: I like pizza.

    Number two: Take a plate of cheese.
    Number two: Take a plate of cheese.

    Number three: Stop it!
    Number three: Stop it!

    Number four: It's empty.
    Number four: It's empty.

---

❷ Say and colour.
Speaking exercise

- Ask the children to look at the pictures again. Explain that if they can say the correct words or phrases for the pictures, they colour the frames in the corresponding colours.
- When the children have coloured the frames, give them an activity from Units 9 or 10 of the Teacher's Resource Pack to work on while you go round and check the individual answers to the colouring activity. Ask individual children to say the colours, e.g.: Teacher: (*Ann*). (Ann): *Go into the kitchen. – red.* Teacher: (*Bastien*). (Bastien): *Stop it! – green.*
- Divide the class into groups of four or five to do this if it is easier to move from group to group to check their work.

III.
Appendix

FLASHCARDS

Unit 1 – Hello

1   one
2   two
3   three
4   four
5   red
6   yellow
7   green
8   blue
9   black
10   white
11   brown
12   bike
13   boat

Unit 2 – School

14   schoolbag
15   pencil
16   pencil case
17   scissors
18   glue
19   book
20   orange
21   pink
22   purple
23   five
24   six

Unit 3 – Fruit

25   apple
26   banana
27   plum
28   pear

Unit 4 – Pets

29   dog
30   mouse
31   rabbit
32   duck
33   cat
34   hamster

Unit 5 – Toys

35   teddy bear
36   train
37   plane
38   car
39   doll
40   computer game
41   ball
42   puzzle
43   seven
44   eight
45   star

Unit 6 – Weather

46   rain
47   sun
48   wind
49   cloud(s)
50   snow
51   frog
52   snowman
53   bee
54   butterfly
55   flower(s)
56   umbrella

Unit 7 – Party

57   sheriff
58   princess
59   bear
60   ghost
61   clown
62   monster(s)
63   nine
64   ten
65   cake
66   plate
67   bird
68   magician
69   crocodile
70   prince

Unit 8 – Health

71   bed
72   tooth/teeth
73   knees
74   (a glass of) milk
75   orange
76   ice cream

Unit 9 – Food

77   butter
78   spaghetti
79   chicken
80   cheese
81   chips
82   pizza
83   cornflakes
84   spider
85   eggs

Unit 10 – Animals

86   lion
87   elephant
88   hippo
89   money
90   snake
91   whale
92   turtle
93   penguin

STORY CARDS

1–9   Unit 2 – The painting
10–21   Unit 3 – The greedy monster
22–33   Unit 4 – The mouse
34–45   Unit 6 – The little seed
46–57   Unit 10 – The lion is ill